The Spiritual Path

the *Spiritual* PATH

An Introduction to the Psychology of the Spiritual Traditions

Han F. de Wit

Translated by Henry Jansen & Lucia Hofland-Jansen

DUQUESNE UNIVERSITY PRESS
PITTSBURGH, PENNSYLVANIA

Published in Dutch under the title
De Verborgen Bloei by Kok Agora
Copyright © 1994 Han F. de Wit

English Translation
Copyright © 1999 Duquesne University Press
All Rights Reserved

Library of Congress Cataloging-in-Publication Data

Wit, H.F. de.
   [Verborgen bloei. English]
   The spiritual path: an introduction to the psychology of the
spiritual traditions/by Han F. de Wit; translated by Henry
Jansen & Lucia Hofland-Jansen.
   p. cm.
 Includes bibliographical references and index.
 ISBN 0–8207–0307–9 (alk. paper)
 ISBN 0–8207–0308–7 (pbk.: alk. paper)
 1. Psychology, Religious. 2. Wit, H.F. de. Contemplatieve
psychologie. 3. Contemplation. I. Title.
 BL53 .W57713 1999
 200'.1'9—dc21
                        98–58115
                         CIP

Printed on acid-free paper.

CONTENTS

v

ACKNOWLEDGMENTS

There is a growing interest in the psychological background and insights that can be found in the great spiritual traditions. This is the result of the perception that these traditions include a peculiar psychology, which not only can enrich academic psychology but can also be of great practical value for those who travel along a spiritual way. Although this psychology is one of the greatest treasures belonging to humankind, it has remained almost invisible beyond — and sometimes even within — the boundaries of the spiritual traditions. A systematic treatment of its insights on the human mind and experience and of the psychological effect of spiritual disciplines and methods is virtually nonexistent.

This book discusses this psychology, on which I have given introductory lectures at different universities for several years. Because of this, this book is very useful both for self-study and courses within and outside of the university setting. In addition, the topics treated in this book are directed at the practice of the spiritual life and this book therefore differs from my earlier, more theoretical work, *Contemplative Psychology*, which was also published by Duquesne University Press.

Without the personal instruction and encouragement of

my own spiritual mentor, the Buddhist meditation master Chögyam Trungpa Rinpoche, I could not and would not have dared to write on this almost invisible psychology. He encouraged me to take up the dialogue between the psychology of the great spiritual traditions and Western psychology and by this means to make others aware of this special psychology. His instruction in the practice of the spiritual disciplines has never been absent from my mind.

The immediate occasion for writing this book, however, was the invitation to give ten lectures in 1991 during the so-called *Magisterdagen* (Magister Days) which the Dutch and Belgian monasteries in the Benedictine tradition organize annually. I readily accepted the invitation, because these lectures offered me the opportunity not only to exchange insights of contemplative psychology but also to further interreligious dialogue. The dialogue conducted by people who lead the contemplative life is, in fact, the cradle of contemplative psychology, for we see this psychology most clearly at work in that life. Therefore, I am grateful to the masters of the novices who were present at these lectures and have contributed to the writing of this book through their special, spiritual hospitality and through the discussions that I could have with them.

The Dutch version of this book could not have been completed without the contribution of my wife, Ineke de Wit-Schaeffer. She turned the tape recordings of the ten lectures into the first drafts of the chapters and also commented on all later versions. I am very grateful to her for this.

Regarding the American version, I would like to express my thanks first to the translators, Lucy and Henry Jansen. Working with them also provided the opportunity for improving the original Dutch text in some respects. I would also like to thank the Dutch Organization for Scientific Research for its willingness to contribute to the costs of translation.

Last but not least, I would like to express my gratitude to John Dowds and Susan Wadsworth-Booth of Duquesne University Press for their willingness to make this book accessible to an English-speaking public.

Oegstgeest, the Netherlands
July 1999
H.F. de Wit

FOREWORD

Having learned a great deal from Han de Wit's earlier book, *Contemplative Psychology*, I was pleased to receive a pre-publication copy of this new book. In *The Spiritual Path*, Dr. de Wit presents an illuminating account of spiritual psychology in both theory and practice. He describes core features of our spiritual nature and then explains how egocentricity closes us to this nature — why, therefore, we need to cultivate openness if we are to rediscover our spirituality, and how spiritual disciplines help us do this. De Wit's perspective is cross-culturally inclusive. His insights are grounded in a respectful, in-depth study of both Eastern and Western traditions.

Of the many valuable ideas in *The Spiritual Path*, two in particular strike me as having special value as guiding ideas for a more comprehensive understanding of spirituality. One of these ideas is that our spiritual nature — which de Wit calls our *humaneness* — has four basic, inseparable dimensions: clarity, courage, compassion, and joy. And the other is that spiritual practice has a twofold character in being both a restraint of the ego and a cultivation of one or more of the dimensions of humaneness. These two ideas, so simple to state, have profound implications, and much of *The Spiritual Path* is a systematic working out of these implications.

Much that seems bewilderingly complex when studying spiritual traditions is coherently simplified when one thinks of spirituality as having the four dimensions of clarity, courage, compassion, and joy. Some traditions stress one of these dimensions while others stress one or more of the others. Almost all traditions, however, acknowledge all four dimensions. Our growth in wisdom is also a surmounting of ego-based fears; our emerging compassion for others is also a discovery of unconditional joy within ourselves. The key notion is that these four dimensions of our humaneness are inseparably linked. Although specific cultural paths and personality types may give primary emphasis to one, the cultivation of that dimension is at the same time a cultivation of the other three. Understanding this intertwining is invaluable in helping us uncover depth commonalities underlying surface differences in spiritual practices. De Wit's idea of the fourfold nature of our humaneness is a powerfully integrating concept.

And so, too, is his idea that spiritual practice is twofold in character in being both a suspending of the ego and an eliciting of one or more of the dimensions of our humaneness. De Wit explains how the ego is prone to remain in the mode of reflection and how it is prone as well to confuse its projected conceptual maps of experience for experience itself. Owing to these tendencies, we live a self-preoccupied, illusioned life, and consequently we lose touch with our humaneness. If, then, we are to recover our original clarity, courage, compassion, and joy, we must learn how to disengage the reflective and projective activities of the ego, and we must work to cultivate the features of humaneness that we have lost. Spiritual disciplines, the author explains, do both of these things — typically first by disengaging the ego and then, as an inner spaciousness is thus opened, by cultivating humaneness. Drawing on both Eastern and Western sources, de Wit discusses meditative (discursive, imaginal, contemplative) disciplines and disciplines of action and speech and shows how they accomplish these ends.

The Spiritual Path has much to offer both theorists of spiritual psychology and travelers on the spiritual path. In matters of theory, it opens up new ways of exploring relations among spirituality, psychology, psychotherapy, and epistemology. And in matters of practice, it clarifies the underlying processes and goals of a wide range of spiritual disciplines. I am honored to have been invited to write this foreword and am pleased to recommend this excellent book to you.

Michael Washburn
February 1999
Indiana University South Bend

INTRODUCTION

THE FLOURISHING WITHIN

Why is it that one human being becomes wiser and gentler during his lifetime while another becomes more hard-hearted and shortsighted to the needs of others? What is it that causes some people to experience and radiate an increasing measure of joy in their lives while others become increasingly anxious and fearful? And why do some people develop the ability to cope with suffering while others fall apart under that same suffering? How is it that these two such divergent psychological developments can occur under similar circumstances, whether favorable or unfavorable? And, finally, can we influence this development or does it lie beyond our control?

These questions are central to contemplative psychology. They are questions that concern an inner flourishing — sometimes willed, sometimes not — which can occur in the depths of our being. It takes place so deeply within our being that its presence or absence can determine our attitude toward our life in its totality.

Even though this flourishing occurs in a certain sense in the hidden depths of our heart, it is, nevertheless, not something abstract and detached from our lives: this flourishing within

1

becomes manifest in how we live our everyday life. Its fruit is visible in the specific way in which we relate to our environment, our fellow beings and ourselves — a way that deepens and elevates our own lives as well as those of others.

We all know or have heard of people who (at moments or perhaps continually) radiate something — a certain warmth, an unconditional interest in their surroundings and a clarity of mind that is catching and inspiring. This is not necessarily because their situation in life provides them with a special opportunity or because these people are especially fond of us, but rather because these qualities of warmth, interest and clarity appear to belong to their very nature. Sometimes we wonder where this mental power comes from, where people find the courage and inspiration to keep going in very difficult circumstances and, even more difficult to answer, where people acquire the power to encourage and inspire others as well.

Here we think perhaps of people such as Nelson Mandela, Dag Hammarskjöld, Martin Luther King, Mother Theresa, the Dalai Lama or Thich Nhat Hanh. Or we may think of United Nations General Morillon, who out of solidarity with the Bosnians refused to withdraw from Srebrnica so that he could witness with them the inhumanities that occurred there. Or we have read, for example, Etty Hillesum's biography on living in Nazi concentration camps and have wondered how she managed to deal with the situations she encountered.

When people deal with a major setback in a certain way, we sometimes say that they "have risen above themselves." By this we mean that such people, who were (or seemed to be) primarily concerned with their own private projects and personal ambitions, suddenly abandoned all of that when faced with an actual crisis situation and began to act from a much broader perspective. The advancement of the well-being of the total situation took precedence, as it were, over that which they initially saw as their self-interest.

Even though we may be pessimistic about people and their abilities, it cannot be denied that such moments occur in our lives: moments when something breaks through, like a flood that washes away our pettiness, moments when the protection or cultivation of the entire situation in which we find ourselves becomes more important to us than our own interests. Or rather, these are moments when the usual distinction between our personal well-being and the well-being of the total situation is no longer relevant. When this happens it is more than "a blessing in disguise": it is a moment of liberation that reveals new possibilities. This also explains why people, even in the most difficult of circumstances, can experience freedom and strength in a very fundamental sense, are even *able* to experience happiness and encourage and inspire those around them.

We sometimes have the tendency to view people who act from this broader perspective as very special and regard them as far above us spiritually, as people who simply possess a spiritual power that is beyond our reach. But even if we view these people in this way, it is because we *recognize* something in them. The spiritual power and joy in life that we recognize in them *is not essentially alien to us*. We ourselves also have our moments when our attitude to life is like this — moments when our own fundamental humanity, our humaneness, is awakened and manifests itself.

FUNDAMENTAL HUMANITY OR HUMANENESS

The inner flourishing of which we have spoken concerns the uncovering of our fundamental humanity. Because this term is a central theme of this book, it is important to know what we mean by it. The term *fundamental humanity*, or *humaneness* for short, may possibly sound quite pompous or theoretical. We may even be inclined at first to view it as somewhat moralistic. In this book, however, we will use this term to refer to a very concrete experience that is actually quite familiar to us. Let us take a closer look at humaneness — not how we think it can be perceived in others but how it is visible in our own lives.

Because fundamental humanity manifests itself under circumstances of both prosperity and adversity, it is difficult to express the way in which it does so in one word. In times of personal adversity it takes the form of *courage in life*. Confronted with the adversities of others it manifests itself as *compassion*, as unselfish caring. It enables us to work with adversity in a way that elevates us and others. In times of personal prosperity or in the viewing of prosperity of others it manifests itself as *joy in life*.

But there is also, in addition to these three forms, yet a fourth aspect: *clarity of mind*. This clarity, which provides insight and allows us to be realistic in our view of ourselves and the world, can occur in both prosperity and adversity. In this sense it is *independent* of the situation. Moreover, this clarity is not intellectual, as we will see in chapter four, but rather appears in many respects to resemble the open inquisitiveness and interest that we sometimes see in healthy young children. Yet age has little to do with it. It is more the attitude we take toward the richness of color and shape, sound, odor and physical touch offered by the world of phenomena. It is the universal human capacity and desire to be able to learn, to see, to be aware. It belongs to all people in all times and cultures. As we grow older, this open, eternally youthful inquisitiveness — if it is not choked — can lead to an increasing understanding of one's own existence and to the capacity for understanding other people and evoking understanding in them.

By means of these four aspects of our humaneness, we are capable of working in a wholesome way with the reality of our existence — with prosperity and adversity, happiness and suffering, love and hate, sincerity and insincerity.

But let us attempt to word this even more concretely: we experience our humaneness at the moment that we feel that we are "at our best" — not in the sense that we could make a topnotch job of something or that we feel happy, but rather in the sense that we experience that we are human beings who have been born *fully equipped* for human life in all of its prosperity and adversity. At such moments, we realize that we are born first and foremost as *human beings* and not as John or Mary. There is a fundamental difference here, which we will examine thoroughly in chapter three. As John or Mary, we often have the feeling that we must justify, explain, defend or earn our existence. And as John or Mary, with our past history and our expectations, with our oversensitivities and insensitivities, we do not always feel capable of coping with life. But at the moment that we experience our humaneness we feel strong and gentle at the same time, filled with youthful vitality and evident self-confidence. We feel strong, not in the sense that we feel "I'm on top of the world!" and could conquer or resist the world, but strong in the sense that we can allow the world to be as it presents itself to us and make room for it. On the one hand, this power lifts us above ourselves as John or Mary and, on the other hand, it brings us closer to ourselves as human beings. It is experienced as a joy and courage that causes us to be open to our surroundings and capable of living with them. At such moments, even if we are in poor health or have other limitations, we still have something to offer — not because we *need* to give something, but because these moments are of themselves *wide of view* and *great of heart*.

These moments of "being at our best" do not occur because we have succeeded in satisfying certain desires or needs or in fending off dangers — although such success could lead to such moments. Rather, it is that in a certain sense such moments *go beyond* or, better yet, *lie hidden under* the satisfaction or frustration of our desires: they occur when every attempt at satisfaction is absent, either because our desire has been met or because we have had to let go. It is as if rich soil for genuine humaneness exists within us *independent* of our desires. We are aware of this soil sometimes in prosperous circumstances, and sometimes in adverse circumstances. More often, however, it does not manifest itself at all, neither in prosperity nor in adversity. Why is this? Let us examine this somewhat more closely.

Joy in Life and Satisfaction

When we are born we know nothing. We are naive, in a certain sense our existence is veiled in darkness, unarticulated. There are no instructions for life lying beside our cradle. But, small and helpless as we are, we are not out of the game: from the very first moment of our birth there is an open, unconditional interest in and devotion to the world of phenomena. We are, apparently, born this way. It is our humaneness and is just as much a part of our being human as are our not being toilet trained and our crying. And it remains a part of us for the whole of our lives, even when we have long outgrown the need for diapers.

With some people it seems that this unconditional zest for life increasingly determines their lives. In contrast, with others it seems to disappear as they grow older. In our own lives as well, there seem to be periods in which it manifests itself in a greater or lesser degree. Why this happens is, as we stated earlier, one of the central questions to which contemplative psychology seeks and also (as we will see in detail in chapters two and three) gives an answer.

But let us give a broad indication of the answer to this

question on the basis of one of the four aspects of humaneness, i.e., *joy in life*, and thereby make a distinction between *satisfaction* and joy in life. By means of the qualification "life" as it appears in phrases such as "joy in life," "attitude toward life," "courage in life," etc., we indicate that we are talking about a state of mind or attitude that is directed toward our *life in its totality* and not toward certain circumstances in our lives. This state of mind or attitude is therefore not dependent on our circumstances. Rather, the connection is the reverse here: the way in which we respond to our circumstances is dependent on this state of mind. It determines how we deal with prosperity and adversity. In this sense it is *independent* of our circumstances.

Thus by *joy in life* we mean a joyful state of mind that permeates the way we relate to circumstances and which in that sense is independent of them. Of course, circumstances can lead to our losing contact with this unconditional joy so that it seldom manifests itself. But at those moments when it does manifest itself, it transcends our circumstances. Such a moment can occur in distressing situations as well as in prosperous ones, on a sunny day, working in a hayfield as well as on a rainy morning in the city. Every human being experiences these moments, although they are often concealed from us because we, driven by our expectations, pass them by. Tolstoy writes as follows about these moments of joy in life:

> They mowed long rows and short rows, good grass and poor grass. Levin lost all count of time and had no idea whether it was late or early. A change began to come over his work which gave him intense satisfaction. There were moments when he forgot what he was doing, he mowed without effort and his line was almost as smooth and good as Titus's. But as soon as he began thinking what he was doing and trying to do better,

he was at once conscious how hard the task was, and would mow badly.

The longer Levin mowed, the oftener he experienced those moments of oblivion when it was not his arms which swung the scythe but the scythe seemed to mow of itself, a body full of life and consciousness of its own, and as though by magic, without a thought being given to it, the work did itself regularly and carefully. These were the most blessed moments. (Tolstoy 1954, 272–73)

But again, one need not be a Tolstoy to know of such moments of joy in life and to experience them *simply* (that is, unconditionally).

Over against this unconditional joy there is also a conditional form of joy, which we will designate here by the term *satisfaction*. We experience this form of joy when we succeed in satisfying our desires. The distinction between joy in life and satisfaction is that the latter is dependent on circumstances, both external and internal. By internal circumstances we mean the wishes and desires that we cherish. By external circumstances we mean the situations to which our desires are directed. Together they constitute the conditions for satisfaction.

Materialistic and Spiritual Views of Happiness

Ordinarily we use the word *happiness* to refer to the satisfaction of desires. Happiness in this sense of the word is dependent on circumstances: certain conditions must be fulfilled if we want to be happy people. Happiness is *dependent on* something that *brings* happiness. Happiness comes from outside of us: "When you are finished school, then you will feel better. When you have a good job, partner or friends, you will be happy. When you are healthy again, when you get along well with your children, when you are free, then you will be happy. Try to accomplish that!" While there is something to be said for this, it is not the whole story. Even more, it is misleading in suggesting that if we could only control our circumstances, we could obtain happiness for ourselves. True, this is an appealing notion: if we do our best and make an effort, happiness, like possessions, esteem and power, can be obtained. It suggests that we are not entirely powerless.

However, the implication of this view is that we can also lose this kind of happiness, just as we can lose material possessions. This is why this *materialistic view of happiness* is the soil for a life dominated by anxiety, by hope for gain and fear of loss. In addition to this, our desires can differ from those of others and become a source of conflict. Finally, our desires themselves can also be unrealistic, so that the attempt to fulfil them plunges us into unhappiness. But even if we succeed, usually through much labor and pain, in satisfying our desires, this happiness is short-lived. It actually consists of the cessation of the tension caused by unfulfilled desires.

When the moment of satisfaction passes we must once again continue the search for happiness. When we reach that which we expected to bring us happiness, it becomes apparent sooner or later that our feeling of being happy does not last. Once again we begin to search for happiness in life or become disappointed and more anxious: we no longer trust life. Our attitude might change from searching for happiness to avoiding unhappiness. We now judge future circumstances primarily in light of the degree to which they can hurt us and make us unhappy. The basic motivation of our lives now becomes the search for safety and protection, for invulnerability. Again and again, when we find that this search is fruitless, our fear increases until it turns into *fear of life*. The world becomes one huge threatening place in which even survival can become too great a task. It then seems that the only way out is death.

The materialistic view of happiness is problematic not only

because it does not fulfil our expectations in a lasting way but also because it severs our connection with our humaneness and thereby our joy in life. Less and less do we experience that joy in life belongs to us by nature and we therefore attach less and less value to it and look for it less often. And because joy in life does not spring essentially from external circumstances, although we do search for happiness there, disappointment is heaped upon disappointment.

Over against this materialistic view there is a *spiritual view of happiness*, in which happiness is not viewed as a moment of satisfaction but as a moment of joy in life. This view does not look down upon striving for satisfaction, but it rejects the high expectations that appear in the materialistic view of happiness, particularly the suggestion that satisfaction *is* joy in life or necessarily leads to joy in life. In the spiritual view, happiness is something quite different from satisfaction. Perhaps, while we are preoccupied with searching for happiness by adapting our circumstances and our desires to each other, we look up for no reason at all at the big fluffy clouds drifting lazily across the blue sky, or we look at a sparrow hopping about on the sidewalk. For a moment, just one moment, our preoccupation is gone and we experience reconciliation and joy in life — just for a moment, but possibly a very intense moment because of the great contrast. It is then possible that we recognize that a change of perception has occurred which places our search for happiness in another light and unmasks this search as fundamentally misleading, because at those moments we experience that that for which we are searching is something we already possess.

In our Western culture with its great material prosperity, we are well aware that favorable material circumstances are no guarantee of joy in life: "Money cannot buy happiness," we say. But even that insight often only leads us to search for happiness elsewhere, for example, in social circumstances or even in internal, that is, mental, states. In the latter case, we might see our desires and wishes as the major causes of unhappiness. We then want to liberate ourselves from our desires, and we search for ways to manipulate our mind to get what we want. Perhaps we think that the practice of spiritual disciplines can help us. But that is not how we can make our humaneness flourish because our basic attitude is still the same here: if only we could attain that which we desire or eliminate that which stands in our way, then we would be happy. The only "merit" of such attempts is that, in doing them, we can learn to see their inadequacy.

Moreover, the belief that the only way to achieve happiness is by manipulating our external or internal circumstances also makes us greatly manipulable: we become susceptible to promises of all kinds, realistic or unrealistic, in material, social, psychological and spiritual areas. If we believe that only riches or social status will make us happy, we are at times prepared to work ourselves to death as well as resort to practices that are less than decent. If we believe that the destruction of our enemies will ultimately bring us happiness, then we will fight. If we see our mind or ourselves as the enemy, we will try to conquer our mind or destroy ourselves.

Many spiritual traditions say that we lose our humaneness by approaching ourselves and our world (including religion) from this materialistic view of happiness. The fruit that we pick personally and communally from this view has a bitter taste. And although, in spite of this, we continue to experience our humaneness at moments, such moments quickly pass. Surmounting adversity or promoting our prosperity soon demands all our attention again. And, in the light of this, such moments seem unrealistic and irrelevant. It is then difficult to imagine that they are the foundation of and the door to a completely different way of living.

The reason we have discussed the aspect of joy in life in

some detail is that the same problem occurs in the other three
aspects of our humaneness — courage in life, compassion
and clarity of mind. These three are unconditional as well:
they are not related to certain circumstances but are independent of them. When we live from the perspective of our
humaneness, then our *compassion* manifests itself freely and
unconditionally whenever suffering appears: we quickly jump
to someone's aid, not because we see it as our moral *duty* at
that moment but because we cannot do otherwise. If we see
a toddler fall into the water, we run to pull her out. At that
moment we are not at all concerned with moral duty. We
have pulled the child out to safety without even thinking
about it. But if we are not in touch with our humaneness, we
might easily come to believe that mercy is a matter of maintaining and propagating good morals. Sermons on morality
have seldom accomplished anything, however, and certainly
not in times of danger. At those times it is only our humaneness that can achieve anything.

When we no longer have *courage in life*, we quickly believe
that toughness, perseverance, persistence in the difficult
struggle to achieve our goal and the defiance of adversity is
true courage. And when we lose our *clarity of mind*, we come
to see it as something vague that cannot compete with being
well-informed and having a great deal of knowledge. Or we
regard it at most as presence of mind, which is useful for the
promotion of our own interests, as a form of cleverness that
prevents the wool from being pulled over our eyes.

Humaneness, when we are no longer in touch with it, seems
to be a beautiful utopia, good for chronic optimists or religious people. There is something to be said for this, because
it is precisely in the great religious traditions that we find
all kinds of indications and insights that refer to our humaneness. We will explore them in the first part of this book. Moreover, we also find instructions in the religious traditions as

to how this humaneness can be cultivated by means of certain disciplines. These we will discuss in the second part of this book. It is for this reason that our investigations into contemplative psychology lead us to consult the religious traditions; they prove to contain quite a bit of psychological insight. For some people this book will therefore resemble a "religious" book; for others, it will be a book that discusses *humaneness* and its cultivation, which the Shambhala tradition calls *basic goodness* (Trungpa 1984, 35) and which those who reflect deeply about our culture sometimes call *spiritual humanism* (Bulhof 1992; Amaladoss 1990). Humaneness is a universal human power that is not associated with a particular ideology or philosophy of life. We can uncover it in our personal lives by cultivating our mind. The fruit of this flourishing within manifests itself in our actions and speech, which in turn are felt in our society and our culture. It is that which is able to elevate our own existence and that of others.

Searching for or Bestowing Happiness?

It is a typically spiritual premise that joy in life, courage in life, compassion and clarity of mind are qualities that do not come from outside but from within — qualities that we do not need to acquire but possess already at birth. The question is how we can develop them instead of smothering them. If this is so, does this mean that we should simply allow our external life situation to run its course, that we can afford to become passive and cease to care about our external circumstances?

That is certainly not the implication. But we *would* have to give up our self-deception, illusions and unrealistic expectations as to what our situation in life can offer us in terms of joy in life. They stand in the way of our humaneness — a humaneness that is by nature (i.e., unconditionally) involved with life and manifests itself in the form of a caring and understanding way of dealing with others and with our external circumstances. And the more it manifests itself the stronger it becomes. Inasmuch as we are able to live from the perspective of our humaneness, we are able to become people who unconditionally *bestow happiness* instead of people who seek happiness. Thus we have not turned away from the world around us but have turned toward the world unconditionally, that is, in a truly human way. Bringing about this turn of mind or conversion is the concern of the religious traditions, and contemplative psychology is concerned with the *how* and *why* of this turn of mind.

But at present most of us are seekers rather than bestowers of happiness. And that is why specific external circumstances are still definitely relevant and cannot be ignored, for to the extent that we *think* that our humaneness is dependent on specific circumstances and the satisfaction of our desires we are no longer able to ignore those circumstances and desires. If we wish to cultivate our humaneness, we will have to face the circumstances of our lives and examine how they play upon our expectations and blind spots, because all of these have become the source, or rather, the focal points of our fear of life. It is possible that we are right to change certain circumstances in our lives temporarily or perhaps permanently, as long as we cannot let go of our expectations of (and our hopes and fears about) them.

We thus give a certain shape to our way of life — a shape that could be called *spiritual*. This is a way of life that allows us space for exploring and penetrating our fear of life. To do so is at the same time the manifestation and essence of courage in life as well. In this way, we also restore our link with our humaneness. This process is quite different from attempting to turn internally away from or becoming insensitive to life. It is the opposite of fleeing from the realities of our existence into materialistic or spiritual fantasy worlds that please our imagination and seem to offer security. Rather, it is the creation of circumstances in which we can rediscover and cultivate our humaneness. In those circumstances we discover that we "are able to rise above ourselves" and how we can do this, how we can be "at our best." The more we grow in our ability to do this, the more independent we become of our circumstances. Our circumstances become less and less effective in destroying the manifestation of our humaneness; they become stepping stones for its manifestation rather than focal points of our fear of life. Psychological factors play a role in this process of inner transformation, and we will examine these factors in the following chapters.

THE CONTEMPLATIVE LIFE

As we stated above, moments of unconditional courage and joy in life belong to life just as much as moments when we are gripped by fear of life. That we have these moments, that they belong to human existence, is beyond dispute. They are present in all cultures, but there are very different ideas as to what value we should attach to those moments when our humaneness manifests itself and what price we would be willing to pay for uncovering it. Such moments often disrupt our customary attitude to life in such a radical way that they seem to be beyond our reach or control while simultaneously belonging to our lives.

At the same time we will continue to long for these moments as long as we live — these moments of courage and clarity of mind, which can appear at any time and for any or no reason. Sometimes we wonder hesitatingly whether it would be possible to live from the perspective of these moments and whether that is what some people do and why they inspire us. Perhaps we then even ask the question of why we do *not* live from the perspective of these moments and ask ourselves whether the causes for this can be removed. But when we look back at these moments and the idea occurs to us, "If only it could always be this way for everyone," then despair and so-called realism takes over: "If that were possible, it would already be so, and because it is not, it apparently cannot be so." Maybe we are willing to acknowledge that such moments do occur, but we are very unsure as to whether we can cultivate them. From the perspective of our usual attitude toward life, we tend to occupy ourselves with keeping our affairs in order. That is in itself already difficult and time-consuming enough.

In every culture, however, there are traditions that apply themselves to cultivating our humaneness with the help of mental disciplines and disciplines in the areas of action and speech. How does this work? These disciplines first reveal the factors that smother our humaneness and then help us to eliminate them. For although we do not control our humaneness itself — we are not capable of manipulating or holding onto the moments at which it manifests itself — we do control the factors that cause it to recede, for we have created these factors ourselves. That is why the cultivation of inner flourishing is more a process of *uncovering our humaneness* by exposing and eliminating that which chokes it rather than directly cultivating this humaneness itself. Subsequently, we begin to (re)discover and trust our humaneness. Finally, we begin to identify with it more and more and live from this perspective.

The desire to realize our humaneness fully and make it manifest lies at the basis of *the contemplative life*. It is the origin of the religious traditions. The desire for a truly human life is universal, being itself an expression and proof of humaneness. But the ways in which that desire acquires form in our lives are extremely varied. It manifests itself in many forms of searching — forms that are wise and foolish, fruitful and sterile. Sometimes people leave the environment in which they grew up, searching for a more authentic existence. All great religious traditions have countless stories of people who have done exactly this. Prince Siddhartha, who would later be known as the Buddha, fled his princely existence with all its comforts and ease when he was 29 years old and already had a wife and child. Because he could no longer bear the hypocrisy of his sheltered way of life, he set off in search of a way of life that could awaken insight into human existence in his heart. Although this was undoubtedly a very drastic approach to the problem, he has not been the only one to embark upon this course of action.

This approach is also abundantly present in the New Testament. A striking story is that of the rich young ruler who asks Jesus what he must do to inherit eternal life. When the ruler tells Jesus that he has lived according to the commandments since he was a boy, Jesus tells him: "You still lack one thing. Sell everything you have and give to the poor, and you will have treasure in heaven. Then come, follow me" (Luke 18.22). This is no small task, but one about which Jesus remarks: "I tell you the truth, no one who has left home or wife or brothers or parents or children for the sake of the kingdom of God will fail to receive many times as much in this age and, in the age to come, eternal life" (Luke 18.29–30).

Others do not break away from their previous way of life in a dramatic way but grow out of it slowly because in one way or another they have kept an ear open to the voice of truth. The life of Augustine is a beautiful and — in all respects — modern example of this — a double example, actually, because as a very young man he broke with the Christian tradition in which his mother had raised him. This break had to do with his desire to "make it" in the world, to acquire honor and fame by shining as an orator and generally respected intellectual. He believed this was the way to find true joy in life. In spite of — or perhaps because of — his success in this, he began to feel the hollowness of his way of life more and more. Little by little, his perspective began to change. He made the fortunate error of listening to a famous orator, Ambrose, the bishop of Milan:

> And I studiously hearkened to him preaching to the people, not with the motive I should, but, as it were, trying to discover whether his eloquence came up to the fame thereof, or flowed fuller or lower than was asserted; . . . and yet I was drawing nearer gradually and unconsciously. For although I took no trouble to learn what he spake, but only to hear how he spake (for that empty care alone remained to me, despairing of a way accessible for man to Thee), yet, together with the words which I prized, there came into my mind also the things about which I was careless; for I could not separate them. And whilst I opened my heart to admit "how skilfully he spake," there also entered with it, but gradually, "and how truly he spake!" (Augustine 1983, 88)

Still others do not break physically with their surroundings or grow out of them as Augustine grew out of his surroundings but seem rather to grow into them. They somehow know how to use their actual situation in life as a means for developing their humaneness. A familiar example from Buddhism is the legendary king Indrabodhi, who did not give up his kingship and the comforts belonging to it but, under the guidance of his gurus, took advantage of his position in the world itself as a spiritual path. In our day and age as well, there are people who live a contemplative life in the midst of the world. We do not necessarily have to think of people in high social positions, such as Ü Thant or Dag Hammarskjöld. Our own lives can be lived this way.

Throughout the centuries people have sought for and found ways of life that strengthen and support the contemplative life. This way of life belongs to all times and cultures. In some traditions it has led to the development of monastic ways of life. In other traditions, such as, for example, the Jewish and Protestant traditions, living spiritually is practiced in everyday life, which is why such traditions have no monasteries. And there are also traditions, such as Hinduism, Buddhism and Catholicism, in which living contemplatively has been given form both in everyday life and in monastic life.

But regardless of how a spiritual way of life is lived and which form it takes in a certain time or culture, it is always based, on the one hand, on the desire to uncover true humanity and, on the other, on deep psychological insight into the human mind and into the ways in which humanity can be developed. This insight is not so much something theoretical or philosophical, attainable only by learned minds, but is a very concrete type of insight into our human nature — both into our humaneness and into that about which we say: "Homo sum; humani nil a me alienum puto" ("I am a human being and nothing human is foreign to me").

In conclusion, perhaps a warning is in order here. Although we are searching for the way in which the uncovering of humaneness has acquired form in religious traditions, this is not to say that all existing religious traditions actually contribute to this. There is much that is ripe and green in this area, and it is also possible for existing traditions to degenerate. Traditions are maintained and passed on by people, and there is no guarantee that every tradition offers an effective support for such cultivation in its present form (see de Wit, 1991a, 171). However, by practicing the disciplines of a tradition and studying its insights, we can establish through experience whether it cultivates our inner flourishing and yields fruit in our speech and actions.

When we refer to religious traditions in the following chapters, we are referring only to particular traditions insofar as they aim at uncovering our humaneness. Traditions with a different aim are not considered here because they do not offer relevant material for the development of a contemplative psychology that has inner flourishing and its fruit as its subject. If we are aware of this restriction, we do not run the risk of forming too rosy an image of religious or spiritual traditions, of assuming that they are more or less understood to be *bona fide* by nature. As history has taught us, they are not. But it cannot be denied that it is precisely in these traditions, more than anywhere else, that valuable psychological insights and disciplines are to be found which are directed toward the cultivation of our humaneness in our concrete existence. This is what we will examine in the following chapters.

I

EXPLORATIONS

ONE

Contemplative
Psychology

INTRODUCTION

Because we ourselves are part of Western culture, we are
perhaps not always aware that in the last half century it has
developed into a distinctly psychological (in the sense of psychologizing) culture. Many things seem to have or do have a
psychological aspect to them — an aspect that we may have
overlooked in the past. People think and speak in psychological terms much more often than they used to in order to
express genuine understanding of their own human existence as well as to give an impression of understanding. We
find it quite normal to speak to one another about our feelings and motivations, including the unconscious ones and
the background of our behavior in terms that, until recently,
did not even exist. We have grown up with this.

Of course, the work of many psychologists has played a
major role in this development. Because of this work, the

psychological vocabulary and the conceptual framework that we use in daily life has expanded tremendously. This development has its pros and cons. For example, we are able to discuss certain psychological issues in a much more nuanced way and with more precision than we could a century ago. Yet this assumes that we are familiar with that new, enlarged conceptual framework, which, of course, is not always the case. At times it is not clear what certain terms mean because they have not been clearly defined or we have only a vague notion of what they mean and communicate by means of them as best we can. This is the case with psychologists as well as laypeople. We then run the risk of lending support to psychological theories when they are posed with a certain aplomb or surrounded with the aura of scholarship, even if we cannot link them with our concrete experience. These theories then begin to function easily as an *ideology*, causing us to try to bring our experiences into agreement with the theory to which we adhere rather than the other way around. We are no longer open to our experience. Entire generations in our culture have grown up with the concept of humanity that was drawn up by Freud and they interpreted their experiences by means of this concept. Moreover, psychological interest is subject to fashion. Some topics are front page news in the psychological journals for a decade or so, only to disappear and sometimes even be entirely forgotten. For instance, research into personality types was still popular up until the middle of this century. Then research into motivation was popular for a while. With the advent of the computer, interest has shifted to the human being as an "information processing system." In any case, the presence of psychology is a fact in our modern society. Whether we like it or not, this is how things are.

Is the contemplative psychology that is central to this book not itself an expression of the psychologizing tendencies in our culture? In a certain sense it is, since it arises from the question of how we can communicate about basic human themes — such as the way in which we concretely experience and give shape to being human — with people who have begun to think more psychologically. In our day and age, how can we speak about spiritual development and all that is related to it?

It is a paradoxal phenomenon in our culture that, in spite of the developments of psychology, precisely the topics that concern humanity are thrust into the background. Our culture considers the satisfaction of (material and emotional) needs and desires of paramount importance. This in turn determines very strongly the direction in which the sciences, including psychology, develop. When opening a standard work on psychology, there are a number of themes that we do not encounter. Theories as to the nature of the mind, consciousness and experience are rarely offered. Self-knowledge, wisdom, compassion, courage and how they can be attained are not discussed. Topics such as how we stand in and over against life and how we must respond to it are relegated in part to the realm of philosophy and in part to what are called "women's magazines." Scientific psychology has little to do with these issues.

Yet there exist — in our own culture as well as elsewhere — other traditions in which these fundamental topics do receive full attention: the spiritual traditions. What is meant by *a spiritual way of life* has been touched upon in the introduction to this book. We will examine it in more detail in the following chapters. For the time being, let us say that this term refers to a specific, disciplined way of life. Discipline is a word that easily scares us. But here it concerns the practice of a *gentle and intelligent* discipline that is directed at cultivating our humaneness — both within ourselves and within others. This discipline is based on an understanding of human nature and awakens such understanding.

In most cultures, the spiritual way of life is discussed in a religious context, which does not always make it easier. This is particularly so when the terms of the religion in question hardly or no longer speak to us precisely *because* we have begun to think so much in psychological terms. Such terms quickly give us the impression of being old-fashioned, vague, unrealistic or excessively moralistic. We are therefore not immediately inclined to lend a listening ear to these great religious traditions where vital questions are concerned.

Yet it is precisely within these traditions that one can find some insight into the human mind and the experience of reality. This being so, it is worthwhile to attempt to express these insights in such a way that they are comprehensible to people (including psychologists) today. Earlier studies (James 1902; Fortmann 1974; van Kaam 1983; de Wit 1991, etc.) have, in fact, shown that many religious traditions do include a *contemplative psychology* — a psychology that can clarify the nature of the mind and spiritual development and the function of spiritual disciplines.

Contemplative psychology has received a strong boost from the recent development of *interreligious dialogue*. When conducted on a practical rather than a theological level (see, for example, Walker, 1987), this dialogue has shown us psychological knowledge that arises from and is relevant to a spiritual way of life.

Expressing this knowledge in terms of a contemplative psychology is in a certain sense like pouring old wine into new wineskins. But it is a wine that we had almost forgotten was stored in the cellar — a very special wine of high quality and, moreover, immense wholesome power: the wine of spiritual development. The new wineskins here represent a psychological conceptual framework. This is already in itself a risky way of expressing it. After all, we could easily read into this that modern Western psychology is able to survey and clarify the nature of the spiritual way of life by means of its own conceptual frameworks. Many psychologists have approached spirituality in this way — certainly not without results, as the work of people like Jung, Maslow, Drewermann and many others who work in the field of the psychology of religion demonstrates. Nonetheless, as we shall see later, this approach has its limitations.

It is for this reason that we will follow a completely different, one could say reversed, approach in this book. We will look for the psychological ideas that have been developed and maintained by the religious traditions themselves, because these traditions have something to contribute to psychology: they contain insights that are of great importance to psychology and thus to humankind. That is why it is important that we first listen to what these traditions themselves have to say. In this way, the psychological approach inherent *in the great religious traditions themselves* will become visible. Thus we will not explore spirituality from the perspective of already existent psychological conceptual frameworks but will attempt to make visible the psychological conceptual frameworks and ways of thinking that are to be found within the religious traditions. This will provide us with a unique psychology — a *contemplative psychology*.

Unfortunately, the distrust between psychologists and those involved in religious traditions is at times so great that they do not want to delve into one another's conceptual frameworks. In itself, this distrust is not completely without grounds. Every now and then both psychologists and religious people have developed and propagated the most absurd, fantastic and even harmful theories about people (on this see, for example, Kouwer 1963). Errors are and will be made on both sides. A critical stance with regard to psychology and religion is necessary. Moreover, it can be fruitful as long as it does not make us so shy of psychological thinking that we are not willing to search for valuable *psychological* insights that are to be found within the religious traditions: insights into the human mind, motivations, emotions, cognition, insights into actions and speech, language and communication and, *last but not least*, insights into how all of these facets influence one's spiritual growth, the inner development of courage, wisdom and joy in life.

The study of the human mind and experience as we find it in academic psychology and in the religious traditions naturally has the same root in spite of the difference in approach that we will discuss below: both traditions attempt to clarify the nature and functioning of human existence.

Allow me to mention a third tradition because of its connection to the contemplative approach: *art*. Like the scientific and religious traditions, this tradition also attempts in its own way to clarify human existence. We could, of course, view art as a purely aesthetic matter, but art also involves attempting to make something visible. Whether this occurs through visual art, music or literature, there is also another aspect besides the aesthetic one: a truth-seeking aspect. In one way or another, the artist attempts to make something clear, to arouse and to communicate — a certain perspective, a certain kind of experience in which something is revealed — so that we, even just for a moment, look at things in a somewhat different way. This is an important motivation for the artist. Art reveals something, clarifies something. Thus, it is not amazing that in many cultures we often see art practiced in connection with a religious tradition. Perhaps "searching for truth" is too grand a phrase in this connection, but, in addition to all kinds of other aspects, art also involves something that lies in this direction — a form of insight into human experiences. In this sense, art is also a tradition that in its own way seeks and contains psychological insights — insight into the nature of human experience. Who knows the psychological significance (and effect) of form and color better than the visual artist? Who knows the effect that sounds and tones have on our state of mind better than the composer? No sensory psychologist can match them. With respect to literature, one of the founders of scientific psychology in the Netherlands, H.C.J. Duijker, used to say, in fact, that it would be very valuable for psychologists to read the novels of Marcel Proust.

In all cultures, we find these three main traditions: the religious or spiritual tradition, the scientific tradition and the tradition of art. Although all three are very different and follow very different approaches, they also have something in common: the desire to explain in one way or another what it is to be human. In this sense, the three main traditions of our culture — science, art and religion — have a common psychological root.

CONVENTIONAL AND CONTEMPLATIVE PSYCHOLOGY

Before we look any more closely at what contemplative psychology has to say on the topic of humaneness and spiritual growth, it will be useful to compare this psychology on a few points with the scientific psychology familiar to us. This can make us aware of the sense in which contemplative psychology is different from that which we normally understand by the term *psychology*, for our general view of what psychology is already strongly colored by scientific psychology.

Allow me to state bluntly that scientific psychology does not, in fact, form one coherent whole. So many theories and so many conceptual frameworks have been developed in the last hundred years that today we could almost say that there are as many psychological opinions as there are people.

Psychology has become a very extensive science with many *fields*. This has led to all kinds of subdisciplines, such as social psychology, child psychology, educational psychology, clinical psychology and research psychology. Many kinds of different *approaches* have also arisen, of which behavioral psychology, depth psychology and cognitive psychology are the most familiar.

All in all, it has not become any less complicated, since one theory sometimes denies precisely that which another theory confirms. Psychologists of various subdisciplines often have little understanding of one another. For example, behavioral psychologists usually want little to do with depth psychologists and vice versa. Some psychologists, like many laypeople, drift eclectically from one conceptual framework to another, depending on the problem with which they are confronted. Others adhere to one framework, as if it were an article of faith, even if the main defects of this framework can be demonstrated. At the same time, many psychologists regret the fact that their science is not a clear unified discipline.

The Plasticity of the Human Mind

But there is also an undercurrent of psychologists who see the large number of psychologies as the inevitable result of the plasticity of the human mind itself. This view is to be found in both the phenomenological and existential corners as well as among psychologists who work with forms of cognitive psychotherapy. These psychologists accept rather than deplore the large number of psychological approaches. In their view, the human mind is capable to a certain degree of creating its *own patterns*. The task of psychology is to attempt to chart these patterns. This chart must be constantly *updated* because people change psychologically, both individually and collectively. This is why more than one type of psychology is necessary. Each of these psychological theories contains a number of useful insights, but these insights cannot be integrated into a unity. This is not a source of contention for this undercurrent.

According to this view of psychology, *plasticity* (the freedom to shape one's psychological existence) and *rigidity* (lack of that freedom) also exist in an interesting relationship with each other: people have the ability to change themselves and, simultaneously, the ability to deny themselves this opportunity by forming habits. Simply put, to a certain degree people have the freedom to form their own mind and the freedom to imprison themselves within this form, to limit their psychological space. Cultural anthropological research has also demonstrated that this freedom is much greater that we normally think. In fact, the great diversity and rigidity of cultures and forms of society illustrate the extent of this freedom.

Religious traditions emphasize the idea of the *plasticity* of the human mind as well. According to these traditions, however, people almost always use this freedom incorrectly. They form certain egocentric habits in which, once formed, they are imprisoned. In the contemplative psychology of Buddhism, these patterns are called *samskaras*, mental conditionings (see, for example, Vasubandhu, book 1, verse 15), that together form the egocentric motivations of a human being and give direction to actions. In essence, they are mental habits in the form of grooves that are practiced and thereby become engraved. Once formed, it is difficult to change these grooves: they become *psychological patterns*.

Not only people but also psychology and an entire culture can become so convinced of the apparent inevitability of the formed patterns that they are viewed as absolute. When this happens they easily become part of a concept of humanity. We then say, "That's how human beings are." This concept of humanity subsequently influences the way in which people raise their children, thus closing the circle. When psychologists study and describe these people, they find *patterns* that confirm this concept of humanity. The conclusion is: "It has been scientifically confirmed. . . ." Within this vicious circle it is very difficult to unravel which is the cause and which is the result.

Religious traditions are concerned with identifying the *mental* habits (*patterns*) that are destructive and blinding in our lives, refusing to allow them to become even more ingrained, and permitting us to let go of them. Inasmuch as these mental habits are the cause of a certain behavior, that behavior also ceases. The spiritual way of life is therefore concerned with uncovering the basic mental freedom of (a) human being(s) — no longer imprisoned by self-made patterns. This is not so much for the sake of a sort of ideal of freedom or even for the sake of a (psychotherapeutic) ideal of health but to open up the mental space in which the Holy Spirit, the Buddha-nature, Allah, Yahweh, Brahma or whatever the particular tradition calls it operates or is able to operate. Formulated in the terminology of contemplative psychology, the contemplative life is directed toward opening a mental space in which our humaneness can flourish. Within this space, the human mind is governed by something other than the *patterns* that conventional psychology holds valid for *humankind*. In this contemplative development, freedom and health are not a goal but a kind of bonus. People who travel this path can no longer be described and explained satisfactorily by conventional psychology. Vergote, for example, illustrates this very clearly in his essay "Jezus van Nazareth in het licht van de godsdienstpsychologie" ("Jesus of Nazareth in the Light of the Psychology of Religion") (Vergote 1987, 31–62). He demonstrates that Jesus cannot be described or explained in terms of the psychology of religion with which we are familiar. The same holds, of course, for the human being on a contemplative path, albeit to a lesser degree. The further she or he goes on the Path, the less she or he can be understood in the terminology of conventional psychology.

In contrast, the religious traditions do so much better by means of their *own* psychological concepts! Why is this? It is because this psychology has an eye for the basic plasticity (freedom) of the human mind and aims at studying the extent of that freedom. It is because of this plasticity that something like a spiritual path exists. Being on the path can even be compared with molding the mind in a number of ways. We will discuss this in the next chapter.

The Objectivity of Research

The difference of opinion on the plasticity of the human mind is one cause for the tension present between much (but not all) of scientific psychology and religion. There are, however, other causes for this tension. One such cause is the fact that psychology as we know it in Western culture has disassociated itself from religion. In one respect, this disassociation was linked with the abandonment of the Christian concept of humanity. Because of this, a number of new *concepts of humanity* were able to develop within psychology — that is, a number of new definitions of the object of study in psychology. These new concepts of humanity deliberately leave out the spiritual dimension (see de Wit 1991, 19f.). This disassociation also offered room for the development of new methods for studying human life. A new *methodology* arose on how to acquire reliable knowledge with regard to human functioning. This methodology specifies an approach known as the *empirical method of research*. De Groot (1969) wrote a classic work on this method, which was originally grafted onto the natural sciences at the turn of the century and in the course of time has come to be applied to psychological research.

The empirical method is quite different from the methods used by the religious traditions for the development of insight into people. The essence of the empirical method is that it attempts to discover patterns between (psychological) phenomena that are *intersubjectively observable* — phenomena that can be observed by everyone. "Observed by everyone" is usually interpreted as that which involves the use of our senses, either with or without the help of technologically refined tools. In this sense, that which is studied is *independent of the researcher*. In practice, this means that the researcher must endeavor to design and conduct his research in such a way that the outcome is in no way influenced by his personal attitude and subjective experience. No matter who conducts the research, if it is conducted (correctly), the results are (should be) always the same. Only then can the results be regarded as *objective facts*. When scientific psychology studies religious phenomena it makes use of the empirical method as well. In that way, it has made an important contribution to the development of the psychology of religion: it has increased our insight into the causal relationships between religious and other (psychological) phenomena (see, for example, Paloutzian 1983).

Yet this methodology is the cause of a certain limitation within scientific psychology. As we will see below, there is a sizeable field that the empirical method of research must leave out — the field of one's own mental or inner life — because it is not *directly* accessible through this method. According to empirical psychology, this field is not independent of the researcher and therefore not open to empirical research. At the same time, it is precisely this field with which the religious traditions are concerned. The advantage of objectivity that the empirical method brings with it is countered by the loss of objectivity in another domain: direct observation of the domain of the mind, the world as experienced subjectively by humans falls outside its range of possible research. Disengaged from the domain of the mind, the remaining domains of speech and actions are cast in an artificial and distorted light. Of course, philosophers of science and scientific psychologists are aware of this but can see no possible solution. The dilemma entails the question of how mental phenomena can be studied without damaging the scientific, objective nature of the method of study. In contemplative psychology this dilemma is formulated somewhat differently, phrased in terms that also direct us toward a certain solution. Let us take a closer look at this point.

Research in the First and Third Persons

As we stated earlier, it is characteristic of the empirical method of research that it can and may be used only for the study of phenomena that are accessible to all researchers. In practical terms, this means that psychological research is restricted to *research in the third person*. What is meant by this term? It refers to the types of study in which individuals other than the researchers themselves are the object. The researchers study *him* and *her* and *them*. This type of study is characteristic of academic psychology, which is why it is usually engaged in the study of the behavior and speech of people, since that is what we can see of others. This is its field of study.

But there is yet another, quite large field: the field of the mind or experience or thought — in short, the field of mental phenomena, which is not accessible in the third person. This mental field is only directly accessible *by me*, that is, it is only accessible to *research in the first person*, to self-examination. After all, I can experience what is going on in *my* mind but not what is going on in someone else's mind.

If we truly wish to study the mental field, we can no longer

use the third-person approach of the empirical methodology. We must use a first-person approach, a form of self-
examination in which our own experience (and our thoughts
and emotions are a part of this!) is the object of study.

In contrast to scientific traditions, study in the first person is central in the spiritual traditions. For this reason many
of those traditions have also refined instructions at their disposal so that this first-person form of study may be conducted
in a thorough and reliable manner. In other words, these
traditions have a *first-person methodology.*

At the beginning of the twentieth century, scientific psychology rejected introspection as a method of research, leaving only research in the third person. Of course, it is possible
to learn (and sometimes also to conjecture by means of analo-
gies) something of what goes on in the minds of others but,
again, we cannot see directly what is happening in someone's mind like we can in our own. Moreover, what others
tell us about their mind or what we conjecture about them is
not always reliable. Distortion is possible when someone attempts to express what is "going on" within himself or herself. For example, in attempting to give expression to one's
feelings, language itself can fail. It is also possible for other
persons to *think* that they are saying what is going on inside
of themselves, whereas this is not the case. And finally, people can refuse to say what they think and choose to say something else instead.

This unreliability is the reason why the student of scientific psychology is reserved about research in which so-called
"self reports" are used as data. There is no guarantee that
the subjects (can or will) give an accurate report about their
mental field. About a century ago, introspective psychologists
like Wundt, Külpe and Titchener attempted to teach people
to be accurate, but these attempts yielded little or no results.
They led only to a conviction in scientific psychology that

stands to this day: reliable introspective research is impossible. For this reason there are few psychologists today who still try to devise reliable methods to study the realm of the mind. An interesting example of this in the Netherlands is the work of Hermans, et al. (1985).

Nonetheless, this conviction has led to a parting of the ways within psychology. On the one hand, it has led to the development of what we now call scientific psychology — a psychology based on the empirical method of research. This psychology attempts to *clarify our thinking about our experience* by testing our thoughts (theories) against our experience. On the other hand, it has led to forms of psychology that bear traces of the old psychology of consciousness. These psychologies attempt to *clarify our experience itself* by transforming our consciousness and our way of thinking. Examples are clinical psychology and many forms of psychotherapy. We will return to these two forms of clarification extensively in chapters four and six.

What is interesting is that according to many religious traditions human beings possess a mental discernment (a *discriminating awareness*) that allows them to clarify their experience — a capacity to distinguish between illusion and reality, self-deception and truth. As a rule, this discriminating awareness does not function adequately, but it can be cultivated. It can be trained in such a way that we are able to view our own mental domain clearly and to recognize patterns in it. Simply put, these traditions claim that we can explore and know our mind! On the basis of this we can also learn to identify the causal connections between what we think, say and do. Religious traditions claim to have the methods for this identification at their disposal. We will investigate them in detail in the second part of this book. These methods have been tested and refined by generations of practitioners and are effective if we train ourselves in them.

Just as the training of our intellectual or conceptual powers requires time, so also the training of our discriminating awareness requires time.

What is the nature of this training? First of all, its purpose is different from that of academic psychology. One could say that academic psychology aims at acquiring insight by collecting *information* about human functioning. Contemplative psychology aims at acquiring insight by bringing about a *transformation* of human functioning. It is, to use Van Kaam's (1983–92) terms, a *formative science*, whereas academic psychology is an *informative science*. Contemplative psychology is not directed exclusively at collecting knowledge in the form of information that is to be carried around like intellectual baggage but is directed at cultivating wisdom. It rather concerns a transformation of the one who acquires knowledge, the *knower*, rather than collecting knowledge. Just as Van Kaam does not reject the collecting of knowledge or information in his *Formative Spirituality*, neither do we. But within a contemplative psychology collecting information acquires a different function: only inasmuch as the collecting of intellectual knowledge or information has a transforming effect on the one who acquires it is it taken into account and studied. The transformation refers here specifically to the transformation of one's own mind in the direction of one's humaneness. So, once again we see here the first-person approach.

The idea behind this (we will return to this later) is, of course, that ignorance and mental blindness do not always arise from a lack of knowledge (or information) but because things escape our awareness or confuse us. If our mind is not clear, the result is a faulty or incorrect way of perceiving and thinking about people, including ourselves. This in turn leads to all kinds of confusing and conflicting emotions, which in turn affect our clarity of mind.

Because our state of mind also determines our experience

of reality, we can also say that contemplative psychology is concerned with clarifying our experience of reality. Spiritual traditions have developed special methods for this purpose — methods that are entirely different from those used by empirical psychology. They are methods directed at discovering and rising above our confusion and ignorance (see chapter four).

These methods are extremely varied, both within as well as between the various spiritual traditions. A factor common to all, however, is that they involve cultivating that which we can indicate as *perceptivity, attentiveness, alertness* or *consciousness*. In the first instance, we think perhaps of disciplines such as meditation, contemplation and prayer. Often these do form the "hard core" of the contemplative life. But there are also many other spiritual disciplines, since in principle *all* activities that require attention can be used to cultivate *alertness*. When these activities are practiced in the context of a spiritual discipline, then the emphasis shifts somewhat from *what* we do to *how* we do it. Suppose we have been assigned as a spiritual discipline the task of trimming the hedge or cleaning the hall every morning. What is important is not that the results be perfect but that we cultivate our attention while performing the task. And the test for this is, of course, whether the hedge is trimmed neatly or the hall is clean. If we are practiced gardeners, capable of trimming the hedge while on automatic pilot and able to daydream during this task, then trimming the hedge is not *per se* the most helpful discipline with which to begin.

What these examples demonstrate is that spiritual methods are *not determined by their external shape* but by the *internal* function that they entail for the practitioner. The empirical methods of scientific psychology can be defined in terms of their external shape, in terms of actions visible to everyone: the researcher posits a hypothesis about certain causal relationships in reality, conducts an experiment (whether in a laboratory or outside of it), manipulates the object of research in a certain way, notes the effects and tests whether or not they support the hypothesis. In contrast, the methods of first-person research that we find in the religious traditions consist of internal (that is, mental) actions, such as systematically directing one's attention, observing one's own patterns of thought, letting go of mental preoccupations, etc. Thus the actions involved are visible only to the researcher and not to others. It involves a first-person approach — a form of systematic exploration carried out in the hiddenness of our own mind. This is the type of research in which religious traditions specialize.

THE CONCEPT OF HUMANITY IN CONTEMPLATIVE PSYCHOLOGY

Scientific psychology and contemplative psychology also differ from each other on another essential point other than their methods of research: their concepts of humanity. By the term *concept of humanity* we mean the idea and collection of views that arise when we ask ourselves what the term *human being* refers to. That idea is not innocuous, because it determines the way in which we relate to people. We form a concept of people and respond from the perspective of that concept.

Human Beings as Objects

The concepts of humanity that we find in scientific psychology are also closely linked with the third-person approach. To a certain degree, they indicate the direction that scientific research can or should take. Concepts of humanity function as a kind of presupposition. An interesting, pioneering work on this is that by Shotter (1975). In scientific psychology, these concepts of humanity are most emphatically *not* based on self-investigation but on what the researcher sees people do and hears them say. The human being is here a third party, the other, a human being as the *object* of study. Its concept of humanity is a scientific version of the *concept of the other*.

Much of the psychological knowledge we use everyday is also based on what we (believe we) see in the people around us. In the way we usually think about people: people are often present as third persons, as *objects*, as the objects of our expectations, desires, thoughts, emotions, our hopes and fears — in short, the objects of our way of thinking and emotional life. All of these mental phenomena lead to the formation of a certain concept of humanity and, in turn, this concept functions as a starting point for our attempts to increase our understanding of human nature. It suggests the direction in which we should look if we want to have a better understanding of human behavior. Our concept of humanity can also be useful if we want to justify our behavior to others: "Because people behave the way they do, that is how they are; therefore, it makes sense for me to respond in the way that I do."

Of course, others in turn have ideas about us. We are also third persons to others, objects for the expectations of others. In this third-person approach, it is also useful to know what ideas others have about us because these ideas determine the behavior that is directed at us. If we know what those ideas are, then we can better judge whether our expectations about them can be fulfilled. Thus we have become *objects* for one another, objects of our mutual expectations, whether realistic or not. Our everyday psychology consists of the art of gauging one another's expectations and gearing them toward one another. Our concept of humanity is often of use to our psychological private politics, which is frequently a politics of (enlightened) self-interest directed at the satisfaction of our personal desires. Actually, we cannot speak of *knowledge* at this point with regard to our everyday psychology because we do not yet know whether the concepts that we hold about others and that others hold about us are correct. This requires systematic study, in which scientific psychology specializes.

We may take this third-person perspective one step further yet: not only can we attempt to gauge the ideas that others have about us but we can also *identify ourselves with* these ideas. We then see ourselves through the eyes of another, as it were, for whom we exist as third persons. This generates a form of *indirect self-knowledge* — "indirect" because the knowledge is second-hand, knowledge from others about ourselves, third-person knowledge. From the perspective of this indirect self-knowledge, we have become *objects* to ourselves. We view ourselves as objects. This indirect self-knowledge exists independently of the way in which we directly experience ourselves as *subjects*. That is why our *experience of ourselves* can also contradict our indirect self-knowledge, causing an inner conflict. Sometimes it seems like we have to enter into a kind of negotiating process with ourselves in order to achieve a "good relationship with ourselves." But there are also times when this indirect self-knowledge can help us to clarify our direct experience of ourselves. Much psychotherapy is based on this.

Human Beings as Subjects

The concepts of humanity that we find in contemplative psychology and also in some forms of psychotherapy have a different origin. These concepts of humanity arise from the *way in which people experience themselves*. Here the human being in the first person is central, and, in this case, the understanding of human nature is based on *direct self-knowledge*, that is, on knowledge that springs from direct observation of *ourselves*, from *self-experience*. This form of self-knowledge is firsthand knowledge, first-person knowledge, based not on "something we heard from others" but on direct observation. It is knowledge in the sense of *being acquainted with* and is not closely linked to concepts (see chapter four). Here as well, however, we cannot speak simply of *knowledge* because, again, we do not know if our observation of ourselves, our self-experience, is biased or not. This is why systematic exploration of our own mind, in which the religious traditions specialize, is necessary.

Direct self-knowledge does not only consist of the knowledge of phenomena that belong specifically to ourselves or our personal situation in life alone. Much of what we see in ourselves is not at all as strictly personal as we often think. Other people frequently experience the same things in themselves. Thus direct self-knowledge contains knowledge of *universally human* phenomena as well. Love or anger, for example, is something we all know from firsthand experience, and we are familiar with it as a first-person phenomenon, a personal experience. We assume that it is also a universally human phenomenon and that other people have had similar personal experiences. Thus our individual self-knowledge sometimes extends beyond ourselves. At times it can also be applied to other people and, in that sense, is knowledge about others. Thus our self-knowledge also broadens our knowledge of others. But this knowledge is an *indirect knowledge of others*, a kind of *empathic knowledge*. It is a form of first-person knowledge in which we see others *as if they are us*. The knowledge of people is in this case an extrapolation of our self-knowledge.

Obviously, *direct and indirect forms of self-knowledge* shape our *self-concept* — that is, the totality of the ideas and views that we have formed of ourselves. This concept of ourselves, especially where it refers to universally human phenomena within ourselves, again offers the basis for the development of a *concept of humanity*. In turn, both our *direct and our indirect knowledge of others* acquires shape in the *concept of the other*. And that concept can also form the basis for our concept of humanity.

Two Asymmetrical Concepts of Humanity

Practically speaking, then, there are *two sources* for the development of our concept of humanity: our *direct first-person knowledge* and our *direct third-person knowledge*. Because of the third-person approach used in conventional scientific psychology and in everyday psychology, the concept of humanity is usually formed on the basis of direct third-person knowledge. This knowledge also shapes our self-concept by means of indirect self-knowledge, by "what they say about me." In contrast, in contemplative psychology the concept of humanity is formed to a large degree on the basis of our experience of ourselves and the direct first-person knowledge derived from that experience.

Because the way in which we experience *ourselves* directly and the way in which we experience *others* directly are basically different, it is not that surprising that the concepts of humankind which arise from both sources are also very different. Our mind — our way of thinking and our emotional life — has a very important place in the way in which we experience ourselves. Of course, others also have an important place in our mind, but that place is fundamentally different from the place that we ourselves occupy: we do not know them as we know ourselves. We know that they have their own way of thinking as well, but that is not part of our direct experience. Other people have a place in *our* way of thinking and experience of reality just as we also have a place in *their* way of thinking, but their way of thinking and experience of reality still does not take place in us.

This asymmetry explains why, if we think and speak about people, we often have ideas that are very different from the ideas we have when we think and speak about ourselves. If we talk about people, they are *objects* for us, whereas we ourselves are *subjects*. For example, if we are regularly disappointed in the expectations we have of people or if they do not satisfy our (emotional) needs, we easily develop a negative concept of humanity. It takes little effort then to speak about "people" very negatively and with contempt. But usually this does not include ourselves or our conversational partner! If people fulfill our expectations, then a positive concept of humanity is fostered. Obviously, the converse is also possible: our concept of ourselves could influence our concept of humanity positively or negatively as well.

The Concept of Humanity as a Challenge

Our concept of humanity is an important factor in our attitude toward life. The spiritual traditions are conscious of this and explore how realistic our concept of humanity is. What if our expectations about people, including ourselves, stem from a lack of understanding and our desires from egocentricity? Will we not often then be disappointed by people and ourselves? And will our disappointment not be expressed in actions that will in turn disappoint others and confirm within them a negative concept of humanity?

Our concept of humanity, whether positive or negative, bears traces of our realistic and unrealistic expectations. It tells us something about ourselves, about the place that *we* give to others in *our* way of thinking and our emotional life. It is this phenomenon — more so than with the so-called "truth" of a concept of humanity — with which the religious traditions are concerned.

When someone asserts that people are basically good or

created in the image of God, it is not simply an assertion with which one can agree or disagree, but an appeal to ourselves — an appeal that challenges us to study thoroughly our expectations of ourselves and others and their effect on our concept of humanity. It is not a naive attempt to deny people's callousness but an appeal to locate and eliminate our *own* callousness and our *own* egocentricity and unrealistic expectations. The possibility then exists that our experience of ourselves will reveal a glimpse of something very fundamental about ourselves and, thereby, about human nature — a different perspective on people, one that the spiritual traditions endeavor to cultivate. In that perspective, we experience neither ourselves nor the other exclusively as an *object*, the object of our expectations and needs, but as a *subject*, a being within whom we can recognize, next to all his shortsightedness and callousness, humaneness. We then experience the other as much as possible as a first person — that is, as we experience ourselves. As far as we can experience the other as subject, the sharp distinction between subject and object becomes transparent. We are able to *identify with* the other. A feeling of relatedness, of fundamental connection begins to color our experience of the other and our concept of humanity. The degree to which we are capable of this is also the degree to which we are capable of loving our neighbor as ourselves. In concrete terms, this amounts to a deep change in our attitude toward life and our concept of humanity. According to some religious traditions, this way of experiencing can even develop into the ability for telepathy.

Thus, in living contemplatively the examination of our own humaneness does not remain confined to ourselves: it leads to the ability and the readiness of recognizing the humaneness of our fellow humans as well. This is not a theoretical matter, not a matter of good intentions; having good intentions is not enough. We need to practice spiritual disciplines that uncover our own humaneness — something that we scarcely believe in at times. Subsequently, we must also practice disciplines that open our eyes to the humaneness of others and teach us to approach others as we would ourselves: as beings who are as kind and sensitive as we are, although they are also (just as we are) dominated by blindness, egocentricity, aggression, fear of life and disappointment about people, about themselves and possibly about life in general. Nearly all the great spiritual traditions provide such disciplines.

Humaneness and the Concept of Humanity

Is it possible to let go of our unrealistic expectations and the concept of humanity that arises from them? Is it not (too) much to ask for a development in this direction? Certainly, if we have a firmly established concept of humanity that, in our view, is based on years of experience with people. Nevertheless, there is a gateway for this development, a gateway that can be found within a human being in the first person, that is, in our experience of ourselves.

Our experience of ourselves contains aspects that we sometimes find difficult to recognize in others. More strongly, we sometimes become aware of these aspects precisely because we are unable to recognize them in others. When someone treats us in a way that we consider (whether correctly or not) callous or shortsighted, we simultaneously experience our own (injured) kindness and insight and vice versa. We are not robots but people, and people are only able to recognize callousness and suffering *because* they are sensitive beings. It is because people have a sense of justice that they are able to recognize injustice. Even when we do something that others consider depraved, there are times we cannot deny we are trying to attain some good, albeit in a clumsy or shortsighted way. We nevertheless try (although not always) to make the best of it. We do not mean any harm. Even when we do mean harm and set out to harm others intentionally, the fact that we know how to do so also indicates that we are aware of what is beneficial. That awareness is an unconditional part of us, in our good moments as well as our bad moments. The desire to cause chaos, confusion and suffering implies that we are cognizant of harmony, clarity and happiness, and the converse is also true. We are aware of both sides through experience: in addition to our most negative and destructive moments, we also have moments of kindness, happiness, tenderness and devotion, moments of appreciation, love and compassion as well as moments of genuine insight and understanding. Such moments are not accidental or coincidental but, in spite of all the negativity that we experience in ourselves, are a part of our being, even though they may last only for a short time and "others are not aware of them." When we examine ourselves it is very difficult, if not impossible, to deny the existence of such moments. They characterize our humaneness and may be incorporated into our concept of ourselves *and* our concept of humanity.

But it is also possible that we banish moments of genuine concern and understanding from our consciousness because, for example, they do not fit in with the concept of ourselves or the concept of humanity that we have already formed. Perhaps we have formed a very negative concept of ourselves on the basis of negative indirect self-knowledge or on the basis of seeing our own egotism. Instead of realizing that the moments in which we are *aware* of our own callousness and short-sightedness are actually moments of compassion and insight *because we are aware of them*, we are so overwhelmed by our callousness and shortsightedness that that is all we can see. Our want of humaneness and the disappointment about this can overshadow our moments of insight and compassion. In this way, our contact with our humaneness gradually fades and, ultimately, we no longer believe that we possess it. We become our own enemy and fear this enemy. Our attempts to deal with this enemy acquire the form of an increasingly bitter struggle. Even if this struggle takes on religious clothing ("armor" would be a better word if we are talking about our heroic struggle against our negativity!), it leads only to our self-destruction. Our spiritual health is in danger. This is not the path to which genuine spiritual traditions point. That path begins with a renewed and frank look at who or what we are at this very moment. There is room for what we have called our negative and positive aspects in this look. We turn back to our experience of ourselves and explore it with the help of the contemplative disciplines. In other words, we start where we are (Chödrön 1993).

Like the concept of humanity in scientific psychology, which stems from the third person, the concept of humanity in contemplative psychology as well as that of much psychotherapy stems from the first person, from our experience of ourselves. This is why, in the concept of humanity in third-person psychology, all of those mental phenomena which are so important in our self-experience and which determine our lives almost never come up for consideration. The possibility and impossibility of experiencing our humaneness, love and hate, devotion and self-exaltation, insight and self-deception are not discussed. In contemplative psychology, these phenomena are essential, for they are directly linked to the inner flourishing of our humaneness.

CONCEPTS OF HUMANITY: CORRECT OR EFFECTIVE?

The problem with concepts of humanity is that one cannot prove whether a certain concept is correct — one can only note its effects in what one does and does not do. Thus, although these concepts have arisen through experience with people, they have, as it were, transcended and separated from such experience and have acquired the status of universal ideas which, together with related concepts, such as those of self, the world and God, play a large role in our world of thought. They have become, to use a philosophical term, *metaphysical* notions. At the same time, however, they do guide our actions, influencing our behavior and the way in which we interpret and assess behavior and situations.

The spiritual traditions have always had an eye for the psychological consequences of these concepts. These traditions are interested not so much in whether such concepts of humanity are *correct* as in the consequences that the *belief in their correctness* has for contemplative growth. And, as we shall see, there are definite consequences. Together with our concepts of the world and of God, they determine our attitude towards and experience of reality.

Scientific psychology also maintains certain concepts of humanity as starting points — concepts of humanity that follow naturally from its third-person form of research. The most well known are the *utilitarian* and *hedonistic* concepts of humanity. What these terms mean can be stated as follows. According to the utilitarian concept of humanity, a person seeks profit and avoids loss: all thoughts, words and actions of people are ultimately guided by striving for that which one wants and avoiding or destroying that which one does not want. According to the hedonistic concept of humanity, people are "pleasure-seekers": human beings seek that which gives pleasure and avoid that which causes suffering. It is ultimately this that guides all one's action. This concept of humanity is found in *behaviorist* and in modern *cognitive psychology* as well as in Freud's *depth psychology*. The problem with these concepts of humanity is that they are presented respectively as the explanation for *all* human action. In itself, striving for profit or pleasure is a very human activity: people do so quite often. Whether the psychology be conventional or contemplative, it must also recognize and acknowledge this striving — but it is something else again to claim that all human actions can be explained by this striving.

These concepts of humanity also play a large role in everyday psychology. We could characterize them as *materialistic concepts of humanity*. In materialistic approaches, all aspects of life are viewed as if they were material goods which we can grasp, reject or destroy. If well-being, wisdom, love, hate, suffering, health, youth, age and such are viewed as material goods of one kind or another, we attempt either to acquire and hold on to them or to avoid and destroy them like we do with material goods. We are then, as we saw in the introduction to this book, attempting to apply a strategy on a level on which it does not work. This is, of course, a source of suffering. Our youth cannot be grasped and hoarded nor can suffering be cut into pieces and destroyed.

As we stated earlier, concepts of humanity are metaphysical notions and, as such, they cannot be refuted by recourse to facts. Allow me to illustrate this by means of the hedonistic concept of humanity. From the perspective of this concept of humanity, the spiritual way of life can always be interpreted as a way of life that is motivated by the search for pleasure and avoidance of suffering. Suppose that John has chosen to enter upon a spiritual path because he believes this way of life can help him find the truth (whatever that may be). A hedonistic concept of humanity does not admit of such a motivation and will instead explain his choice as arising from the fact that he finds it pleasant — it satisfies him. From John's perspective, however, other factors come into play. After all, there are times when the contemplative life does not appeal to him at all and, moreover, he will maintain that seeking pleasure is not one of his priorities. He is not interested in that at all; his concern is to find wisdom, to find truth. But the hedonist psychologist is not to be put off by

one obstacle: he can continue to maintain that John has chosen to seek truth because he likes it. John can then explain
that his basic motivation for practicing the contemplative
life has much more to do with the discovery that his life and
the lives of others are dominated by a serious kind of blindness and callousness — a blindness and callousness that may
be *comfortable* (which is something that the hedonist likes
to hear) but at the same time causes us to be completely
unrealistic. And he can add that he is motivated by the desire for truth even if it causes him pain. The hedonist psychologist will then say: "I know all about it. We call it *delayed
need satisfaction*. Ultimately, you assume that the truth will
be pleasant; otherwise you would not seek it. You are not a
masochist, I hope?" And John, somewhat hurt, will lash out:
"My search is unconditional! It is not tied to hopes and fears,
pleasure or suffering, profit or loss. Only if you seek in this
way will you find!" But the hedonistic interpretation leaves
no room for the authenticity of a power like the search for
truth. This power is constantly reinterpreted as the search
for pleasure and the avoidance of suffering and therefore
viewed as nonexistent or illusory.

We could tell the same story, replacing the hedonist with
a utilitarian psychologist, who assumes that John seeks the
truth because he believes it will benefit him. And if John
should say, "I want to seek the truth even if I am hurt by it,"
a utilitarian psychologist could still maintain that John is so
perverse and confused that he sees profit in loss!

No real dialogue takes place here because the starting
points do not share any common ground. Nevertheless, these
starting points play a role in the dialogue between materialistic psychology and contemplative psychology. In the view
of the contemplative traditions, materialistic psychologies are
profane psychologies: they are based on a concept of humanity that allows no room for a spiritual or religious dimension

as an authentic power. Therefore, the objections that the contemplative traditions have against academic psychology are
not only directed at the *method* of academic psychology but
also at the materialistic concept of humanity that, intentionally or unintentionally, is a factor in many of its theories.
Not only does the materialistic concept of humanity impov-
erish our human existence but adhering to it also prevents
us from seeing the relativity of this concept of humanity and
freeing ourselves from it.

Concepts of Humanity as Gauges

Concepts of humanity have an entirely different function
within the contemplative traditions. Here they do not function as theoretical presuppositions but as gauges for the development of the mentality of people on the Way. Concepts of
humanity are not fixed notions but change in relation to the
contemplative development. The concept of humanity that
we have now is a creation and therefore an expression of our
mind as it is now. It concurs with a certain phase in our experience of ourselves and our experience of reality. Thus the
contemplative life is concerned with becoming conscious of
these concepts of humanity, recognizing them and transforming them in a direction that causes our fundamental humaneness to flourish. Its concern is not to provide a *different and
more correct concept of humanity* or a new *ideology* but to
offer a concept of humanity that awakens a concrete *experience of our fundamental humaneness* within us. That experience itself is not a theory or a presupposition.

To that end, it is inevitable that we come face to face with
aspects of ourselves and others that are callous and shortsighted. If we should be asked at that moment what kind of
concept of humanity we have, it would be relatively negative. Rather than constituting a problem, entertaining such
a concept is a necessary stage along the Path: there must be

room to recognize and study negativity. After all, negativity is a part of us.

Precisely because it is a stage, we do not, however, see our negative concept of humanity as absolute. If we did so, we would certainly become depressed. Because it is relative, something that we can let go at any moment or place in a broader perspective, viewing our negativity (sin, sinfulness or whatever we want to call it) is a step — as inspiring as it is painful — along the contemplative way. When we find the courage to see our negativity clearly, another aspect is simultaneously revealed: namely, that we have the ability to face our negativity. Apparently, this clarity of mind is also a part of us. We do not have a heart of stone, even though we may have thought so at times. Is it not precisely because we are gentle in heart that harshness hurts us? Is our suffering not the expression of frustrated joy in life? Our negative self-concept and our concept of humanity ends up, as it were, in a broader context, thereby losing its depressing characteristics without forcing us to deny our negativity. Thus an entirely different, much more nuanced self-experience arises that also changes our concept of humanity: we discover that we can deal with our negativity in a very productive way, that our negativity is not our destiny but a challenge. At this stage we discover that it is, as Buddhism expresses it (see Trungpa 1969, 19ff.), like manure: it has a ghastly smell, but it is fertile — it is useful to spread it over the field of the *bodhi* (the enlightened state of mind). In Christian terms, we could say that the farmer who works this field is an individual who is created in the image of God. This view of our humanity is now brought more into the foreground. So, the concept of humanity that is progressively formed along the spiritual path is based on concrete experience — experience that rises far above the negative concept of humanity that we often initially perceive as our inevitable destiny.

THE VALUE OF DIALOGUE

We have seen that contemplative psychologies and the psychologies with which we are familiar (both in their scientific and everyday versions) differ from each other on fundamental points. This is exactly why contemplative psychologies have something to say to us. They offer their psychological insights and their own methods of research. Perhaps one contemplative tradition has developed its psychological insights somewhat more than another and possibly one tradition places somewhat more emphasis on them than another, but in all cases we find *universal* insights into human experience and the human mind — insights that nowadays are called psychological. This is not so surprising for, although there are major differences in the *theology* of the great religions, religions are always practiced by human beings. Whatever the culture or period into which people are born, they all have two eyes and two hands. They all have a human mind. Thus there is a very broad, common ground: all people must deal with such fundamental concerns as fear of and joy in life, compassion and callousness, insight and ignorance. And greed, jealousy and aggression as well as their opposites emerge among people of all cultures. The objects toward which these emotions and attitudes are directed are, of course, different but the psychology of the profane or materialistic way of being exists in other cultures just as it does in our own. It is for this reason, therefore, that all great world religions attempt to transform or liberate that way of being. This is also why the contemplative way of life can be found in all cultures.

All contemplative psychologies ask what happens to an individual along the contemplative way and how he or she can watch out for pitfalls and dead ends. To answer this question we must look closely at the human being from the first-person perspective, as we will in chapter three. We will have to explore how the profane, egocentric mentality and the accompanying psychology arises and continues to exist. How does the individual maintain his or her state of "brokenness" from day to day or even from moment to moment? How does he or she do this and why?

Of course, we could avoid these practical questions by, for example, placing the rise of the profane mentality in a historical context. Then it becomes something that happened in the past and which we are now powerless to fight against. Formulated in Christian terms, people were driven out of Paradise when they fell into sin. Such a historical interpretation then immediately compels additional historical interpretations — for example, that Jesus at one time, about 2,000 years ago, took away the sin of humankind.

We also find historical interpretations in other religions. And yet these interpretations do not affect the core of those religions, i.e., the core that is important to those who live a contemplative life. They do not affect our personal and daily experiences in life; they are ideologies rather than instruments by means of which we can find traces of our egocentric experience of reality. This is why the contemplative life puts more emphasis on a psychological interpretation. Thus within the Christian tradition one can, for example, view the Fall as something that takes place each and every moment again and again and, *in principle*, can also be undone each and every moment. From this point of view, the Kingdom of God is not something that is far from us but something that we tend to hold at a great distance from us again and again. When we are capable of allowing Christ into our hearts or of discovering Christ, then we can work with our sin: our heart then becomes so spacious that it is capable of taking up our sin. This is a Christian formulation of this problem, but the same theme can be expressed just as well in terms of the other great religions. This has been clearly revealed by interreligious dialogue in recent years.

Stated in contemplative psychological terms, our fundamental humaneness is never actually absent but can be made to flourish and that which obscures it, our negativity, is not only not fundamental but can also be overcome. This is the concern of the practice of every spiritual discipline. This view is the foundation of the contemplative way and we also encounter it, although in other terms, in a great many traditions.

With the notion that such a flourishing is possible, the spiritual traditions knowingly fly directly in the face of the profane concept of humanity found in materialistic psychology. With this, they also oppose the depressing and destructive view of people, which sees the fulfillment of human happiness in the satisfaction of desires. This is why the spiritual traditions are a provocative as well as valuable partner for the dialogue with our conventional psychology and with every materialistic culture.

Of course, contemplative insights are often embedded in a religious way of thought and terminology. For example, the Christian tradition states that people are made in the image of God, whereas the Mahayana Buddhist tradition asserts that people possess Buddha-nature. Without further explanation, such statements can often lead to misunderstanding among regular psychologists and laypeople. This is why a dialogue between theology and contemplative psychology is also needed. That dialogue can help us to see through worn or seemingly inaccessible theological and religious packaging. In this way, we can discover whether certain religious concepts and faith statements function with respect to cultivating the flourishing within and, if so, how.

In the dialogue with theology, however, we must not forget that contemplative psychology, like all psychology, is anthropocentric, whereas theology is obviously theocentric. A *theological psychology* does not exist; it is a contradiction in terms. Contemplative psychology does deal with people — people who might well experience their reality from a theocentric perspective. Allow me to add immediately that the term *anthropocentric* must not be confused with the term *egocentric*. Contemplative psychology is not an egocentric psychology but it is, as we will see, a psychology that studies our egocentrism and offers various means for transforming it. What this means will be discussed in the following chapter.

Two

Experiencing Reality and the Spiritual Path

INTRODUCTION

We have frequently referred above to the *Path*. The Way or the Path is a very universal metaphor encountered again and again in the great world religions. The term *journey* is also used to indicate actual progress along the Way. In this chapter, we will examine what this metaphor has to tell us. We will first look at a number of fundamental aspects that the meaning of the metaphor itself entails. Next, we will explore what appears to be the essence of the reference of the metaphor: the constantly changing *experience of reality*. Finally, we will make a few comments on the limits suggested by the metaphor of the Path.

ASPECTS OF THE METAPHOR OF THE PATH

What does this metaphor mean? Why is the use of this metaphor so widespread? The first reason is that the contemplative life or spirituality has to do with the *develop-ment* of our being human in a certain *direction*. The spiritual traditions point to this direction: they claim that they are able to show us the Path. Secondly, the metaphor suggests a *continually changing perspective* on the landscape. We will discuss this suggestion below in terms of the *changing expe-rience of reality*. Thirdly, the metaphor also suggests that there are *stages along the way* and that it is possible to obtain guidance and guides. We will return to this in the chapters below. Finally, the idea of a way or path suggests *a certain constraint*: a path is bounded by sides, and we can wander from the path or stay on it. The two sides also suggest that one can speak of a double-sided development (see below).

With regard to the first point, the notion of direction, we may ask: to what does this refer? Some say that life itself is a journey, regardless of whether we belong to a religious tra-dition or not: is our passage from the cradle to the grave not a journey? The spiritual traditions, of course, do not deny this, but their message refers to yet another journey that we as humans can make — a journey whose beginning and end are different from those of our biologically determined jour-ney through time. This journey can lead in different direc-tions: a direction in which we become entangled in the grip of callousness, shortsightedness and fear of life or one in which kindness and insight, joy in life and wisdom increas-ingly guide our attitude.

The essence of this message is that we need not leave the direction and progress of this journey entirely to chance. It is possible to live in such a way that the realities of life — birth, sickness, old age, death, interaction with our environ-ment, one another and ourselves — make us gentle rather than callous, do not compel us to stick our heads in the sand out of fear but make us more realistic, more honest. This is a hopeful message. In the following chapters we will consider, from various perspectives, the question of whether this message is in itself realistic or not.

The Viability of the Path

Development toward compassion and wisdom in life has to do with the development of a basic attitude to life *as a whole*, that is, inclusive of its adversity and prosperity, its happiness and sorrow. It has to do with the creation or discovery of a certain mental space, a fundamental *magnanimity* or mental openness that gives insight and ennobles ourselves and our fellow beings.

That it is actually possible to uncover such a space in our own concrete existence and to continue to develop it is the inspiration for the contemplative life. At bottom, this inspiration does not arise from what we see as our final goal nor from our circumstances in life but from each step that we actually take along the Path. Such steps show us that the Path is actually viable and that the obstacles we encounter can be overcome. Thus the metaphor of traveling along the Path does not refer, as is sometimes thought, to a life in which the satisfaction of needs is delayed. The delayed satisfaction of needs is simply not a strong enough motivation for bringing about a real transformation. Moreover, it is easy for us to ignore ourselves if we are fixed on a certain goal. We then tend to dream about that goal and do not keep in touch with our actual situation in life, that is, *ourselves as we are*. Instead, we dream about ourselves as we would like to be. So, even though the Path leads to a realization or fulfillment, reconciliation, liberation or whatever the tradition calls it, in practice that final goal does not function as the source of inspiration. The inspiration lies in the progress that we make in the way we deal with our everyday circumstances, both good as well as bad.

In religious terms, the theistic traditions speak of the restoration of our relationship with God or the divine. Journeying along the Path, then, is often phrased in terms of obedience to God. But it is not necessary for this kind of inspiration to be understood in religious terms *per se*. After all, it has to do with the development of something that belongs to our being human. In contemplative psychological terms, we could describe this development as a liberation from all of those attitudes and views that cause us to be callous, defensive and blind to the realities of our lives and to reality as a whole. This development is central to the great religions and is thus also the focus of the spiritual way of life, in both its monastic and secular forms.

We will return later to the question of the degree to which such a development is a matter of human action or grace. I wish to stress here only that all spiritual disciplines of the contemplative life (the mental exercises, the performance of work and study) are practiced in order to give our fundamental humaneness space and to cultivate it in our speech and actions. It is possible and inspiring. People are capable of doing this, as attested in all times and cultures, although it cannot be achieved without pain and effort.

The Sides of the Path

The metaphor of the Path also includes the idea of certain borders or constraints. After all, a path has two sides that serve as borders on the left and the right. These borders point to the spiritual practices that place certain restrictions on us, a certain form of discipline that influences the cultivation of our mind and our actions. With respect to the mind, it is chiefly the development of insight into life or wisdom that is involved; with respect to actions, it is the cultivation of mercy, compassion or love. Mercy or compassion refer here not only to feeling but to *actual* mercy, that is, mercy *in speech and actions*. Thus we could also interpret the left and righthand sides of the Path respectively as the *side of insight* and the *side of loving care*.

This interpretation also emphasizes that in the actual progress along the Path there is *simultaneous* growth in insight and in mercy. We cannot travel the spiritual path without having these two sides. We need them in order to stay on course. In concrete terms, growth in genuine insight is accompanied by growth in one's dedication to one's fellow human beings and, conversely, genuine care is bound to give us insight. The reason for this is simply that care turns us toward reality, and we can see everything to which we turn more clearly than that from which we turn away or wish to keep at a distance. The converse is also true: insight leads to understanding and understanding leads to loving care and compassion. It has been said that to understand everything is to forgive everything. It is very striking that we find both aspects continually emphasized in the great religious traditions — but not as opposites. We cannot practice the one without the other.

And yet insight and loving care are viewed by some as opposites and are even sometimes pitted against each other, as if they were two distinct ways: a pure *mental* way of insight and, in contrast, a practical way of care, love of neighbor and charity. Sometimes both ways are linked with the idea of a *vertical* religiosity (directed towards God) and a *horizontal* one (directed towards human beings). Social action (working towards a better world) is then viewed as distinct from — and therefore placed on a plane other than — the transformation of our profane experience of reality. At most, the practitioner is urged to balance these two different dimensions. But the image of two perpendicular dimensions suggest a false opposition. The lines are not perpendicular but parallel. Some years ago, H.M. Kuitert made a number of comments well worth our consideration on the danger of the Christian tradition *going off the rails* if it ignores "the fundamental question of the perspective in which that work of making our world worth living in is to be placed" (Kuitert 1993, 216).

It is this pairing of insight and loving kindness that makes us capable of actually dealing with moments when we must intervene, even if the intervention is painful and results in tears. If we attempt to cultivate both aspects independently of each other we run the risk of developing *shortsighted care* as well as *callous insight*. When we act out of shortsighted care, or *blind compassion* as it is called in the Buddhist tradition, we often only help people go from bad to worse. We may behave in a very friendly and tolerant way, but we do so at the wrong moments with the result that we cause rather than prevent suffering. Callous insight may help us to see more clearly the shortcomings, sins and other such things in ourselves and others, but we are not capable of dealing with them in a caring, compassionate way that leads to their disappearance. Rather, we become enmeshed in an increasingly aggressive struggle against *evil* in ourselves and others. This is pouring oil on the fire. Insight without compassion is like a sharp sword wielded by an uncompassionate hand.

Thus, even though loving care and insight develop simultaneously just as the two sides of a way run parallel, there is still this difference between them: insight is something that grows within us and, in a certain sense, is concealed from others. Conversely, growth in care or compassion is visible to others. Through this visible growth, it is possible to perceive in an indirect way whether the flourishing within with respect to insight is real or imaginary: a tree is known by its fruit. Effective charity and care is the visible fruit of a flourishing within and, at the same time, this fruit is the seed of the flourishing within.

THE PATH AS A CHANGING EXPERIENCE OF REALITY

Another aspect of the metaphor of the Path is that it entails a continually changing perspective on the landscape. Of course, it is not only our perspective that changes. The landscape itself changes, whether we are traveling or not. Here, the "landscape" is a metaphor for the events in our lives, the continually changing situations in which we find ourselves. Thus we have two sorts of changeability: the (external) changeability of our concrete situation in life and the (inner) changeability of our shifting perspective on it.

The spiritual traditions are preeminently concerned with that shifting perspective on our situation in life, for this perspective determines how we *perceive* the events of our lives. Moreover, this perspective and the way in which it shifts differ with every individual. Two people involved in the same event each experience it in their own way. We know all of this from our daily lives, although we still do not know how *consequential* this fact is from moment to moment.

If we now ask what actually "travels along the path," we could say that it is our *experience of reality*. This concept is a basic notion of contemplative psychology. What makes the term *experience of reality* such a useful term for contemplative psychology is the fact that the word *experience* highlights the subjective side of what is happening while the word *reality* emphasizes its objective side. The construction gives a good indication that that which we experience as real is something that is *subjective* but experienced as *objective*. On close inspection, the reality in which we live is, in fact, reality as we experience it *personally*. This reality is *relative* to us, although in terms of our daily lives we regularly lose sight of this fact. We experience our situation as if it were not relative but *absolute* in the sense of being objective and independent of ourselves. This is why, instead of the term *experience of reality*, we could also use terms like *relative, subjective* or *personal* (in the sense of *individual*) *reality*. The articulation and communication of our personal reality to others might give rise to an *intersubjective* experience of reality that people share with one another but it remains dependent on the individual and, in that sense, relative.

For many people, including philosophers and psychologists, the story ends here. They view the unmistakable relativity of our experience of reality as a fact that cannot be tampered with. Their final conclusion is: "All experience is interpreted experience." In other words, in their experience of reality the fact that we live in a relative reality has become an absolute given, an indisputable fact. At most, we can attempt to understand one another's relative realities to some degree, to grasp them by means of what is called *hermeneutics*. Hermeneutics is the science of explanation, of interpretation. The possibility of a stance or, better yet, a *mental space* within which our experience of relative reality is completely exposed so that its relativity is visible in detail then and there is rarely acknowledged. As a consequence, the possibility of a mental development that would allow us to see, and see through this relativity, is not acknowledged, either.

This, too, is quite different from the spiritual traditions. These traditions not only acknowledge this relativity but also assert that humans possess and are able to develop a discriminating awareness that allows them to discover and completely eliminate the blinding effect of this relativity. For the spiritual traditions, therefore, this relativity is not an *absolute* given to which we should resign ourselves but a *factual* characteristic of the blinded individual. Many spiritual disciplines are therefore directed at developing a *clarity of mind* that enables us to discover where and when this relativity in our experience of reality happens and how to free ourselves from it. Thus the recognition of relativity here neither leads to a "worldly" despondency nor remains an intellectual relativism. Rather, it is an incitement to travel along the spiritual path.

Experience of Reality Along our Way of Life

Let us attempt to make this possibly rather abstract concept *experience of reality* more concrete by means of some examples. Let us look at an earlier phase in our life — our childhood, for example. If we look back at our experience of reality as a child, in as far as we remember it, there were certain aspects present that gave our experience a sense of reality — trusted and familiar (though not necessarily always pleasant) aspects that acted as buttresses for our childish experience of reality: the way our house smelled, certain corners in the room where we played, perhaps the open door to the garden, certain objects such as the large vase with sunflowers on the dresser, our mother's box of buttons, the bear that we took to bed and, *last but not least,* our parents themselves, the sound of their voices, the way in which they moved and held our hand. And all of those were immediately surrounded by the house with the sidewalk as a boundary beyond which we were not allowed to go by ourselves. Together, these aspects formed the reality in which we lived. Some of them were so important to us that our reality would have collapsed if they disappeared. These foundational elements therefore also formed the object of our anxieties and delights, our hopes and fears. If our mommy or daddy stayed away too long, we were scared that they might never return. Then we felt (our existence) threatened. Or we could not sleep if our teddy bear was missing. All these certainties and uncertainties that belong to childhood formed the world of experience that we perceived then as reality: our childish experience of reality.

Let us look at our experience of reality on the basis of a classic North American example. As children, most of us believed in Santa Claus. This produced a certain experience of reality around Christmas. Everything was permeated by it and directed at it. This childish experience of reality no longer exists for us now because we no longer believe in Santa Claus; we now see that he is simply a man dressed in a costume. Our awareness of what reality is, i.e., what is real and not real, has changed. The person dressed in a costume is more real to us now than Santa Claus is. In this respect, at least, we have become more realistic, and this can be seen in our behavior.

The question asked by contemplative psychology is, of course: how many Santa Clauses have we held on to in a metaphorical sense? Perhaps we still view every day as the 25th of December with different illusions but ones that are just as powerful as those which played a role in our childish experience of reality around Christmas: illusions about birth, parenting, society, sickness, old age and death. Nor should we forget illusions about ourselves. Even if we are academically trained psychologists, theologians or philosophers, there is no guarantee that we are not subject to all kinds of illusions in our daily (including our professional) lives — illusions that determine our experience of reality with all their emotional reactions and the ways of acting that follow in their wake.

In any case, we know that our childhood world is gone. We no longer live in that world. And yet, when that world did exist, it was absolute reality for us, actual and real. If we look back now, we realize that it was a *relative reality* — relative to our mode of experience as a child. The elements to which we then held on in order to maintain our sense of reality have lost their function. Our teddy bear no longer comforts us and our mother's hand has long been replaced by other buttresses. When we look back to our puberty or young adulthood, we see that the buttressing elements, the building blocks of our experience of reality, have been changing constantly. Those realities were relative as well.

Of course, we have not yet reached the end of this development: what we experience as reality now will be gone in the course of time. There will then be other aspects from which we will derive our sense of reality and orientation. The reality in which we live from day to day now is also relative to the way of experiencing that is peculiar to us *now*. The problem is that it is difficult for us to see at this time exactly *where* that relativity is and just *how extensive* it is.

The Experience of Reality Along the Spiritual Path

Why are the above examples that illustrate the relativity of our experience of reality in our life significant? Their significance is due to the fact that the contemplative traditions are primarily interested in the development of our experience of reality. But their interest does not involve so much the transformation of our childish experience of reality into a more mature form as the fact that our experience of reality can develop in a direction that makes us wilt mentally — a direction that makes us callous and defensive, increases our shortsightedness and fear of life, thereby causing endless suffering for us and our fellow human beings — or in the opposite direction — the direction of an internal flourishing — within which the visible fruits in our speech and actions are those that the contemplative traditions seek to ripen. When we go in this direction — either within or outside of the context of a religious tradition — we find ourselves on the Path of the contemplative life.

In spiritual terms, this concerns the transformation of our *profane experience of reality* into a *sacred experience of reality* — a development to which many traditions refer as a (continuing) *conversion*. This conversion is also characterized as the transformation of a *materialistic* attitude towards life into a *spiritual* one. In more philosophical terms, one can refer to *appearance* and *reality* or also, as Lacan does, of *the imaginary (l'imaginaire)* and *the real (le réel)*. The nature of appearance is to present itself as reality (see, for example, IJsseling 1990). The contemplative transformation concerns freeing ourselves from *appearance*, i.e., fictions, self-deception and illusions, by learning to see them for what they are. Another both philosophical and contemplative formulation is one that uses the terms *relative reality* and *absolute reality* or, as abbreviations, *the relative* and *the absolute*. Progress along the Path means that we learn to recognize and let go of our *relative reality* as such. In this way, we begin to live more and more within *absolute reality*. In contemplative psychological terms, we speak of the *egocentric experience of reality* and the *egoless experience of reality*. We use these terms in a spiritual sense as well: we can see our egocentric experience of reality for what is it only from an egoless perspective.

These terminological pairs, however, easily lead us to believe the misleading suggestion that we must abandon the one and embrace the other. But we do not, in fact, really go anywhere. Nor, in the *contemplative sense*, do these pairs refer to two different areas. They do not form an *opposition* but are each other's *complement*; they entail each other in the same sense that the separate terms of conceptual pairs like pleasures and unpleasures entail each other in Derrida's thought (cf. Bennington and Derrida 1993, 141–42). Thus, concepts such as the absolute and the relative, appearance and reality are also *relative concepts*, as the Madhyamaka philosophy of Buddhism also asserts (see, for example, Inada, 1970). This is a typical spiritual insight, and it is therefore important to know what the transformation of our relative reality into absolute reality means. It means that our experience of reality, which initially *appeared* to be absolute reality, later turns out to be relative. A typical contemplative twist (see also de Wit 1991, 53) is that the moment when we no longer see our relative reality as absolute but recognize it for what it is *is* the experience of absolute reality. Thus the pairs of terms refer *not to two different realities* but to one and the same reality viewed from two different perspectives.

Yet, whatever terms we use for the mental transformation at which the spiritual traditions are directed, they always refer to a change in our experience of the concrete events in our lives — a change that leads to the flourishing of our fundamental humaneness. Thus the image of stages that follow one another, suggested by the metaphor of the Way or Path, represents a *sequential experiencing of reality* that carries us further and further away from a development that chokes our joy in life, our compassion and clarity of mind.

Such a development is, of course, no small matter. After all, our experience of reality does include *all* aspects of our lives. Our emotional life, our way of thinking, our expectations and memories, our mental values, our concepts of ourselves, of humanity, of the world and of God — all these internal aspects are just as much a part of this development as our external circumstances in life. And because we perceive our experience of reality as real, letting go of it seems like letting go of reality itself — a form of mental suicide that can only lead to our downfall or to psychosis. This is why we often prefer to change our external circumstances rather than our way of experiencing them. For example, we tend to destroy or acquire the *objects* of our aggression or greed rather than give up our aggression or greed. That often seems the only possible way for us to live. But it can cause us to adhere to certain ways of experiencing even though we (rationally) know better and understand that these ways of experiencing are harmful to us or to others. The power or motivation to let go of a destructive way of experiencing reality often escapes us precisely because we cannot recognize its illusory, relative nature.

As we stated above, the contemplative traditions are directed primarily at a transformation of our *experience* of reality and not at a transformation of reality. Both are distinct from each other *and* are connected with each other. What I mean is this: the more transparent our perspective on (our) reality becomes, the more mental freedom we have to work with our circumstances. Within that freedom lies an element of increasing selflessness because our desires and interests have also become more transparent. In this way more room is created for a less compulsive and more open way of working with our circumstances in life. This selfless openness unlocks possibilities, but, one may ask, possibilities for what? These are possibilities for changing something in our reality for the well-being of all. Thus the transformation of our experience of reality becomes manifest in the world as *involvement*. The less we are of the world, the more we can do something good for the world. This also means that our contemplative development is increasingly less determined by our external circumstances and increasingly more by how much openmindedness and mental freedom we have attained.

This does not detract from the fact that circumstances in life, especially in the contemplative development toward this openness, can be helpful as well as harmful. We cannot close our eyes to this fact. The contemplative traditions do not do so either. Just as a mother does not attempt to force her newborn baby to walk, neither does a competent mentor (immediately) ask the impossible from the new student. It is considerations such as these that determine the concrete form of guidance along the Path. But the development to which the Path points is ultimately one that leads to an unconditional wisdom in life and loving care — a form of wisdom and compassion that can manifest itself freely and that *is continually active regardless of the circumstances.*

The Stream of Experience

We will examine what the contemplative psychological aspects of both a profane and a spiritual experience of reality are in the next chapter. And, of course, we will look at how the one can develop from the other. These issues are of fundamental importance. Because we speak and act *from the perspective of* as well as *within* our experience of reality, the effects are far-reaching, both for ourselves and for our fellow human beings and surroundings. But before we take this up we must ask a very practical question: how does our (continually shifting) experience of reality, whether it be profane, spiritual or something in between, actually come into being from moment to moment?

Within the spiritual traditions, the answer to this question is not informed by theology or philosophy but by a psychological insight that has been acquired through the practice of observing one's mind. This answer begins with a very concrete observation: the form or content of our experience of reality arises through the confluence of six sources of experience. Of these six sources, five are linked to our senses, which together provide us with the stream of *sensory experience.* The sixth source, which we could call our mind or psyche, supplies the stream of our *mental experience.*

All our sensual experiences — what we hear, see, smell, taste or touch physically — combine from moment to moment with our mental experience, that is to say, with what we think, find, feel, desire, with our hopes and fears, our fantasies, our imagination and everything else that we can conceive of and goes through our mind. The six streams of experience constantly merge together into our experience of reality of the moment without our being aware of the precise contribution of each source. In this way, an imagined reality arises that we cannot recognize as such (see also Kaufmann 1971). Allow me to give an example. If we hear the *sound* of a car, we often have the *experience* of a car going by. Although in fact we only hear the sound of a car, we mentally augment that sound with the image of the car. This mental image can be so strong (when, for example, we recognize the sound to be typical of a truck) that it is as if we *see* that truck go by, whereas in fact we experience only the sound of its engine. In the same way, the mental stream can be mixed with the sensual streams without our knowledge. In the words of Marcel Proust:

> Even the simple act which we describe as "seeing some one we know" is, to some extent, an intellectual process. We pack the physical outline of the creature we see with all the ideas we have already formed about him, and in the complete picture of him which we compose in our minds those ideas have certainly the principal place. In the end they come to fill out so completely the curve of his cheeks, to follow so exactly the line of his nose, they blend so harmoniously in the sound of his voice that these seem to be no more than a transparent envelope, so that each time we see the face or hear the voice it is our own ideas of him which we recognise and to which we listen. (Proust 1954, 19)

We can gain a good view of the stream of mental events if we keep the sensual stream of experience constant — for example, if we perform a very monotonous physical task or sit still, so that the situation of our body and our senses is more or less constant and peaceful. All that moves then is our stream of thoughts, allowing us the opportunity to see this stream more or less *in vacuo*. We can learn something from this — namely, what it is that our mind in fact constantly produces and how that contributes to the establishment of our experience of reality. The possibility of learning in this way is also the basis of many spiritual disciplines or mental practices. We will return to this in later chapters.

A Metaphor: The Film of Experience

What we mean by the term *experience of reality* can also be clarified through the metaphor of a movie. When we watch a movie, we see a visual stream of images and also almost constantly hear a stream of voices and sound, often accompanied by music. The more we become involved in the movie and are caught up (!) in it (assuming it is a well-made movie that appeals to us), the less we distinguish those streams from one another, which is what allows a reality to unfold that engrosses us for an hour and a half. During the making of the movie the director has consciously distinguished between these streams of experience. The director's art consists of allowing these streams to flow together in such a way that they present the viewer with an experience of reality. The director knows that, with the addition of a certain kind of music, the image of an old car driving slowly down a shaded lane toward a lonely, abandoned house can be the opening of either a comedy or a horror movie. The director's skill allows us to forget that we are sitting in a large room with other people, listening to noises and watching moving pictures. A certain kind of *discriminating awareness* is switched off within us and, as viewers, we are all too prepared to go along because we want to get our money's worth: we want to become "caught up." It is because movie directors make use of their own discriminating awareness that they are able to control our discriminating awareness. A good director knows the mental effects that the viewer attaches to the visual and auditive impressions offered, and knows how to combine them in such a way that the viewer experiences them as reality.

Our six sources or streams of experience operate in approximately the same way. Our sensual experience — that which we collect through our senses — flows together with and combines with givens from a mental source. In contrast to the production of a movie, however, we are simultaneously our own director and audience. Moreover, the production and the observation of the product take place at more or less the same moment. The movie is not fabricated beforehand in a studio but is more or less improvised on the spot with the material on hand. The "director" in this case operates so unnoticeably and quickly that we are seldom aware of our own activity. We are much too caught up or captured by the self-created experience of reality to see the activities of our director, our mind. We lack the space or distance (Greek: *anachorese*) that allows us to see the director in action. Concretely, the mindfulness or discriminating awareness (see chapter eight for this) that is needed for this does not function.

The Stream of Thoughts as Internal Reporter

Although we lack the distance characteristic of openness when we are caught up in our experience of reality, there may be another kind of distance at work: an intellectual or conceptual distance. This distance does not introduce openness but binds us even more firmly to our mental stream. The distance at which we aim here consists of the internal commentator, which usually provides a running commentary on that which we undergo. It is as if an "internal reporter" is at work in our mind, telling us and explaining to us what we see, hear and experience. A contemporary term used in psychotherapy for this is *self talk*. To continue with the metaphor of the movie, we experience our reality as a documentary or news program that uses a voiceover or subtitling to explain our experiences from a distant position.

This internal reporter is familiar to all of us. He or she or it is almost always speaking: it informs, evaluates, warns and lectures. It admonishes and encourages us. All of this occurs with an urgency that implies that it is guarding our interests. Now it is active with respect to the situation in which we actually find ourselves and later with respect to situations in which we do *not* find ourselves — situations that are both possible and impossible, both in the future and in the past. This so-called reporter is, of course, a metaphor for the internal commentary that takes the form of a stream of thoughts that fills our mind from early in the morning until late at night (and even in our dreams). It is this commentator, these ideas "which we recognise and to which we listen" (Proust 1954, 19).

The distance that our mental stream appears to take in the form of an internal commentator with regard to our actual experience is an apparent distance because, regardless of the content of our commentary, *it is part of our situation of this moment*. Even though this commentary is *about* our actual situation (see chapter four), it is also part of our total stream of experience and colors it. In the guise of an apparently distanced subtitling with regard to our subsequent experiences, it gives our experience of reality its subjective character. Because of this commentary, a certain situation can become irritating to one person, while to another the same situation can be reason for joy. If our internal running commentary about someone is aggressive, then we believe we see an enemy; if our internal running commentary about someone is friendly, then we believe we see a friend. Consequently, we also believe that that enemy or friend exists outside of ourselves and has an objective existence. But since one individual's friend can be another's enemy, the existence of that friend or enemy is not as objective as it seems. To put it even more strongly, matters are not settled once and for all in our own experiences either. We are continually occupied with making adjustments. For example, when we believe we recognize someone from a distance, the history that we have had with that person comes to mind and we experience that person in that context. We approach that person from the perspective of that context in which he or she is a friend or an enemy. For us, that person is who we think he or she is. If that person comes closer and turns out to be someone else, then our experience of the reality of that same person shifts again.

Direct Self-Knowledge

The examples above are familiar enough, but it becomes more difficult to determine the influence that our commentary has on our experience if we look at ourselves rather than at someone from our surroundings. Then, as well, a commentary emerges (whether well-documented or not) that causes us to "see" and deal with ourselves in a certain way. But are we who we *think* we are? If so, then we can never be mistaken about ourselves. If not, how do we determine whether, when and to what degree we are mistaken? This question is not irrelevant because the answer determines the way in which we relate to ourselves. Shall we ask others and involve them in our self-examination? That could be risky: "I think I'm like this but you think I'm like that. This is because I think you simply cannot see me in any other way than the way in which I think you see me." The ensuing discussion could go on into the wee hours of the morning, the goal being to build a common intersubjective experience of reality in which our concept of ourselves and our concepts of others acquire an acceptable place.

But have we ever examined ourselves, the activity of our mind, *directly*? Or have we only *thought* and speculated about ourselves with others and identified ourselves with the results of our speculations — in other words, identified ourselves with who we thought we were? Have we examined the commentator — our stream of thoughts — itself rather than listened to the commentary and allowed ourselves to be swept along with the stream?

How Real is our Experience of Reality?

It becomes even more difficult if we attempt to trace the influence of our stream of thoughts on the *totality of our experience*. What is our relationship to reality as a whole? How real is our experience of reality from moment to moment? Do we perceive reality as friend or foe, as threatening or benevolent, as workable or overwhelming? Is it corrupt or sacred, and how real is this kind of experience? Does our experience of reality tell us something about reality or about ourselves, our way of experiencing? Or does it say something about both at the same time and to what extent? Although we are groping in the dark here, these questions are important because our experience of reality affects our speech and actions, our concrete working with the world and our fellow human beings.

The point that the spiritual traditions never tire of emphasizing is that we do not actually know the precise area of our *blindness* or *darkness*. We do experience moments at which we (perhaps briefly) become aware of some aspect of our blindness: moments at which we "wake up" to our self-deception or illusion. There is no guarantee, however, that we will not immediately become submerged in a new one. Nor do we know just how many illusions we have that are still in progress. But we *are* able to cultivate that "waking up," thereby becoming more familiar with that typically human discernment — to wake up in a space in which we have a clear view of the nature of our experience of reality. And it is precisely that capacity that the spiritual traditions systematically attempt to cultivate.

Spiritual traditions view the nature of the unenlightened individual as that of a blind man in the sense that he believes in the reality of his self-created experience of reality. This experience of reality is perceived not as relative but as absolute, which is why he does not see the possibility of — let alone the need for — freeing himself from it. Perhaps only those few (usually unsolicited) moments that briefly reveal something of that relativity (moments that form the basis of what we will discuss later within the framework of conversion) allow him to see this possibility.

In short, our experience of reality is permeated by an unknown degree of blindness or, if you wish, self-deception. Blindness or self-deception is one of *the* major spiritual themes. Thus the spiritual traditions make use of various terms such as darkness, confusion, blindness, ignorance as well as their opposites: light, clarity of mind, insight. The *Tenach* (the Old Testament) of the Jewish tradition speaks of opening one's eyes. In the New Testament Paul prays for the enlightenment of "the eyes of your understanding" (Ephesians 1.18). Islam praises Allah as "He who blesses you, and his angels, to bring you forth from the shadows into the light" (Sura 33.43). The Hindu tradition speaks of the "third eye" opening. The Buddhist Sutras refer to the rousing of the mental discrimination awareness by the phrase "the opening of the eye of Wisdom" (see also Dalai Lama 1981). That light or open eye makes us see the *degree to which* our experience of reality is our own misleading creation.

GUIDANCE

A mentally open eye is, of course, essential for guiding people along the spiritual path — a theme we will discuss in

greater detail in the chapters below. In contemplative guidance, our guide is constantly and with great care engaged in
creating a space in which we are able to let go of apparently
necessary buttresses of our experience of reality without pan-
icking uncontrollably. This cannot always be done without
pain but can be done in such a way that an individual does
not lose his nerve entirely.

It is cruel to ask a child who, in her own experience of
reality, perceives her mother's place in her life as absolute
and is unable to relativize it to any degree: "Do you know
that in ten years that place will virtually no longer exist?"
We would never do that while raising a child; it would only
make the child fearful and increase her tendency to hold more
frantically on to that which she thinks she has. And yet, as
parents we guide a child in such a way that it gradually out-
grows its child's world, creating space for other elements so
that an experience of reality gradually develops that is closer
to our own — whatever that is worth. For a degree of openness is often lost if, while raising our children, we ourselves
absolutize our *own* experience of reality and believe we must
introduce our children to it as well.

With respect to care, however, a knowledgeable guide along
the spiritual path takes up this task much as a good parent
does with his or her child. Now, however, the goal is not to
replace one experience of reality with another but to expose
the student's experience of reality and to make it transparent.

Let me add immediately, however, that such a development is not solely dependent on the guide. It is only natural
that, in shifting the experience of reality, we might encounter moments where a total collapse does occur, an internal
breakdown, a *contritio cordis*. Then it might be better for
our guide to offer a (temporary) buttress to make the *contritio*
bearable. This buttress can prevent the student from fleeing,
becoming enmeshed in blindness and defensiveness and can

promote his or her growth in realism and compassion. We
will return to this in chapter ten.

THE HAZARDS OF THE METAPHOR OF THE PATH

Finally, something must also be said about the hazards of
the metaphor of the Path. The strong imagery of this metaphor includes so much that we might be tempted to absolutize
the metaphor itself. Precisely because of this, it would be
easy to allow it to function as a new buttress in our spiritual
experience of reality. For this reason we will now discuss its
weak points.

The metaphor suggests that the Path or Way has a starting point and an end to which it leads. There is something
very linear in this that cannot always be found in our experience. A weakness of this metaphor is that it could encourage
too strict a view of the sequential stages: "What stage am I
in now? Let me consult the literature of my tradition." This
is something that occurs among practitioners in many traditions and arises from the desire to acquire certainty, to find a
new buttress for our experience of reality at that moment
and possibly to evaluate ourselves through comparison with
others. Because of this, we no longer look openly at the whole
of our experience but only at the aspects that we think are
relevant for a comparison. This actually impedes further
progress along the Way.

The metaphor also suggests something that resembles our
(Western) faith in progress or advancement. A Cistercian
abbot, André Louf, delves into this in his volume *Tuning In
to Grace: The Quest for God*. He states that the old Renais-
sance humanist ideal of progress is completely different from
that of the Christian tradition. The Way excludes ideas such
as climbing up the social ladder or having a successful career.
Although many traditions make use of such imagery (think

of climbing Mount Carmel or ascending the ladder of the Benedictine tradition), at the same time they stress that this ascension must occur *humiliando*, through (the practice of) humility. The practitioner experiences journeying along the Path more as a descent. Practitioners in the Buddhist tradition sometimes say that one travels along the spiritual path walking backwards. That awareness of a reversed direction and the sense of going backward rather than going forward arise precisely because, as we journey along the Path, we progressively acquire a better view of our egocentrism and our blindness that frustrates our naive ideas and ambitions for self-improvement (if not self-advancement). Traveling on the Path is as if we are removing ourselves further and further from that which we have naively set as our ideals and from that which we expect of the Path itself.

Our ideals and expectations quickly become new buttresses, thereby becoming obstacles to contemplative development. Our ideas about the goal (holiness, perfection or fulfillment) can become a new theme on which and by which we model and measure everything around us. Because of this, we are no longer free to look openly at ourselves because we may see things that do not fit in with our travel plans and destination. Dom Louf expresses it in this way: "Obedience, self-discipline, even prayer — these can all be directed away from the living God and become subordinated to an ideal of perfection that in essence barely differs from a secular ethics" (Louf 1992, 51). Thus we have once again climbed up the ladder of spiritual ambition and success. Chögyam Trungpa introduced a term for this branching away or perversion of spirituality: *spiritual materialism* (Trungpa 1973). It is a provocative term — especially since we tend to view spirituality and a materialistic attitude as irreconcilable opposites. And they are, indeed, such. Yet that does not prevent us from perverting authentic spirituality by viewing it materialistically as something that we must draw toward ourselves in order to enrich or "save" ourselves. We have then arrived at the utilitarian mentality (see chapter one) in which we allow our lives to be led by striving for that which we see as advantageous. We make our decisions on the basis of an analysis of profit and loss: there must be some *spiritual* profit. The more human actions are based on this mentality, the better economics is able to describe the behavior of these people, as Becker (1968), for example, demonstrates.

It is very easy for spiritual ambition to float along in the wake of the materialistic approach to spirituality. The metaphor of the Path appears to allow room for it, which is one of its weak points in addition to the linearity that it seems to suggest. We could view the spiritual path as a racetrack where it is possible to win honor and wonderful prizes. Spiritual ambition and the resulting spiritual pride is something that plays a role not only at the beginning but along the whole length of the Path. There are those moments at which some insight about the Way (our experience of reality) dawns upon us. At times we cannot resist the temptation to display the insight we have developed like a feather in our cap. At other times we do not do so openly but tuck that insight away in a little box. And at those moments when no one is watching, we open the box so that we can savor its contents. This is how we feed our spiritual pride.

When we begin to perceive our pride about our progress, we may initially be somewhat shocked. But the more often we see it the more it begins to rouse our sense of humor: all that spiritual pretentiousness is so naive and so childish. At the same time we begin to see the seriousness of our situation: it is risky to feed our spiritual pride, for it causes the flourishing within to wilt. We then slowly outgrow our tendency to exalt ourselves and develop a very natural and true humility — a humility that arises not out of feelings of guilt or self-reproach but out of self-knowledge. Here this self-knowledge is the awareness that the fruits of our contemplative practices are in us but not of us. It is not surprising that the contemplative traditions include many remedies to alleviate the development of spiritual pride.

Lastly, included in the metaphor of the Way or Path is the suggestion that we are concerned with a road that has already been paved. This is because our thinking about a road in our day and age is very different than the thinking of people in the time when this metaphor arose. There were almost no roads as we know them today. Going on a journey meant putting oneself in danger. It also meant leaving a familiar neighborhood without any certainty of ever seeing it again. It was also impossible to obtain a reliable or detailed map or preview of the road. Information about what more or less lay in the direct future was gathered day by day. The metaphor of the way does not express this aspect of uncertainty and risk as well as metaphors such as journey or mountain climbing, which is used in the tradition of, for example, the Carmelites. The contemplative life or spiritual growth is a risky business because it amounts to a departure from our familiar, conventional experience of reality. And, with regard to the traveling instructions that the traditions give, they only illuminate the Path a little beyond that which lies directly before us at every step. Or, as it is expressed in Psalm 119.105: "Your word is a lamp for my feet and a light for my path."

THREE

The Development of Ego

INTRODUCTION: SELF-EXPERIENCE AND EGO

A central theme in the psychology of the spiritual way of life is the restlessness within our own hearts, which arises from uncertainty about our existence and ignorance as to who or what we are. In a variety of ways, the spiritual traditions state that this is connected with an *egocentric* mental attitude — an attitude that makes it impossible for our fundamental humaneness to flourish. Thus, there appears to be something the matter with the place that the *I* or *ego* assumes in our experience of reality. This chapter will acquaint us with the many aspects included under this theme. Before we go into more detail as to what the contemplative psychological meaning of the term *ego* is and how *ego* develops, we will first define it roughly by contrasting it with a related concept — namely, *self-experience*. The latter term refers to all those phenomena that occur, as we called it in chapter one, *in the first person*, that is to say, to phenomena that are not directly visible to others because they occur in what we could call our *internal landscape*. In that landscape, everything and anything is to be found: our thoughts and emotions, expectations, memories, dreams, impressions, images and anything else that we can think of. Our *I* or *ego*, as it is viewed in contemplative psychology (de Wit 1991, 167), is to be found there. It lives in this mental domain, as do the accompanying phenomena such as our self-image, our self-love and self-hate, etc.

Thus, the contemplative psychological term *self-experience* refers to a *mental domain* within which our *I*, as well as other phenomena, is present. In this domain the *I* or *ego* can be present to a greater or lesser degree and can influence our self-experience. And, as we will see, it can even be *absent* from our self-experience. Thus the term *self-experience* is much broader and certainly not the same as the experience of our *I*. By *self-experience*, therefore, we do not mean something like I-experience or I-awareness but the experience of our mental domain with everything that occurs within it from moment to moment.

According to the spiritual traditions, our self-experience and our experience of our surroundings include many blind spots that result from *ego*. These blind spots are the cause of a way of life that brings with it immeasurable psychological and social suffering. What is at stake here, therefore, is no small matter. We do not know ourselves and, what is more, we are seldom aware of this fact. As a result, during our lives we travel regularly in directions that cause harm to ourselves and our surroundings without being aware of it. These directions can lead to or end up in a destructive darkness and fear of life that seemingly can only be eased by escaping into fantasy worlds, into dreamlike states. Even if these dreamlike states should be about wisdom, goodness and spiritual flourishing, they would still obscure our vision because we cannot live on dreams. They cause us to wither spiritually. Confronted by reality, dreams only make us more fearful and callous. In this chapter we will study the nature and cause of the blind spots in our self-experience.

Before we begin, we must return for a moment to what we discussed in the previous chapter: our experience of reality. This includes our self-experience. After all, we are part of reality. We have seen that our experience of reality is neither completely objective nor completely subjective. Nor is it invariable. It is actually similar to a living organism, to something that grows and flourishes but can also die off or calcify, so that all life and flexibility ebbs out of it. It is in a state of constant change. By change we do not mean that certain situations appear in and disappear from our lives but that the *way in which* we experience our situation in life is constantly changing. It is true that our childhood toys have disappeared from our lives, but, as we said, that is not the primary concern of contemplative psychology. We are concerned with the shift that causes our childhood toys to have another *experiential value* when we look at them today. The shift has to do with the development of a continually changing perspective of what may well be the same world of phenomena.

As we stated above, there is an aspect of blindness to our experience of reality. Actually, a more appropriate word would be *darkness*. A well-known spiritual metaphor is that, like a caterpillar, we spin a cocoon around ourselves out of our experience of reality. We begin to live within its seemingly pleasant but actually oppressive limitation. Not much light penetrates into this cocoon, but at least the situation is orderly, precisely because it is limited. In any case, we have the feeling that we know where we are (heading). When this cocoon becomes damaged or even touched, panic arises within. We become aware that the world is larger (perhaps very much larger, possibly dizzyingly so) than the cocoon and that, because we live in the cocoon, we have no influence whatsoever upon it. Encased within the cocoon, we cannot make contact with or even anticipate that which is outside. We cannot give way to and dance with the wind like a vulnerable butterfly, but must hope that the cocoon, spun onto a twig in the shelter of a leaf, can withstand the gusts of wind. The only possibility for self-preservation appears to be to strengthen the threads of the cocoon. In concrete terms, this means that we begin to spin new threads of thought in order to keep our *personal reality* — as we have called it — intact and inhabitable.

If we want to use a philosophical term, we could say that our experience of reality is *solipsist*, meaning that our experience of reality only (*solus*) exists as long as I myself (*ipse*) exist. In other words, it is born and dies with us. Not only our friends and enemies, what we like and what we loathe, come and go with us but our entire experience of reality, including our self-experience, appears and disappears with us. This is why we, just as the spiritual traditions themselves, cannot avoid the psychological question of who the creator or what the creative power of this solipsist world is. After all, we suffer under (and in) this world, this restrictive cocoon that gradually deadens our joy in life. Where did this world come from? How did it come into existence and why? What do we mean when we say that we have created it ourselves? How, in concrete terms, does that work? What is the psychological process that leads to it?

A Spiritual View of Ego

Before we give a more concrete psychological analysis of ego, we will look more closely at how this concept is commonly used in a spiritual context. But first we must understand that the use of the term *ego* does not refer simply to a purely grammatical category; ego is not the same as the personal pronoun "I" that people use to refer to themselves. The use of this pronoun does not imply that the speaker has an ego. Conversely, that there are languages that do not even have the pronoun "I" does not imply that the speakers of these languages do not have an ego.

In a spiritual context, the concept ego (although it is often indicated by other terms) refers to a certain mentality: an *egocentric* or *egotistic mentality*. This mentality is considered to be the cause of spiritual blindness and callousness and must therefore be overcome. Ego is that which prompts each one of us to create, defend and enlarge our own realm of influence. This ego sees self-exaltation as self-development, impulsiveness as spontaneity, and confuses the power to fulfil one's desires with freedom. This is why many traditions speak of the spiritual path as *transcending ego*. Some Christian traditions use the phrase *crucifying ego* here. Ego is the hardened *sinner*, the center of our self-conceit, the center of our egotism. Hindu traditions speak of *jivanmukta*, the liberation (*mukta*) of ego (*jiva*), the transcendence of the *false self* and the discovery of the true Self (*brahman*). Buddhism speaks of the realization of egolessness (*anatman*), seeing through the *illusion of ego* (*atman*). The Chassidic tradition of Judaism considers *bittul*, the erasing of the self, to be a condition for the highest *unio mystica* (Mindel 1985, 12).

Is it really possible for us to free ourselves from our egocentric experience of reality? According to the spiritual traditions, it is. They point to certain moments of experience, moments in which our internal commentary with all its images and fantasies about reality is silent for a moment. In a famous passage, Augustine writes about a conversation he had with his mother:

> We were saying, then, If to any man the tumult of the flesh were silenced — silenced the phantasies of earth, waters, and air — silenced, too, the poles; yea, the very soul be silenced to

herself, and go beyond herself by not thinking of herself —
silenced fancies and imaginary revelations, every tongue, and
every sign, and whatsoever exists bypassing away. . . . If this
could be sustained, and other visions of a far different kind be
withdrawn, and this one ravish, and absorb, and envelope its
beholder amid these inward joys, so that his life might be
eternally like that one moment of knowledge which we now
sighed after, were not this "Enter thou into the joy of Thy
Lord"? (Augustine 1983, 137–38)

The moment at which our internal commentary, our speaking to ourselves, ceases and all conceptualizations, all conceptual frameworks within which we define ourselves and our reality, sink into nothingness is given many different names: nakedness, liberation, candor, enlightenment, openness, truth, wholeness. But from the perspective of ego, such moments are associated with death and destruction. The mystical tradition within Islam calls the fulfillment of the spiritual journey *fanaa*, which literally means "destruction." In Buddhism it is said: "The attainment of enlightenment from ego's point of view is extreme death, the death of self, the death of me and mine, the death of the watcher. It is the ultimate and final disappointment" (Trungpa 1976, 6). In the Zen tradition, enlightenment is also called *taishi*, the Great Death (Nishitani 1982, 21). A well-known Zen poem puts it:

Die while you live,
be completely dead,
then do as you wish,
all is well.

The last two lines of this poem are interesting because they demonstrate that these "moments of death" of ego have also to do with joy in life or, even more strongly, they are the only moments when we are truly alive. In Buddhist terms, the moments of egolessness are at the same time the moments in which (our) *buddha nature* is able to unfold and to permeate our life. This double-sidedness is encountered again and again in various spiritual traditions. For example, in Vajrayana Buddhism this two-sidedness is evident in images in which the enlightened state is depicted as a naked royal individual or couple dancing on a corpse — the corpse of ego. It is through the "destruction" of ego that the purified Muslim "becomes so concentrated on God that 'He becomes the ear with which he hears, the eye with which he sees, the tongue with which he speaks, the heart with which he observes,' as expressed in a well-known *hadith kudsi*" (De Bruijn 1987, 200). And then, of course, there is the familiar double-sided passage from the Bible, which proclaims the liberation from ego not simply as a possibility but as a fact: "I have been crucified with Christ and I no longer live, but Christ lives in me" (Galatians 2.20). In Christian terms, we could say that these moments create room for the activity of the Holy Spirit.

But people know of these things outside of religious traditions as well. In "The Eighth Elegy" of *The Duino Elegies*, Rilke expresses the double-sidedness between *we*, that is, ego and the space of the flourishing within as follows:

> *We*'ve never possessed, not for a day,
> the clear space in front of us, in which flowers
> constantly open. We have the world with us, always,
> never that unnamed place which is no place: the pure,
> undefined air we breathe and intimately
> *know* and never yearn for. A really young child
> can get lost in that silence, must be shaken
> back to itself. Or, someone dies and *becomes* this.
>
> (Rilke 1993, 45)

On the one hand, *ego* has a rather negative ring about it. For this term refers to the psychological basis of egocentrism and egoism. Ego is the basis of our profane, that is, nonenlightened mentality and the cause of blindness, fear and strife. As such, it chokes the flourishing of our humaneness. On the other hand, according to many contemplative traditions, ego only *seems* to be something negative, just as the contents of a bad dream seem to be negative. That is why ego is not something tangible and concrete against which we can and must fight but rather a state of mind from which we must try to awaken ourselves.

Psychotherapeutic and Spiritual Views of Ego

The section above has already made clear that the contemplative meaning of the term *ego* is very different from the meaning it is given in much clinical psychology and psychotherapy. There it is often stated that a person must have a strong ego in order to be able to function in a healthy way. The concept *ego* is then linked with the idea that one must be able to have confidence in oneself, confidence that one has the right to exist.

The spiritual traditions also speak of this type of confidence in a positive sense, but they do not use the term *ego* for it. Why not? Because these traditions believe that at its core this confidence is not a confidence in what we ordinarily call "ourselves" but that it is unrelated to this. It is a confidence in the fundamental ground of our existence. Simply put, it is a confidence in ourselves as human beings, confidence in our truly humane qualities. This kind of self-confidence is something very different from that which the spiritual traditions call *ego*. In the spiritual traditions the term *ego* refers precisely to that which undermines our self-confidence and our acceptance of ourselves and makes us anxious, constricted beings.

It is necessary to keep this difference in meaning in mind when we speak of ego in the contemplative sense. It will then also be clear that it is misleading to say with regard to the psychological development of people that one must first build up a strong *ego* before one is able to begin the spiritual process of letting go of this *ego*. It is misleading because in this statement the term ego, which is used twice, refers to two different things. The first time it refers to ego as it is defined in psychotherapy and the second time as it is defined in the spiritual traditions. The strong ego about which psychotherapy sometimes speaks is *not* the ego about which the spiritual traditions speak. If that were the case, then this statement would mean that it is healthy to develop a strong measure of selfishness, blindness, arrogance and fear of life first before we can begin the process of letting go of them. This is not something that clinical psychology wants to encourage in us. Or else the statement would mean that we first have to develop a strong dose of fundamental confidence in our own humaneness and, subsequently, to let go of this confidence. This is certainly not the direction in which the spiritual traditions want to lead us.

Thus the meanings of the term *ego* in both traditions are almost diametrically opposed to each other, even though in some forms of psychotherapy (see, for example, Epstein 1996) and anthropology (see, for example, Campbell 1988) that take spirituality into account, we find ideas concerning ego that lie very close to its contemplative interpretation.

The reason that some spiritual traditions say that ego must be transcended, "crucified" or "humbled" is not so much moral as psychological. Ego must be transcended or let go, not because it is necessarily *bad* (such a moral judgement is of no help to anyone) but because it is psychologically destructive: the cultivation of ego does not lead to a flourishing of our fundamental humanity but chokes it. The mental attitude that considers self-exaltation to be self-development does, after all, rest on the notion that we must try to be *on top of things*, must build a strong position for ourselves so that we can remain in control of things, including our emotions and even, yes, ourselves, our cursed ego! When we attempt to travel along a spiritual path with this attitude, then a bitter battle takes place within ourselves in which we, for the sake of spiritual development, manipulate ourselves with the threat of hell and damnation — a battle that is nothing other than an attempt to get on top of ourselves by subjugating or even destroying ourselves.

Ego and Egolessness

Where do ego and the egocentric experience of reality that accompanies it come from? Do spiritual traditions have answers to that question — answers that, psychologically speaking, are somewhat more precise and informative than a reference to the Fall or related theological concepts? It appears so. We will trace the origin and development of ego step by step, not by *thinking about* ego but by trying to *look* as openly as we can at our self-experience, our mind. We will thus follow in the footsteps of the practitioners of the spiritual traditions, those who have thoroughly examined and searched their mind by means of meditative disciplines. What do we actually see when we look at our mind? As we discussed in chapter two, there is continuous activity in the form of a running commentary or subtitling, a stream of thoughts, which more or less randomly and almost continuously merges with our sensory stream of experience. This is how our solipsistic experience of reality arises.

This stream of thoughts creates a mental world, a world consisting entirely of thoughts with all their emotional coloring. If we look at it more closely, we can see that in that mental world there is someone who plays the lead, a person who answers to the name *I*. When we examine the contents of our thoughts we frequently encounter this *I*. We often think about *ourselves*, about ourselves and others, about ourselves and the world around us, ourselves and our past, present and future, about ourselves and our body and mind. Almost all aspects of our experience can be reflected in our stream of thoughts and, as a reflection, can be related to thoughts about *me*. It is when the egocentric stream of thoughts formed in this way merges with our sensory experience that our egocentric experience of reality arises.

Thus it is not only the cocoon woven by the threads of our thoughts that can obscure our view. The *egocentric structure* of our way of thinking also works in a biased way, adding a measure of confusion to all of this. This confusion has far-reaching consequences because this *I* or ego, which plays such a prominent role in our thinking, offers a fixed reference point to which we are very attached — not necessarily because it is pleasant (after all, we can think negatively about ourselves) but because it offers security. We would not miss it for the world. We would even be willing to give our lives or take the lives of others for it, fighting with fire and sword if necessary. As we will see, it is the basis of our aggression and greed.

We are so used to and attached to this egocentric way of thinking that we find it inconceivable that this *I* should play *no* part in our experience of ourselves. What would remain of our way of thinking and our emotional life if this leading character should turn out to be a character that plays a role in the first scene of our lives only to disappear for the rest of the play? Do we die, cease to exist? Can we still function, or would the words of Paul which we quoted earlier, "I no longer live, but Christ lives in me," become meaningful to us? Or, to put it in spiritual terms, it is then no longer ego but fundamental humaneness that lives in our self-experience.

The idea that, in addition to habitual and almost ongoing egocentric moments of experience, we also have moments in which our egocentric experience is absent may sound abstract or elevated. And yet something very concrete and familiar is involved here, although it is not easy to express because it is very subtle. It is something which we can easily pass by without noticing it. Perhaps an example can clarify matters. Suppose we are doing something that requires our attention, such as playing the piano or painting a cupboard. If we are really "into" it, if we are really involved in what we are doing, we forget ourselves — that is, we are not preoccupied with ourselves (for as long as we are doing this particular activity), with the question of whether we are a good pianist or painter. It is not ourselves but the situation or the activity that directs our actions, our observations. Sartre wrote (1972, 32): "In fact, I am then immersed in the world of objects; they constitute the unity of my consciousnesses [that is, moments of consciousness], which present themselves with values, attractive and repulsive qualities, but *I*, I have disappeared, I have been annihilated. There is no place for *me* on this level, and this does not prove to be coincidental, a momentary lack of attention, but the very structure of consciousness." Phenomenological psychologists say that we *coincide* with our actions at such moments. Contemplative psychologists would say that in that situation the mental separation between the action and the one who carries it out *is absent*. In Buddhist psychology, this way of experiencing is called *three-fold purity*: the mental (and psychological) separation between the actor, the action and that which is acted upon does not (yet or no longer) play a role in one's experience.

As Tolstoy describes so clearly (see above introduction, pp. 7–8), the effectiveness and flexibility with which people are able to function and the absence of uncertainty are characteristic of these moments of experience. The notes on the paper, our understanding of music, our concentration, our hands and the keyboard all work together in an effective unity. It is not *we* who make (the) music, but all of *them* together.

We would only get in the way. *We* would only fret about a certain passage coming up, worried that we would not get through it without making a mistake. Or, if things go well, we would pat ourselves on the back and thereby lose contact with the keyboard. In the same way, the surface of the cupboard, the thickness of the paint, the stiffness of the brush, our awareness of and experience with these qualities determine how we paint. *We* are outside of this; at most, we can only sit and watch.

And then the moment occurs in which this clear, efficacious, intelligent unity of conscious experiencing and acting breaks down: suddenly, we are overcome by the fear that we may have lost control of the situation! We have not paid attention to ourselves! We have lost sight of ourselves! A subtle panic seizes us and we ask ourselves: "Where am I?" or, "How am I doing?"

Many spiritual traditions stress that there is something abrupt about this moment, that it is a fracture of some sort, or even an infraction, that seems to occur involuntarily. In the first instance, this fracture is not much more than an awareness of *this* over against *that*, a psychological dualism of *me here* and *that there*. This is the conception of a reference point, something we could possibly hang on to. It is the birth, or rather, the conception, of *ego* that occurs here, the starting point of the development of ego. Let us look at this development now in more detail.

A CONTEMPLATIVE-PSYCHOLOGICAL VIEW OF EGO

In Christian traditions, the origin of ego and our egocentric experience of reality is usually spoken of in terms of the Fall and being driven out of paradise. Of course, these are typically religious and theological concepts, but they also have a contemplative psychological interpretation. Here, the Fall refers to the origin of the egocentric experience of reality, which is the result of a certain movement of our mind. Contemplative psychology is concerned with the question of how this initial mental movement develops further into our egocentric experience of reality.

We will describe the development of ego here in terms of four subsequent mental movements. Let us begin with exploring the state of mind that exists *before* ego. Before any of these mental movements occur there is total openness — an open space in which all phenomena interact with one another according to their own nature in a certain equality, without commentary, without the illusion of distance created by a mental *reporter* (see chapter two) as described in the examples of playing the piano or painting a cupboard. This openness is "like a spacious hall where there is room to dance about, where there is no danger of knocking things over or tripping over things, for there is completely open space. We *are* this space, we are *one* with it, with *vidya*, intelligence and openness" (Trungpa 1973, 123). We all have these moments of openness — moments which, from ego's perspective, as we stated above, are unfathomable and threaten chaos but which, from their own perspective, are as clear as water, true and full of joy. These moments form the underlying basis on which and over against which the development of ego takes place.

The Dualistic Split

The first movement is that in which our mind reflects back to itself as it were, withdrawing into itself and thereby separating itself from all the other things that manifest themselves in the open space of experience. Through this one mental movement arises the duality of *I* and *the other* in our experience. It is the starting point of the development of ego in the contemplative sense of the word. Psychologically, it can be characterized as a moment of mental constriction or drawing back. But why do we draw back? What has happened?

> Nothing has happened, as a matter of fact. We just became too active in that space. Because it is spacious, it brings inspiration to dance about; but our dance became a bit too active, we began to spin more than was necessary to express that space. At this point we became *self*-conscious, conscious that "I" am dancing in space. At such a point, space is no longer space as such. It becomes solid. Instead of being one with the space, we feel space as a separate entity, as tangible. This is the first experience of duality — space and I. (Trungpa 1973, 123)

Carried away by our own energy — of dancing, of playing the piano — the fear suddenly arises that *I* have lost control. Fear is a poor advisor, and because of this we do not see that we never actually had control in the way we thought we had, that, secondly, we will never be able to have that kind of control and, thirdly, that we do not need it in order to live, to dance. And so we proceed mentally along a road that is disastrous and a dead end in all respects, since this ego is not the basis of our existence but the creation of our fear and contraction. This fear does not trust the nature of the fundamentally open space, which is nothing other than the state of total openness of mind. The open space is now experienced as something obscure, as an area external to "I" (see Fortmann 1974, 1:349). For this reason we begin to look for something to hold on to.

Ego Identification

There is nothing to hold on to in this open space. Frightened by that, we engage in a search for something to hold on to, and this becomes a huge and neverending task at which we must continually work. We have the feeling that, in order to be, we must be *someone*. But who? It is as if we must create and prove our existence as *I*. Existing — being human, being a creature — is no longer good enough. Our continuous attempts to find or create something to hold on to themselves become something to hold on to. These attempts form the second step in the development of ego. They are directed at giving *substance* to the as-of-yet abstract and naked *I*. This occurs by a subsequent mental move which divides the field of our experience into what I am or what belongs to me on the one hand and what I am not or what does not belong to me on the other. Expressed more concretely, the move the mind makes after the dualistic split is to identify with certain phenomena and call them *I*. This happens differently each moment, which is why we see that what we call *I* is something that continually changes. For example, one moment we identify ourselves with our body, as when we say, "I fell down." The next moment we identify ourselves with the feeling of pain that we had when we fell and say, "I hurt myself." At another moment, again we identify ourselves with a certain emotion, such as when we say, "I am angry that I hurt myself." Are the one who fell down and the one who is hurt and the one who is angry about it one and the same *I* or not? If I say "I fell down," then it is actually my body that falls down, but it is not my body that is angry about it.

However, we do not even identify ourselves with our emotions all the time. Sometimes we see them as an object, as something outside of us, such as when we say "I was overcome by grief." In a certain sense, these emotions have then become part of the world around us and our *I* withdraws to another point. This point can be our body, our sensations, perceptions, our thoughts themselves or our consciousness. The scope of ego varies: it expands and contracts according to the situation. Thus we see here that that to which the word "I" refers is not something fixed but something that continually changes. The meaning of the word "I" shifts continually. For at each moment, the actual substance or content of ego is something different again.

Because we execute this mental movement of ego identification very quickly in each moment of experience, a certain continuity and stability is suggested — the feeling that this *I* is always there and is something fixed even though it is never the same. We could compare it to walking on ice floes: we cannot stay on one floe too long because otherwise it will sink; we have to jump across to another floe quickly in order to maintain the illusion of firm ground under our feet.

In our experience of reality, these first two mental movements — the dualistic split and ego identification — together constitute the appearance of ego as a thing or object. Around it lies the phenomenal world, which is then equally experienced as a collection of objects or things. We can refer to these two movements together as *object-formation*, as the mental move that causes the *I* to appear as an object or thing in the midst of other objects. In Western philosophy and psychology, this particular thing is often referred to as *the subject*. But this *subject* is something quite different from the notion of subject that contemplative psychology uses and that we discussed in chapter one under the heading "The Human Being as Subject."

The metaphor of swimming in an ocean may be able to clarify both these movements. The process of anxiously looking for something to hold on to can be compared with grasping a piece of driftwood out of the fear that we cannot swim. Landing in the vast ocean of experience and thinking that we cannot swim, we grab hold of whatever we can find. We grasp what we *think* is a piece of driftwood, whereas what we are actually grasping is our own limbs, which makes swimming extremely difficult. Because of the fear that we cannot swim, we grab hold of ourselves and discover that we can indeed barely swim, which feeds our fear and causes us to tighten our hold on ourselves. We will not drown, however, because we actually *can* swim. When the water gets as high as our chin, we are forced to let go of our "driftwood" (that is, our limbs). At that moment there is the possibility that we become aware of our situation and realize that we can swim, that we do not need the driftwood, that our fear was groundless and that the driftwood *does not even exist*. But it is also possible that we believe we have been very clever in the way we have dealt with the driftwood. By letting go of the driftwood for a moment in order to find a different hold on it, we have still managed to save ourselves! We have once again succeeded in continuing to float, thanks to the driftwood's ability to float and our cleverness in taking advantage of it!

Here the continually renewed hold on the driftwood is, of course, a metaphor for the ongoing creation of ego. It clarifies that ego is in fact sustained only as a mental activity. The swimmer is our mind which, when it is directed toward the development of ego, grabs holds of itself, creating the illusion of having something to hang on to. The ocean represents the phenomenal world and the (nonexistent) driftwood represents ego.

In contemplative psychology, subject and object are therefore not established facts, but the continually changing result of the way in which we divide the open space into two, into "me here" and "that there." We could also characterized this mental movement as one that attempts to turn all phenomena (internal and external) into objects, things that we can hold on to: it creates the illusion of the *I* being a thing in relation to the other things.

Dressing Up Ego

Nevertheless, in this phase ego is still very unstable and naked. Thus, the third mental movement is one in which we, as it were, dress up this naked ego. How do we do this? Our mind generates an enormous mental activity in the shape of a continual stream of thoughts *about ourselves* in relation to that which we see as not being ourselves — a kind of internal administrative process in which we keep track of who we are and how we are doing. This administrative process consists of the internal dialogue that we carry on with ourselves (see chapter two). Even though we do not do this out loud, is it not true that we often talk to ourselves? We admonish and encourage ourselves, explain things to ourselves and form many opinions about ourselves. It is not clear whether in this process we are the one who listens to this internal dialogue or the one who speaks. We experience a kind of mental division, as if there were two of us within. Why should we say something to ourselves if the person who speaks is also the person who listens? We already know what we will hear, and thus there is no real need to do so.

However, from the perspective of our struggle toward a stable *ego*, it is literally and figuratively necessary for us to fill the open space with something that we seem able to hold on to: a running commentary. This commentary seems to define and explain the world and our place within it, which is why the maintenance of this internal administration about ourselves seems very useful. But at the same time this commentary also *creates* a world: our ego-centered experience of reality. With the help of this commentary, which serves as a mental garb covering the nakedness of ego, we begin to dress up our still naked *ego* with all kinds of ideas — ideas *about* ourselves. We have a wide range of ideas available and a great deal of freedom in selecting from among them. There are as many ideas as we or others can think up about ourselves: accurate ideas, foolish ideas, happy and discouraging ideas, ideas that are superficial, deep, philosophical, psychological and social, ideas that are borrowed from our personal history or from our expectations of the future. In short, we can dress up our naked *ego* with a *definition of who we (think we) are.* We then form what we called in chapter one a self-concept or self-image. Our self-concept contains the information about ourselves which is registered in our internal bookkeeping system. It offers us a certain security, a certain structure and a feeling of having an overall picture of things.

Ego Identification with the Concept of Self

Finally, there is a fourth, very ingenious and subtle mental movement in the development of this ego which is no longer so naked. This movement increases the stability of ego in particular and the driftwood's buoyancy. In order to describe this movement, we will briefly restate the three previous steps.

The first mental movement toward the development of ego is the dividing of and thus the splitting up of the open space of experience into "me here" and "that there." It gives rise to the dualistic mode of experience. The second movement is that of ego identification: grasping on to certain aspects in the swirling stream of experience as a temporary basis for this *I*, so that we can declare, "I am this and not that." Together, these two movements transform our experience of reality into the experience of *identifiable things.* Ego, then, is also experienced as an internal entity or "thing," as something that is related to the things around it. The third mental movement is that in which we construct a story about ourselves, our self-concept or self-image. The older we become, the more stories we have and the more — perhaps fortunately for us — we forget. In any case, a concept arises that is considered a faithful concept or image of our *ego.*

Because of these three movements, it is now possible for a fourth movement to occur. The third movement has introduced a new phenomenon into our world of experience: our self-concept, a mental construction that we are able, with periodic mental bookkeeping, to keep relatively stable. This self-concept is now part of our stream of experience. Why then, in our search for a stable idea as to who or what we are, should we not identify with this construction? The fourth mental movement is just that: it is once again a movement of *ego identification* which we discussed above but now takes our self-concept as the object with which to identify. That is, we identify ourselves (our ego) with our self-concept. From that moment on we are who we *think* we are. We believe that our *concept* of ourselves is *ourselves*; it is from that position that we now deal with the world around us.

These four mental movements lead to the construction of ego in the contemplative-psychological sense of the word. But we must not view these movements as a mental activity that occurs only once in our lives, after which we are irrevocably trapped in a dualistic experience of reality. In contemplative psychology, these movements are viewed as an *activity* that *reoccurs* in almost every moment of experience (this is strongly emphasized in, for example, Buddhist psychology). We are concerned here with very swift, usually unnoticed and, as a rule, habitual mental movements. Nonetheless, they can be made visible through the practice of meditation. In sum, these four movements show us in what sense ego is *not a thing*, although it is usually experienced as such by us, but a mental *activity* that through its continuity provides the illusion of permanence. This is also why we have not used an article in front of the word ego: we do not speak of *the* ego, but of *ego*.

THE CALLOUSNESS AND VULNERABILITY OF EGO

Thus, at last, we know who we are. It is registered in our mental notebook! The notebook contains ego's version of our self-knowledge, that is, the *indirect knowledge of ourselves* that we discussed in chapter one. It is an impressive mental achievement, but one that has taken us far from the open space of which Augustine and many others of the contemplative traditions spoke. Expressed in stronger terms, *ego*, which has arisen as a result of the four mental movements, conceals the entrance to that open space in which the illusory nature of *ego* would be crystal clear. It leads to what we will discuss in the following chapter: *perceptual confusion*.

Moreover, at the moment that we identify or equate our self-concept with ourselves a new kind of vulnerability arises — perhaps irritability is a better word — because whoever now affects our self-concept affects *us*. If our mental notebook contains the entry, "I am a patient and charming person," and we hear someone (perhaps behind our back) say, "You have to watch out for him. He always goes off the deep end. He's bad news," then not only is our self-concept hurt but we also feel hurt personally: *we* are hurt. We can brood on it for days, intent on revenge at one moment, anxious at others. We become so lost within ourselves that we do not notice the summer wind that makes the poppies in the garden flutter or our little daughter's cheerful, affectionate glance, inviting us to play with her.

If we further elaborate and modify the self-concept with which we identify, so that ultimately all aspects of our world of experience are related to it in one way or another, then almost nothing can happen or be said without our self-concept (and thus ourselves) being at stake. Everything refers back to us — whether for good or for bad, whether as something that confirms or something that hurts. Our egocentric experience of reality has become fact.

Thus the range of the egocentric experience of reality can continually expand. Ego can act as a web, continually spreading out over the field of our experience: more and more of which comes under the domain of ego. The psychological field that we feel we must control in order to safeguard our ego becomes bigger and bigger. This also has an effect on our speech and actions. Now we can be open and unselfish only as long as our ego is not at stake, as long as it feels little or no threat. In other words, our fundamental humanity can only manifest itself under certain conditions, and those conditions are dictated by ego. Moments in which we *rise above ourselves* become rare, even though there is a great deal above which we must rise — so much, in fact, that it drags us down. Our fundamental humanity has become *conditional humanity*. If, for example, we have the idea that, in order not to feel threatened, we must have $50,000 in our savings account, then our generosity, our willingness to give to a good cause will manifest itself only when that condition is met. Likewise, we will be able to extend friendship and care to people only if our ego is not essentially threatened, or even not threatened at all. The development of ego chokes the hidden flourishing of our fundamental humanity and, thereby, the development of its fruits as they become manifest in our speech and actions as well.

IMPRISONED IN EGO

Ego, the development of which we have described and in which the spiritual traditions are very interested, is like a structure that is erected within our hearts. No one may enter. We do not really know why this is. Nor do we know what is behind the walls of this structure, that is to say, behind our self-concept, or even whether there *is* something to be found. We do not know whether the structure protects our joy in life and gentleness or whether it confines our fear of life and callousness so that we are not too troubled by them. Is it possible, as many spiritual traditions maintain, that the same open space resides in it as that space in which we lived before the structure of the ego was erected? What else could it be?

Whatever the case may be, the development of ego is directed at building an impregnable fortress to which others are seldom admitted and then only when blessed with our permission.

But there is another side to the closed nature of our ego, to the impenetrableness of this mental structure: it is also impossible to get out of it. The stronger and more invulnerable ego becomes the more it becomes a prison. This is an inadvertent and certainly not consciously desired side-effect of the development of ego: we have imprisoned our fundamental humaneness. We feel deeply dissatisfied and do not see that we have caused this imprisonment ourselves, that it is our own personal "Fall." As we have already stated with the metaphor of the cocoon, the impenetrability of ego only causes us to feel our separateness more keenly. True, we are provided with much psychological comfort, since we have our own interpretation for every possible situation in life which renders it harmless, but the atmosphere within this structure is particularly stale and dark. There is no window that we can open and we suffer greatly because of this.

Obviously, the concrete form of ego varies in every person since each individual constructs it with his own mental material. The complexity of each structure varies as well. Some people maintain a small hut and, precisely because it is so small, it is easy to build it out of concrete. Other designs include huge palaces with tall splendid towers that reach high into the heavens and extensive additions that take up much space; in short, a construction that is very impressive but also very vulnerable: extra measures are necessary to guard against collapse and possible intruders. Guards must be employed to watch the gates of this structure so that no one enters and throws everything into confusion or steals everything. In all cases, ego and our egocentric thoughts isolate us from direct naked experience. Proust expresses it in this way:

> And then my thoughts, did they not form a similar sort of hiding place, in the depths of which I felt that I could bury myself and remain invisible even when I was looking at what went on outside? When I saw any external object, my consciousness that I was seeing it would remain between me and it, enclosing it in a slender, incorporeal outline which prevented me from ever coming directly in contact with the material form; for it would volatilise itself in some way before I could touch it, just as an incandescent body which is moved towards something wet, never actually touches moisture, since it is always preceded, itself, by a zone of evaporation. (Proust 1954, 85)

Buried deeply in the fortification of ego, we intensely desire open space, playfulness and freedom. We suspect that they are to be found outside of our structure. This desire is our natural and original desire to see life flourish — Thomas Aquinas called this the *desiderium naturale*. Now that our separation has become a psychological fact, this desire manifests itself as the desire to *unite* with our world. Thus, simultaneously with the rise of ego, there is the desire to undo this separation. It increases our restlessness within this split. It motivates us to make many attempts to break out. These attempts go in two directions.

In the one direction, these attempts take on the nature of attempts to change or destroy our concrete everyday situation: a different, job, partner or environment. We tend to think that there is something in our surroundings that must change in order for our original warmth in life to be restored — that warmth that we suspect always exists even though we do not know where to find it.

In the other direction, we attempt to change or destroy our ego: we search for another concept of ourselves, another state of being, try to become another person. Whatever direction we go in, these attempts are fundamentally ineffective precisely because at each moment they recreate again and again the dualistic experience of reality of ego. Thus the result of these attempts is the opposite: the battle against "this" or "that" only intensifies our preoccupation with and belief in the existence of this and that. And that belief intensifies our imprisonment and pain. It intensifies an aggressive and defensive attitude toward life.

THE DEVELOPMENT OF EGOCENTRIC EMOTIONALITY

Thus even though the "blueprint" of ego differs for every person, its appearance is still based on universal psychological principles. We have described a number of those principles in terms of mental movements that lead to a more or less solid ego. But there is more: these mental movements also form the basis for the development of an egocentric emotionality. How does this work?

To answer this question, let us return for a moment to the process of ego-identification within the development of ego. In this process, external or internal phenomena alike are those with which we do or do not identify ourselves (our ego). Sometimes we identify ourselves with our bodies and at other times we do not. The same happens with our perceptions, our emotions, ideas or consciousness. But in all of these cases a dualistic experience of reality emerges within which ego is defined as a sort of entity over against its world.

Things can attract or repel one another or move alongside one another without exerting any influence on one another. Analogous to this, between the *I* conceived as an entity and the other things a game of attraction, repulsion or indifference begins. It is as if ego approaches every situation with the question: shall I draw it toward me, repel it or ignore it? Is this situation important to me because I can get something out of it or repulsive to me because I am threatened by it or is it not important to me at all? Stated in psychological terms, with the appearance of ego in our self-experience, greed, aggression and indifference come into play with respect to the surroundings of ego. In Buddhist psychology, these three emotions are called *poisons* (Sanskrit: *kle'sas*) because they poison our mind. They are the basic emotions of a mentality within which ego is present. The egocentric emotionality of the profane mentality has made its entrance.

It is interesting that emotions (and thoughts, as we shall see in detail in chapter four) are directed at something. We call this the intentional nature of emotions — that is, emotions have an *object*. Thus a person or situation can be the object or target of our aggression or passion. We have also seen that we do not always identify with our emotions and ideas: "I was carried away by my emotions; the idea came to me. . . ." At that moment we perceive our emotions (and ideas) as external, thus belonging to the world outside of our ego; they themselves have become objects to us. Therefore, emotions not only have an object but can also be an object themselves.

When we conceive of an emotion as an object, our self-experience once again undergoes a dualistic split, a further fragmentation and complication: I and my emotion. The question can then arise as to what I think of my emotion, how I must react to it. Once again the three poisons reveal themselves: shall I foster my emotion (indulgence), fight it (repression) or ignore it (denial)? At that moment *emotions about emotions* arise. We are all familiar with this internal fragmentation and complication: "I enjoyed my burst of anger." "It angered me that I desired her so." These mental moves by which we make internal phenomena objects of other internal phenomena (emotions about emotions, ideas about ideas, ideas about emotions and *vice versa*) open up far-reaching perspectives for the building of ego. We can complicate our mental life — our way of thinking, our emotional life — as much as we want or are able to.

Thus, we are dealing here with the phenomenon of *conflicting emotions*: at times we like becoming angry and at times we are angry precisely because we enjoy something. We become a mass of contradictions. Apparently, our emotional life is not a simple affair but includes emotions about emotions about emotions. We can always add to that which we have: at times we are irritated by something but have forgotten what it was. We regret this later on, although we feel it to be childish, etc. In this way we can develop very complex emotional lives and ways of thinking with more or less fixed patterns of emotional reactions toward other emotions. At times those patterns of reaction are so automatic and quick that the emotion that causes them no longer even penetrates our consciousness. We gradually become lost in the structure of ego. Our bookkeeping system becomes hopelessly confused. At a given moment, if we feel a certain dissatisfaction with ourselves, we no longer remember its source. This dissatisfaction is, as it were, the final, visible, exterior wall of ego. We suffer because of it and wonder whether or not it is time for psychotherapy.

Moreover, psychological research has proven that people who possess a very rich vocabulary and conceptual framework (and can therefore utilize a more detailed system of mental bookkeeping) have a greater range of emotions as well. Thus, there is also a connection between the conceptual framework that we have and the emotions that we can distinguish. Therefore, with the help of this conceptual framework and the possibility of viewing emotions as the object of other emotions and ideas, we can create a very elaborate emotional life. We can also identify with this and include it in our self-concept. We might even be somewhat proud of our nuanced emotionality and our ability to maintain order over such a demanding matter.

One might feel that there is something almost denigrating in the way in which we speak about the emotional life here. This would be incorrect, because something very important is involved: the development of ego's emotionality, that is to say, development in the emotional relationships between ego and its objects. And yet, in many contemplative traditions, we find that this internal development is not taken *entirely* seriously. It is acknowledged as something that appears and in that sense must be respected (this is always stressed), but we do not have to allow ourselves to be intimidated or guided by it either. That would be going too far. On balance, this development is the result of an unfortunate *turn of mind*, a *metanoia* or *conversion* in the wrong direction that distorts the emotional energy of our fundamental humaneness into egocentric emotions and thus chokes any mental flourishing.

In other words, there are real tears and crocodile tears: tears that we shed out of compassion and tears that we shed because our ego is hurt. Augustine goes so far as to wonder whether the latter are tears of real grief. When he loses his mother, he wonders whether the welling flood of tears is not an expression of a certain spiritual immaturity, of the desire to hold onto a piece of ego's territory of which his mother was a part, so that the flood of tears wells up more out of self-pity than out of love for his mother. He wonders whether, by shedding tears out of frustrated self-interest, he does not harm himself and others. Later he cries freely out of love and compassion for his mother, because of her minor sins and the life that she had led. Those tears are completely different from the ones he had shed earlier.

Thus in the spiritual traditions there is indeed a certain

hesitation with regard to emotionality of ego and further indulgence in it. But in addition to this, we also see a very strong interest in emotion because ego's emotionality is a very fertile area. Ultimately, all egocentric emotions, although they are distorted, contain the energy of our fundamental humaneness. The mental movements that lead to the rise of ego bring our emotional energy and humaneness under the control of ego. The energy of care is perverted into self-preservation, that of dedication into self-interest. Love shrinks to self-love, unconditional joy in life turns into the satisfaction of desires, equanimity is transformed into indifference and inspiration becomes ambition, power becomes high-handedness and freedom imprisonment. This is how the emotionality of the egocentric mentality arises.

FIRST-PERSON PSYCHOLOGY AND "EGO PSYCHOLOGY"

The development of ego not only leads to a cessation in our experiencing of our humaneness, so that in addition to no longer living out of that experience we also find it to be a perfectly normal, very human state of affairs. It also has consequences on the level of actions and speech, impeding our fundamental humaneness from becoming *visible* to others as well. On the level of speech, we tend to maintain our position as *I* and, if possible, strengthen it by doing some advertising for ourselves — making some slighting remark about others, satisfying our ambition and jealousy in order to extend our own little kingdom. Our egocentric mentality is also expressed in actions: taking things that are not ours, creating situations by which we please our ego, destroying that which does not satisfy us or threatens us. And so we slip into various egocentric patterns of behavior — behavioral patterns under which we and others suffer. Perhaps in our interaction with people we have acquired the idea that, with regard to protecting our ego, it is better to strike the first blow. In new situations we then immediately tend to assert and display ourselves, to dominate the situation. Or perhaps we are of the opinion that we can best protect our ego by going through life in as inconspicuous a way as possible so that no one will take aim at us. These behavioral patterns are the externally visible, bitter fruits of our internal attitude. They can be so deeply ingrained that they persist even if we have lost faith in their effectiveness as protectors of our ego. That is why the spiritual traditions not only provide mental disciplines that are directed at recognizing and letting go of the mental movements made by ego but also offer disciplines that are directed at transforming actions and speech. We will focus on this in the second part of this volume.

From the perspective of ego, the egocentric mentality, emotionality and way of functioning is self-evident. Psychology that arises from this perspective is a sort of *ego psychology*, according to which certain emotions are self-evident: a human being is a creature that . . . and then a catalogue of the basic qualities of the egocentric mentality follows that portrays the human being as a selfish creature that seeks satisfaction, personal comfort and the fulfillment of its wishes. However, this apparently obvious and therefore appealing psychology is not harmless: based on a concept of humanity in which self-interest is the main motivation, it works its way through to our personal as well as our social lives. From the perspective of that concept of humanity, "egoism is seen as the most normal thing in the world. As a social power it has indeed brought us to material progress. But a society whose only standards for human actions are self-interest, usefulness and economic efficiency will fall apart" (Queen Beatrix of the Netherlands 1992).

Viewed from the perspective of the spiritual traditions, this ego psychology is no less and no more than the psychology of the hardened sinner. Thus this *ego psychology* is very different from the first-person psychology that we encounter in the spiritual traditions.

We have already commented that the term *ego* is not the same as the personal pronoun "I." This pronoun is a very useful term and we use it in this text regularly in order to refer to people in the first person. The human being in the first person is central in contemplative psychology — a psychology that has the egoless, open space of experience rather than the ego as its starting point. It is an egoless psychology that studies both the phenomena of ego in our self-experience and the dynamics of its disappearance. This is why the psychology that we encounter in the spiritual traditions is so different from our conventional psychology, which is not only largely a third-person psychology but also for the most part *ego psychology*.

It is not only because the spiritual traditions are directed at transcending ego (and its psychology) that their psychologies are distinct from conventional psychology. The first-person perspective also leads to a very distinctive view of the nature and function of the human mind and knowledge. Because of this it also has its own psychology about thinking, experience and awareness. This psychology lies at the foundation of the spiritual disciplines themselves. Before we examine the spiritual disciplines in the second part of this volume, we will look more closely at this psychology of mind and knowledge in the following chapter.

FOUR

Mind and Knowledge in Contemplative Psychology

INTRODUCTION

In the previous chapters we used a number of terms — *experience, thinking, stream of thought, discernment*, etc. — somewhat loosely, and also differently from the ways in which we normally use those terms. This follows from the typical first-person perspective of contemplative psychology. Before we look in the second part of this book at how the contemplative disciplines work with our mind, we should clarify the use of these terms in this psychology, for all these terms are related to *aspects of our mind*. They are also related to the question of *knowledge*. Clarifying these terms can also help us to see what is understood by *mind* and *knowledge* in contemplative psychology.

Generally speaking, in our ordinary use of language, terms

such as *mind, understanding, consciousness, insight*, etc. are somewhat vague. The concept *mind* is certainly used somewhat casually. It is difficult to put one's finger on what is meant by the term. We use it in various ways in everyday life: "He changed his mind"; "Let this mind be in you" (Phil. 2.5); "mind and body"; "She kept it in mind," etc. *Merriam-Webster's Collegiate Dictionary* lists nine different meanings:

> 1. recollection, memory; 2a. the element or complex of elements in an individual that feels, perceives, thinks, wills, and esp. reasons; 2b. the conscious mental events and capabilities in an organism; 2c. the organized conscious and unconscious adaptive mental activity of an organism; 3. intention, desire; 4. the normal or healthy condition of the mental faculties; 5. opinion, view; 6. disposition, mood; 7a. a person or group embodying mental qualities; 7b. intellectual ability; 8. Christian science: god; 9. a conscious substratum or factor in the universe.

In short, the term is too multifaceted to be reduced to one, comprehensive definition.

The results of modern academic psychology are not any more helpful. In this *psychology* the use of the term *mind* or *psyche* was — amazingly enough — almost taboo until recently. During the first decades of the twentieth century, the term disappeared from the vocabulary of psychology. This is a direct consequence of the third-person orientation typical of this psychology. After all, no one can experience our minds other than ourselves. Nor do theological and religious interpretations offer any kind of concrete understandings of these terms. In these fields, one does find discussion of the human soul and the mind and there are also extensive theoretical discussions in which all kinds of connections between the soul, the intuition, the intellect, the mind, etc. are outlined. Nevertheless, the emphasis in theology is not on the contemplative-psychological dimension but on the construction of a consistent theology. Answers to the practical issue of how we, as practitioners of a spiritual way of life, can work with our mental domain and the experience of reality that arises from it are not discussed.

We can, of course, find answers to concrete questions in psychotherapy, but in that field the questions are posed with an entirely different aim. Such questions are directed not at spiritual liberation but at the resolution of psychological problems.

The approaches to religion in depth psychology have provided us with suggestions for a more psychological interpretation of terms that often appear to have only a theological connotation. Examples of such can be found, for instance, in the work of Carl Gustav Jung (e.g., 1938) and more recently that of Eugen Drewermann (1990, 1991). Particularly when a religious tradition has lost its contemplative psychology, depth psychology can open our eyes to a more psychological point of view. It is here that we find the great value of, for example, Drewermann's work for the Christian tradition. But this approach also carries the risk of importing a terminology that is essentially alien to the spiritual tradition itself. Because of this, depth psychology can obscure precisely that which contemplative psychology has to offer us. This danger looms large, especially with respect to those non-Western or non-Christian religions that are rich with contemplative-psychological insights. The particular danger here is that one believes that the insights of other religions confirm one's own already existing psychological conceptual framework. The contemplative-psychological insights that do not fit into that framework are easily overlooked or considered to be irrelevant. Jung's "Foreword" to *The Tibetan Book of the Dead* (Evans-Wentz 1927) is a typical example of this, as Reynolds (1989, 71ff.) has pointed out.

It is therefore wise to take a different step first, i.e., to show what particular kind of psychological interpretation the spiritual traditions themselves employ with respect to terms such as *mind, consciousness, thinking, knowing*, and *experiencing*. We need to ask these traditions: how do the practitioners of the spiritual disciplines themselves use the terms? And what does the practice of these disciplines actually do with, to or in their mind? What do they *see* when they focus their attention on their mind *by means of the spiritual disciplines*? Just as we have already seen in our discussion of the term *ego*, we will now also see that, in answering these questions, contemplative psychology appears to give meanings to these terms that are different from the meanings we usually give them and which we encounter in contemporary academic psychology.

MIND IN CONTEMPLATIVE PSYCHOLOGY

In the previous chapters, we used the term *mental domain* a number of times. This term gives a first clue as to what contemplative psychology understands by the concept of *mind*. We also saw that contemplative psychology is primarily a first-person psychology and this means that according to this psychology the mental domain can be *experienced*. We can "experience" or "see," in a certain sense, our mind. Our mind is thus not a domain about which we can only think, speculate and imagine — as if it was the other side of the moon — but we can see our mental activity and experience it consciously.

We have also used the terms *thinking* and *stream of thought* in a very broad sense. Everything that occurs within us — what we think, imagine, remember, feel, hope and fear — is found within this stream. And this stream, with all its turbulence, is not something separate from experience but constitutes a part of it. Our stream of thoughts, or our thinking, is one stream next to the stream of sensory experience. They merge together to form what we have called our *experience of reality*.

What else has arisen in the previous chapters that is relevant for the question of what is meant by *mind* in contemplative psychology? In chapter two, we discussed the contemplative view that people have at their disposal a kind of "internal capacity for perception," that is, that they are in a position to see clearly the movement of their mind. In that context we already spoke of the "enlightened eyes of our understanding" (Ephesians 1.18) and the "eye of wisdom" (Dalai Lama 1981). In ordinary language, as well, we speak of the "mind's eye." The word *eye* is of course a metaphor for an aspect of our mind. Which aspect? It has something to do with mindfulness, with awareness or consciousness.

We now have three terms relating to our mind: *thinking, experience* and *consciousness*. We will analyze more closely the contemplative-psychological meanings of these terms, starting with the relation between thinking and experience.

The Relation between Thought and Experience

The contemplative view that our *thinking* — the movement of our mind, our stream of thoughts with all its ideas, emotions and desires — can be experienced deviates from the approaches of academic psychology, as well as from our everyday psychology. In the latter two types of psychology, thinking is viewed as something that more or less stands *outside* and over against experience. Elsewhere (de Wit 1991, 95f.), I have used the following metaphor to characterize this view: we often have the feeling that our thinking — our stream of thoughts — occurs, so to speak, *backstage* of our experience, as if this thinking, separated from the theatre of our experience, leaves our experience undisturbed. We then look upon it as an activity that is carried out in a kind of private space.

On stage we have our world of experience (about which we have our thoughts) and backstage we have our thoughts.

The view that thoughts and experience are two separate phenomena is widespread, also in Western philosophy. This idea rests on the apparent distance that our internal commentary seems to take with respect to our experience. We discussed this in the previous chapter. Within the contemplative-psychological perspective, in which thinking is something that can be experienced, thinking no longer stands backstage. Rather, both what we experience via our senses and our thoughts about what we experience happen on stage.

This metaphor does not only indicate that thinking is seen as something to be experienced but also that there is a reciprocal relationship between thinking and experience: not only can we *think about our experiences*, but we can also *experience our thoughts*. This is a key point of contemplative psychology (see de Wit 1991, 78).

Consciousness

Let us now look the contemplative-psychological term *consciousness*. We saw that we can be either conscious or not of our thoughts. Sometimes we notice that we are sitting somewhere thinking and at other times we are so lost in thought that we do not even notice that we are thinking. Our mind's eye closes, as it were. Mentally, we are asleep; we have drowned in our stream of thoughts. We are not awake mentally. Afterwards, when we come to our senses again, most of what we thought about has been forgotten. We remember, perhaps, that we thought of an errand we had to run and possibly the last link of the chain of thoughts — a memory of someone from the third grade — is still vivid in our mind but we no longer know how we arrived at that thought.

But our mind's eye can close not only with respect to our stream of thoughts. The same phenomenon also arises when we speak, act or perceive with our senses. It can be that we are doing something — perhaps talking out loud to ourselves — and yet do not notice that we are doing it. It is as if an automatic pilot has taken over. For example, we might be following our usual route to work and, when we arrive, we realize that we managed to do so unscathed, with stoplights and crosswalks, etc., but cannot remember how. Our senses have obviously been working — nothing has happened to us — but we have *not been conscious* of the route we have taken. We were, as is well expressed by an interesting word, *absentminded*. We were not "there." We were, as it were, carried along unconsciously by the stream of our sensory experience.

What does this phenomenon say about our mind? We can formulate it very briefly as follows: we are obviously capable of experiencing our sensory and mental stream *consciously* or *unconsciously*. Here a new term has come into our analysis of mind: *being (un)conscious*. This way of speaking reflects the fact that the term *consciousness* in contemplative psychology refers to a *quality* of experience or perception. Its use is linguistically similar to terms like *naked-ness, happiness, eager-ness*, etc. Therefore, *consciousness* does not refer to a mental faculty or region. This is why we will also avoid the use of a term like *the unconscious*, which suggests a kind of region in our mind of which we are not conscious. Instead, we will use the neologism *unconsciousness* as shorthand for the *absence of the quality of consciousness*. We will also use related terms such as (lack of) mindfulness, mindlessness and (lack of) awareness in the same way. When discussing the mental disciplines in chapters seven and eight, we will introduce mindfulness and awareness as two aspects of the quality of consciousness.

In terms of the metaphor of a play, then, unconsciousness refers to the moments when the audience dozes off during the performance or when it only has attention for the star and does not pay any attention to the other players. "All the world's a stage," said Shakespeare in *As You Like It*, "and all the men and women merely players." But what kind of play would it be if we — simultaneously the audience and the players themselves — sat in the theatre and dozed off? Or did we come to the performance in the first place hoping that there would be seats comfortable enough for us to take a nap? The contemplative traditions have quite a bit to say about this and, as we shall see, the practice of the mental disciplines have everything to do with this.

Experience and Consciousness

We have seen that we can experience things both consciously and unconsciously and that this applies both to the mental domain as well as the sensory domain. We find this view not only in the contemplative traditions but also in the old European psychology of consciousness. We will not go into the latter in detail, but some terminological connections are perhaps worth mentioning.

Let us first say something about modern psychology. In modern psychology, the experience of events in the sensory domain is often referred to by the term *perception*. The connection with consciousness is that perception is selective: not all impressions that we undergo receive the same amount of attention. Here a mental process called *selective attention* (Gleitman 1986, 219) plays a role. Moreover, the phenomenon that people can direct their attention to something subconsciously, i.e., without being yet aware of it, is as well-known to this psychology as it is to the driver who drives automatically. So-called *anticipation* can be done unconsciously in traffic. To notice something (consciously) and to perceive something are two different mental events in modern psychology.

In Wundt's early psychology of consciousness, this distinction was also made *vis-à-vis* the mental domain. Wundt used the term *apperception* to refer to "the directing of the attention to psychological content" (Duijker et al. 1964, 424). In Wundt, "psychological content" can be both an element from our stream of thoughts and an element of perception, that is, an element derived from the stream of sensory perception. For him, perceptions also count as mental content. If we direct our apperception to a thought or perception, they then lie within what Wundt calls the "focus of vision" (*Blickpunkt*). They are then conscious. What falls outside this focus lies in the "field of vision" (*Blickfeld*) of which one is only vaguely aware. *Blickfeld* and *blickpunkt* together determine the range and focus of our awareness or apperception. We are not aware of whatever thoughts or perceptions lie beyond them. In short, Wundt's term *apperception* lends itself well to what we intend by the *conscious perception* of mental content. Also, according to Wundt, perception itself can but need not be conscious.

It is interesting that Wundt's terminology is closely related to that found in Buddhist contemplative psychology. The noticing of mental content is there called *manovijnana*. *Vijnana* can be translated by "consciousness" and *manas*, of which *mano* is a declension, by "mind" or "the mental." *Manovijnana* is therefore a moment of consciousness that has mental content as its object. In this psychology, sensory perceptions are events of which we can be aware as *mental events*. At that moment, they lie within the range of *manovijnana* and are then *apperceived*. We will not go any further into these connections. For those who wish to explore Buddhist psychology more deeply, Komito's *Nagarjuna's "Seventy Stanzas": A Buddhist Psychology of Emptiness* (1987) offers a good introduction, as does Geshe Rabten's *Mind and its Functions* (1992).

To return to our main theme, what is concretely meant by the term *(un)conscious experience*? We already gave an example of unconscious experience of sensory phenomena: we can, without noticing, i.e., without paying attention, see, hear or do something, as the example of walking to work illustrates. Conscious experience is then the opposite: we notice the stream of our experience. We are not absent but present.

But there is also the (un)conscious experience of our mind, of the *mental domain*. Let us look at two situations familiar to all of us: we can *be in thought* and we can *see our thoughts* (cf. De Wit 1991, 111). If we *are in thought* and carried along by our stream of thoughts, we often do not notice that we are thinking. We then live in our world of thoughts which we experience at that moment as reality. We undergo all kinds of imaginary joys and sorrows. At such moments we have to do with the *unconscious experiencing of our thinking*.

When we awaken from our stream of thoughts, we then notice that we were thinking and we see often only the tail end of our stream of thoughts. At that moment we have to do with what we will call the *conscious experiencing of our thinking*. Then we experience our thoughts no longer as reality but truly as thoughts. Practically speaking, there are all kinds of gradations between conscious and unconscious experiencing of our thoughts. They can be completely transparent and we see them for what they are. Sometimes they are a veil of clouds that places our experiences in a certain light. And often they are like a thick fog that obscures our view completely, so that we live completely in our world of thoughts. We can also formulate it as follows: our consciousness has a *degree of clarity*. But we can just as well say that this clarity is a *quality of our experiencing*: phenomena are continually *experienced more or less consciously*. And this applies to the experiencing of both sensory and mental phenomena.

Two Aspects of Consciousness

With respect to the functioning of consciousness, two closely connected aspects are quite generally distinguished from each other within the spiritual traditions: one more static and the other more dynamic.

The first aspect is indicated by terms such as *mindfulness, attention, concentration* and *one-pointedness*. It is the ability to direct our attention to something and to continue to keep our attention on it. It is the opposite of absentmindedness, of a restless, chaotic state of mind. This aspect confers a certain *stability* and *precision* to our way of experiencing: mindfulness counteracts the tendency to jump from one thing to another. It creates space for us to recognize the details of our actual situation. Thus, many of the spiritual traditions also emphasize that the cultivation of mindfulness is at the same time the development of a certain mental calm. We are not talking here of a spasmatic, forced form of mindfulness but of mindfulness that finds its natural resting place in itself. Stability, precision and rest are all indications of this first aspect of consciousness. We will discuss how the spiritual disciplines can help us develop this aspect in chapter seven.

This first aspect of consciousness is the basis for the development of the second, which we indicated already in previous chapters by the term *discernment*. This aspect is a *discriminating awareness* which offers an overview of and insight into the coherence of phenomena (both mental and sensory) which surface in the stream of our experience. This aspect is the mobile, dynamic quality of consciousness. It has a quality of inquisitiveness or interest — not an intellectual inquisitiveness but one such as displayed by a young and healthy child for what he or she sees around him- or herself: he or she looks around with an open mind and in a carefree way. Therefore, this aspect of consciousness is also indicated by terms such as openmindedness or clarity of mind. It is an intelligent, alert openness, which is not hindered by biases, preoccupations or prejudiced ideas — in short, a way of being aware that is *free from fixation* on our conventional experience of reality with its running commentary in the form of a stream of thoughts. The stream of thoughts need not be absent for this. To the contrary, precisely because this alert intelligence is not inhibited or caught by our stream of thoughts it can perceive its effect on our experience of reality. This kind of discriminating awareness gives us knowledge and insight, and it is cultivated by the practice of the spiritual *disciplines of insight* which we will discuss in chapter eight.

An image sometimes used for this aspect of being conscious is that of a bird — an eagle or *garuda* — that glides through the air with great ease and silence, almost without moving its wings, and has a perfect view of the world of phenomena. This image thus represents those moments when our awareness is free from fixation.

Such moments sometimes arise spontaneously when the intensity of our experience is very great, as in stirring moments. Our perception then changes as a result of an extremely *energetic alertness*. Through this we experience more quickly and more per moment than is usually the case when our consciousness is conditioned by our stream of thoughts. It is as if time stops or slows to a crawl. Filmmakers are also acquainted with this: they attempt to awaken the suggestion of intensity through *slow motion*, which they use during certain events in the film: an accident, a first embrace, a death scene. The filmmaker thus appeals to what we recognize from our own experience of intense situations — situations in which our consciousness is torn loose, is free and because of that is often capable of seeing the smallest details of a situation for a brief moment with an unbelievable clarity. Because of this ability, this being freely aware, people have sometimes been able to save lives: during the *slow-motion* experience of a threatening accident they appear to have been able to find the time to perform the action that saves a life.

This discriminating awareness, which is free from all inhibition or fixation, is an *unconditioned awareness*. It constitutes the *seed* as well as the *fruit* of what the contemplative traditions seek to cultivate (see chapter eight). This awareness, when cultivated fully in all directions, has been given many names: enlightenment, fulfillment, abyss, death, eternal life, surrender, etc. We spoke of this already in chapter three. Whatever name we give to it, it is these moments of intense, unconditioned awareness when our mind's eye opens — initially perhaps only for an instant. Those moments make us capable of disentangling illusion and reality and seeing human life unveiled. The discernment that is then active is nothing else than the *clarity of mind* of our fundamental humaneness, of which we spoke in the introduction to this book.

The Relation between Stability and Discernment

There are many metaphors available that indicate that the two aspects of consciousness discussed above belong with each other. Discernment or discriminating awareness — the ability to see our true face, as is sometimes said — is developed only on the basis of mental stability or calm: a calm that results from letting go of our fixation on our turbulent stream of thoughts. This calm makes the mind (consciousness) function like a mirror, clear water, the motionless flame of a candle, etc. Calm is not an aim, as is sometimes thought, but a means, i.e., a means to insight. In the sayings of the Christian desert fathers, we find the story of two monks who visited another monk and asked him what his progress consisted in. In his answer he illustrated the importance of rest for the development of insight:

> [H]e was silent for a little, and poured water in a cup. And he said: "Look at the water." And it was cloudy. And after a little he said again: "Now look, see how clear the water has become." And when they leant over the water, they saw their faces as in a glass [mirror]. And then he said to them: "So it is with man who lives among men. He does not see his own sins because of the turmoil. But when he is at rest, especially in the desert, then he sees his sins. (Chadwick 1958, 43)

The same idea, but formulated somewhat more optimistically, is expressed as follows: "Without tranquillity and mind stirs, like water, and cannot settle in tranquil absorption. Such a mind cannot attain a true understanding of its inherent purity" (Namgyal 1986, 33); "When the mind settles naturally in quiescent absorption, free from dullness and sensual incitement, it vividly perceives its very essence" (Namgyal 1986, 35, quoting the third *Bhavanakrama*). We thus see here the interesting paradox that the more restful our mind is, the more mobility and room for mobility our discernment has.

Rest, in the contemplative meaning of the word, is therefore certainly not the drowsy, uninterested calm of which we most often think when we hear the word. In a spiritual sense, calm is a form of mental *stabilitas*, a form of internal stability. This is a steadfastness that does not allow itself to be carried along or away by our turbulent stream of thoughts and precisely because of that makes the stream visible or conscious. For that reason, this calm is at the same time the basis of open insight. The less our awareness is pulled along by our stream of thoughts, the more we can see this stream of thoughts in an unbiased way. And the more open our awareness is, the more energetic and lively our discernment, our insight, begins to manifest itself. Mental calm, of which the spiritual traditions speak, thus appears to contain a great deal of energy. When this energy of wakefulness begins to function, the calm appears to be a very *dynamic* one, which in one single movement furnishes a view of *both the totality and the details* of each moment of experience. This wakefulness incinerates every distortion and self-hypnosis that belongs to our usual, fixated consciousness. We will discuss later how these two aspects are cultivated by the practice of the mental disciplines.

THE CONTEMPLATIVE PSYCHOLOGY OF THOUGHT

Let us now further explore the concept of *thought* as it is used in contemplative psychology. The way in which this concept is employed in spiritual traditions is different from conventional psychology in an interesting way. I will discuss three points here.

The Broad Meaning of the Term "Thought"

First of all, in most spiritual traditions the meaning of the term *thought* is very closely associated with the term *stream of thoughts*. The term *thought* is often used as a general term for all mental movement, for *everything that occurs within our head*. This broad definition entails that the term *thinking* is almost synonymous with *mental activity*. This broad use is not dissimilar to the way we use the term in everyday life. If we say, "I am thinking about it the whole time," no one is surprised to hear that our stream of thoughts includes images, desires and possibly even strong emotions. In academic psychology the term "thought" is not defined this broadly: it is defined as a cognitive activity that does not include emotion and will or feelings and desires.

The Content and Object of Thought

The second important point has to do with the ambiguity of the term *thought* in our everyday language. If, for example, we ask John, "What are you thinking about?" and he answers, "My work situation," we can interpret this answer in two ways. First, we can interpret it in the sense that John is referring to a situation outside of himself, outside of his thoughts about it, a situation that we, as his colleagues, also know. In a certain sense, the situation is independent of John's thinking about it. It is that *about which* John is thinking. This situation is, we then say, the *object* of his thought, that which the thought is about.

This way of interpreting it also lies at the bottom of the idea that thoughts are separate from the object of thought. The object of John's thoughts, his work situation, exists separate from his thoughts about it. Whether John thinks about it or not, the work situation itself does not cease to exist. Even when we think about our *actual* situation at this moment, we can have the feeling that our thinking is something separate and does not influence the situation. We often believe that we influence our actual situation only when we begin to act. But our thinking is of course also part of our actual situation. By thinking about it our actual situation *has* already been changed. We discussed this point already previously in terms of the stage metaphor.

But there is still another way to understand John's answer. If John says that he is thinking about his work situation, we can look at it this way: John is telling us about the *content* of his thinking. He is telling us which formation of thought is occurring in his head at that moment. His thought has a certain form: images of his desk, conversations with colleagues, etc. The content of this thought does not lie outside of John or outside of his thought but within it. In short, we have two interpretations: one that refers to the *object* of a thought and one that refers to the *content* of his thought. The object lies *outside* the thought and the content lies *within* it.

The *object* and the *content* of thinking are therefore two *very different things*. There is often, though not always, a relation between the object and the content of a thought. The image in John's thought of his desk and his colleagues can, for example, be a more or less faithful mental likeness of his desk and colleagues. We then say that the content of the thought is a *mental representation* of the *object* of the thought. Stated conversely, the object is represented in thinking by the *content* of the thought.

Not all such contents are mental representations. We can, for example, think of a situation that does not exist: "I am thinking of a sunny island where I am lying in the shadow of palm trees, while eternity unfolds before me." If that is John's answer to our question, then we view it simply as an answer about the *content* of his thoughts and not about the object. We do not proceed on the basis that this thought is a mental representation of a certain object.

Therefore, the contents of thought do not need to have any relation to an object in experience. Also, the wealth of their forms is not determined or limited by these objects. They are determined by the wealth of our imagination, by our mental creativity and the material that is available in the form of memories in our stream of thoughts. That this creativity can also be destructive and make us believe in ghosts, devils and even worse has been noted in our discussion of the development of ego. We saw there that we can form contents of thoughts about which we consequently make the incorrect claim that they have an object: our ego and egocentric world of thought. We begin to feel anxiety and fear with respect to imaginary dangers. We then engage in tilting at the windmills of our egocentric experience of reality.

The Contents of Thought are the Forms of Thought

A third characteristic of the term *thinking* in the spiritual sense is that it refers to a dynamic or fleeting phenomenon. The contents of thoughts are *not mental entities*. What, then, are they and how do they come into being? They are shorter or longer phases or moments in our stream of thoughts. In that stream, which cannot be observed by our eyes or ears, all kinds of *mental formations* in very flexible and continually changing forms are almost constantly occurring. The *contents* of thought are the *forms* of thought.

In Buddhist psychology, thoughts are often compared with cloud formations: clouds come and go, form and dissolve again into the sky. Their forms are continually changing yet follow certain patterns. For example, a cloud does not completely dissolve from one second to the next but gradually. Our mental clouds have their own dynamic as well. They can arise and evaporate slowly but also appear and disappear from one moment to the next, as when our mood suddenly changes or something just occurs to us. This dynamic shows us the nature of our stream of thoughts. Another metaphor is that thoughts are a kind of "mental clay," a soft, pliable mental "substance." In the mind, they are continually reshaped: now a horse, then a human being, an ashtray and finally perhaps just a pancake or a rolling pin. These metaphors emphasize that the *contents* of thoughts do not exist as things but as *forms* of thoughts, as thought formations. This concludes our discussion of the term *thought* in contemplative psychology for now.

CONNECTIONS BETWEEN THINKING, EXPERIENCING AND CONSCIOUSNESS

On the basis of what we have said about thoughts, their content (= form) and their object we can indicate two important differences between thinking and experiencing. The first difference is simply this: experiences have content (form) but no object, while thoughts can have both content and an object. If I experience pain or see a cyclist, then the pain or the cyclist is *that which* I experience — that is, it is the *content* of my experience. That is why we can say that we think *about* something but not that we experience "about something." Experience does not have an object in the way that a thought can have one.

When I think about an experience, then the experience is the *object* of my thinking. And *what* I think about the experience is the *content* of my thinking. Conversely, I can also experience a thought. Then the thought is the content of my experience. To give a concrete example, if I see a blackbird, the bird becomes the content of that experiential moment. If I then think, "Ah, a blackbird," this is a thought about the experience. The experience itself is then the object of the thought, whereas the mental form "Ah, a blackbird," is the content of the thought. Or, if I recall a precious memory at a certain moment, that memory is the content of that mental experience. It is also possible that I begin to reflect on that memory and that, for example, the content of my thinking is something like: "That was indeed a very special moment in my life." Here the memory itself is the object of the thought.

Precisely because the content and the object of thinking are two different things, the one can *represent* the other, that is, the content of a thought can be a mental representation of the object. In the case of experience, it is different. We do not have two separate things (content and object) here by which the one can be a representation of the other. Experiences therefore do not represent things. That which we experience is not a representation of something else, as the content of thoughts can be. That which we experience simply *presents* itself. It is not a representation but a *presentation*.

If we experience something — either mentally or in a sensory way — the experience *simply* is; it is not only a presentation but it is also *present*. It does not represent something else but is directly present to us at this moment. From a first-person perspective, the content of experiences is the only thing that we experience. Thoughts can thus be representations, but experiences — including the experience of a certain thought — cannot.

An example here will perhaps help to clarify matters. Let us return to seeing the blackbird in the tree. The tree and the blackbird form the content of our experience. If we turn around, so that we no longer see the tree, we can still think of the blackbird in the tree, we can still form the representation. At that moment, the blackbird and the tree are the content of our thought or representation. The object of the thought — the blackbird and the tree — is then absent from our experience. We can at best only claim that our representation is one of the object, if the blackbird has not — startled by so much philosophizing — flown away.

A second difference, connected with the first, between thinking and experiencing is this. The term *experience*, as used in the first-person perspective of contemplative psychology, is related to what is present in the here and now. *Experiencing* is always *here and now*. This is a somewhat more limited use than that which we find in ordinary usage. There we do speak about "having experience with something" and we mean then that we have become acquainted with something in the past. The meaning of the term *experience* then approaches that of the term *remember*. In contemplative psychology, however, experience has to do with what we *now* undergo. For example, what I experience now is that I am writing. What you, the reader, experience now is that you are reading — this very sentence in fact. But you are now already experiencing a different sentence. It is quite nice to communicate with you for a moment between the lines. But allow me to proceed with the argument.

We cannot experience that which is past nor that which is to come. Experience is, by definition, experience of what is now *present*. In other words, we cannot experience the past nor the future. In that sense, experience has no temporal dimension, no extension in time. It is different in that respect from thinking. Even though a thought always occurs only here and now, its content does have a temporal dimension. The *content* of a thought can, at any rate, very well be a memory or an expectation, that is, a mental representation of something that has been or is still to come. But, again, the experience of the memory or expectation occurs only here and now. It would be a mistake to believe that the *experience of a memory* is the *experience of the past* or that the *experience of an expectation* is an *experience of the future*. It is true that in everyday usage we play fast and loose with this distinction. But if we think about it, then we understand that we cannot experience the past and the future. The past no longer exists and the future does not (yet) exist. What does exist at the moment they appear are memories and expectations as the contents of thought. And those we can (consciously or unconsciously) experience. In our discussion of the mental disciplines of the spiritual way of life we will see that their focus on experience and experiential knowledge (perceptual knowledge) coheres closely with their focus on experience and life here and now.

The I as "Ding an Sich"

Let us take up a related question that often arises in this context: what about the *I*? Does experience not imply *someone who experiences* and does thinking not imply a *thinker*? In everyday language, we are indeed inclined to smuggle in a subject: we are inclined to think that there must be *some-one* who is aware, thinks or experiences. If by *someone* we mean a (human) being here, we must admit, of course, that this is so.

But most of the time by *someone* we mean something else, namely our *I* or ego. And this way of thinking can occur, of course, only within a dualistic way of experiencing reality. In the sense in which the term *ego* is used by contemplative psychology, however, it is the *content* of a thought and not the thinker. The assumption that there is a thinker is also a thought. Apparently, we identify this thinker by means of the thought, "*I* think about something." But if we (that is, human beings) consciously experience this thought, then we see that it shows nothing more than the thought itself. By itself, it proves nothing: neither the existence nor nonexistence of an entity called *I* nor of any entity that we can call the thinker or the one who experiences. In short, if we presuppose the existence of an *I*, then the presupposition is still nothing more than a thought. In itself a thought has no demonstrative power. We can think what we want.

We already saw in chapter three that, from the perspective of contemplative psychology, the *I* is not presupposed as something that precedes our experience of reality. The *I* is not presupposed as an invisible entity *behind* the experience: it is seen as a mental construction that can or cannot be present *in* our experience.

The idea that something exists or must be presupposed behind the experience is an old philosophical theme. Some philosophers have questioned not only the existence of the *I* but more generally whether there was something outside the realm of experience, whether our experience could, like our thought, have an object after all, even if it was an object that we by definition could not experience. Assuming such an object, Immanuel Kant christened it the *Ding an Sich*.

From the perspective of contemplative psychology, the answer is that we can at most imagine — that is, conceive of — the existence of such an object. But as we already saw above, such an object exists, from a psychological point of view, only as a thought, a thought that we might or might not — depending on our philosophical views — want to carry along in our stream of thoughts. The *Ding an Sich* itself — whether we believe in its existence or not and whether we mean by it a subject, an *ego* or an object — we have never seen and will also never experience. For if we could experience it, it would no longer be the one who is experiencing but that which is experienced.

Thought and Consciousness

Finally, a remark about the influence that thought and consciousness can have on each other. A feature of our stream of thoughts is that it flows on seemingly uninterruptedly. This impression arises because of its speed. As soon we wake up in the morning it seems to set its course and carries us along, so that we miss much of life. Because of this running mental commentary, there are a great many aspects in our stream of experience of which we are not aware. The metaphor of the film — now a metaphor for our stream of thoughts — is also helpful here. Films, which consist of separate images, suggest through their speed an uninterrupted movement, a continuous cinematic reality, which weakens the intensity of our being aware of the theatre and the chair on which we are sitting. Our discriminating awareness decreases and we become dependent on the limited space allowed us by the movie. Similarly, this narrowing of our awareness leads to our viewing our stream of thoughts as real. It is, at any rate, the only reality that we have at that moment, the only one of which we are aware. (See the earlier quotation from Proust in chapter three).

We may already suspect that the spiritual *disciplines of mindfulness* undo precisely this narrowing of our awareness and the fixation on our stream of thoughts by first of all decreasing the speed of our thinking. The *disciplines of insight* subsequently cultivate in us our ability to recognize the nature of our mind and experience of reality. Stated in another jargon, these disciplines make us aware of the way in which we interpret our experience. They are not directed at replacing one interpretation by another, a bad one by a better one. The spiritual traditions do recognize that we engage in an almost uninterrupted interpretation of our experiences. But their disciplines are directed at cultivating a *discriminating awareness* that allows us to see the *effect* of our interpretations on our experience of reality *from moment to moment*. For this reason, in many contemplative traditions it is said that this discriminating awareness leads to wisdom. What kind of wisdom is this? It is wisdom that causes us to recognize the confusing and painful illusion of our egocentric experience of reality and liberates us from it. In the Christian tradition it is called *diakrisis*; the Mahayana Buddhist tradition calls it *prajna* (literally: higher knowing). *Prajna* cuts through our being caught in *samsara*, our egocentric experience of reality, and makes *samsara* visible to us. It shows us the true nature of *samsara*: a self-created illusion. When this illusion is recognized as an illusion, it loses its hold on us. Then the world of phenomena, including all our illusions that have been recognized as such, appear to us in a different way, as *nirvana*. The egocentric experience of reality with its accompanying emotionality is extinguished and robbed of its power. The self-deception is broken. That is the kind of wisdom or, rather, the state of wisdom that spiritual traditions seek to cultivate. Then our fundamental humaneness comes to full bloom and can manifest itself in the world for the well-being of all living beings.

The development of wisdom by means of this discriminating awareness is described differently in the various contemplative traditions. But they all emphasize that the cultivation of awareness is a way to wisdom, insight or *contemplative knowledge*. We will discuss the nature of this contemplative knowledge below. In Part II we will see that all this is needed for a good understanding of the mental disciplines that we find in the contemplative traditions.

KNOWLEDGE AND INSIGHT IN CONTEMPLATIVE PSYCHOLOGY

Concepts such as *knowledge* and *insight, ignorance* and *confusion* have their own meanings in contemplative psychology. These meanings also clarify once again an aspect of what is meant by the human mind in this first-person psychology. One of the things with which the practice of the mental disciplines is concerned is the cultivation of insight into the nature of the human mind and experience. It is also said that this insight transforms our mind and experience. What kind of insight and knowledge do we have in mind here?

This is a question about the *epistemology* of the contemplative traditions. The old Greek word for knowledge is *epistèmè*, and *epistemology* means the theory of knowledge. A theory of knowledge explains what knowledge is and when something can be called "knowledge." In chapter three of de Wit (1991), we devoted a great deal of attention to this issue. Here we will summarize some of the key points of that chapter.

The reciprocal relation between thinking and experience (we can think about our experience and experience our thoughts) suggests two ways in which we can acquire knowledge. If we *think clearly about our experience*, this undoubtedly leads to a form of knowledge. We are wiser because of it. The kind of knowledge that we acquire thus is *conceptual knowledge*, for we think in ideas, in *concepts* — which is also the term used in psychology. As we saw above, concepts are elements in our stream of thoughts.

But this is not the only way to knowledge or insight. We can also try *to experience clearly* what goes on in our minds, our stream of thoughts by using our discriminating awareness, our mental discernment. This, of course, also yields a kind of insight or knowledge. This knowledge is not conceptual. We could very well call it *perceptual* knowledge: it comes into being not through thinking but by looking with our inner eye. This gives us a form of knowledge or insight that is *nonconceptual*, not based on concepts. It relies on clear vision and recognition rather than on concepts. In the Buddhist tradition it is said that it is a form of knowing, similar to a mute's knowing what sweetness tastes like but is unable to describe it. In the same vein, it is said that the knowledge that an enlightened person has of enlightenment is perceptual and inexpressible.

In contrast to modern psychology, which only considers conceptual knowledge to be scientific, these two forms of knowledge were recognized in early Western psychology and considered to be valid. William James called them respectively *knowledge-about* and *knowledge of acquaintance.* James writes: "I am acquainted with many people and things, which I know very little about, except their presence in the places where I have met them. . . . I cannot *describe* them. . . . At most, I can say to my friends, Go to certain places and act in certain ways, and these objects will probably come" (James 1981, 216). Thus, for example, we can describe only in a very limited way those with whom we are well acquainted. We may know hundreds of people by face but cannot give hundreds of different descriptions of faces. Our terminological apparatus and conceptual framework simply fall short. If we are asked, "What does the person look like?" we do not proceed much further than: brown eyes, quite tall, male, curly grey hair. We can perhaps say something in addition about the nose or the way he walks, but beyond that we have nothing left to say. Nevertheless, we would immediately recognize that person among a thousand. It is a very different kind of knowing than conceptual knowing.

Bertrand Russell would later refer to James's *knowledge-about* as *knowledge by description*. Because this form of knowledge is conceptual, it is closely bound up with the possibilities offered by language for describing something. I have gone deeper into this elsewhere (de Wit 1991, 124).

In almost all spiritual traditions, we find this distinction between these two forms of knowledge. Within the Christian tradition, one often finds a distinction between knowledge of the head (or understanding) and knowledge of the heart. The knowledge of the heart is understood as a form of perceptual knowledge, it is *acquaintance with*. Knowledge of the head is a form of conceptual knowledge: it is *knowledge about*.

The Function of Knowledge in the Spiritual Traditions

If there are two kinds of knowledge, we can also expect two methods for acquiring knowledge. Let us, before we look at this, first investigate what the *function* of conceptual and perceptual knowledge is within the spiritual traditions. Why are these traditions interested in knowledge? The scientific traditions (including scientific psychology) look for knowledge with the aim of *manipulating* the world of phenomena. But what purpose does the acquiring of knowledge within the spiritual traditions serve?

The aim of the spiritual traditions (including their psychology) is not to acquire a great deal of knowledge about the world in order to rule over it but to *change* the human being. In what respect, however, are human beings to be changed? The spiritual traditions focus on the opposite of knowledge: they are concerned with removing blindness, ignorance, darkness and confusion. To that end, knowledge — both perceptual and conceptual — is therefore ultimately only a useful instrument. The contemplative approach is not directed at gathering a great deal of information, for that can be as confusing as it is helpful (see below). The ultimate aim is the elimination of the confusion and ignorance that comes with our solipsistic and egocentric experience of reality. The human being who has accomplished this is a wise person, a person who *knows life* in the spiritual sense of the word.

Confusion and Ignorance

With what kind of blindness or confusion are the spiritual traditions concerned then? What is the nature of our ignorance and blindness? How can we characterize this in the terms of contemplative psychology?

First of all, we can be confused because we use the concepts we possess in an illogical way. We make mistakes in our reasoning and thus arrive at wrong conclusions. This is a form of *conceptual confusion* with which we are all too familiar. We can also be confused not because we draw the wrong conclusions but because we lack the concepts or information required for having insight into something. It can, for example, simply be that we lack the conceptual framework for understanding how a tape recorder works or how the human mind works. We simply do not know. Elsewhere I have called this *conceptual ignorance* (de Wit 1991, 87).

Of-old science has had a keen eye for both conceptual confusion and ignorance. That is the reason for its interest in *logic* — the theory that teaches us how to reason properly — and for the gathering of reliable *information* by means of empirical research.

But there are, in addition, other forms of confusion and

ignorance that lie not on the conceptual level but on the perceptual level, on the level of how we perceive something. We touched on them already briefly above. There are situations in which something escapes us; we do not pay attention. Someone leaves the room and we do not notice. That is a moment of ignorance in our perception. We call it *perceptual ignorance*.

There is yet another, very important phenomenon that also appears on the level of perception and about which we have already spoken extensively: the phenomenon that we mistake our *thoughts about a situation* for *the situation itself*. We confuse the map with the landscape itself. Or, in the terms that we used for this, we mistake the *content* of our thought for the *object* of our thought; we confuse the mental representation with that which is represented. This form of confusion we call *perceptual confusion*. (For a more extensive treatment, see de Wit 1991, 81ff.)

Within the spiritual traditions we find many examples for characterizing perceptual confusion. The most well-known in the Hindu and Buddhist traditions is perhaps that of the snake and the rope. When, in a dimly lit room in India, we step on something thin and round, we immediately think, "I have stepped on a snake," and recoil, shrieking. We *experience* a snake. But when we turn on the light, we might see that there is a rope on the floor and our experience changes at once. When we stepped on it, we actually had the experience of stepping on a snake. Our experience of reality was thus confused. In short, we have returned to the fundamental theme of contemplative psychology: the way in which we experience the world is also dependent on how we dress it up mentally, that is, with our thoughts.

The metaphor of the map, which is not the landscape, has yet another instructive side. Suppose we are sitting in a car next to the driver. The driver asks us where we are. We unfold the map and point to a red stripe: "Here, somewhere between Atlanta and New York." But the map reader could also have pointed outside and said, "Here — just look out the window." That is a different type of answer, perhaps somewhat less informative but certainly not incorrect. There is a world of difference between these two answers and in some cases the one answer is more adequate than the other. In answering the question "Who am I?" would we be better off consulting our self-concept, the map we have developed about ourselves than "looking out the window," that is, looking directly at ourselves, our mind? The latter is a metaphor for the practice of the disciplines of insight (see chapter eight).

The problem highlighted by the spiritual traditions is that we are not aware of when and where we use an internal map. We can no longer distinguish clearly whether we look at the map or out the window. The discernment of which we spoke above and which is necessary for this is often inactive, let alone developed. We live in our dressed-up experience without being able to recognize its magnitude and extension. The situation with the snake and the rope seems to be clear enough, but in everyday life the magnitude of the problem is often much more obscure. Our enemies and friends, for example — do they exist outside of us or only in our mind? The fact that John is a friend to someone and an enemy to another should make us think. Where is the enemy: within or outside of us? From the contemplative perspective the answer is that he is within us: he is the product and the object of our passion and aggression.

The enemy seems to be outside of us only because we *project* the idea that John is an enemy upon John. We dress John up as the enemy and thus ourselves as well: we become aggressive because we see John. This phenomenon is also recognized in clinical psychology and psychotherapy. Han Fortmann wrote an excellent work concerning the role this plays in the religious context. He remarks: "If I experience myself as the persecuted, I must interpret the image of the other, who is so multifaceted in many respects, in such a way that he is my persecutor" (Fortmann 1974, 351). This, of course, does not mean that if someone follows us with a knife and eventually threatens us physically, we do not have to take action. More strongly yet, if we should at that moment become lost in the thought, "Here is an enemy," we may well be a fraction of a second too late in grabbing the knife and defending ourselves effectively. Such a thought tears a hole in our attentiveness and readiness to fight. The basic discipline behind the Japanese martial arts is not to lose ourselves in such thoughts in dangerous situations. The consummate master in these arts "is not encumbered in any way, be it physical, emotional, or intellectual" (Suzuki 1970, 62). He sees the knife attack and reacts to it. He is not preoccupied with enemies.

In a classical metaphor, the nature of our perceptual confusion is compared with the mixing of oil and water. Stated in more modern terms, our dressed-up experience is a sort of skin lotion. This lotion consists of two clear liquids, oil and water. If we mix them up, we get a somewhat more solid substance, one that is no longer clear but murky. It actually consists of very small droplets, all of which are clear, but because both liquids are so mixed together we can no longer distinguish which is oil and which is water — we cannot tell which is our mental stream of experience and which is our sensory stream of experience. Because of this, we find ourselves in a self-created world, in which in addition a number of illusory personages and events, including ego in the sense in which we spoke above, appear. That experience dressed up by concepts, that skin lotion, contains our self-concept, our concept of the world, our concept of God and all the other concepts that we have developed. And as long as our discernment, our discriminating awareness, is not active, we cannot distinguish our self-concept from our true nature, our concept of God from God nor our concept of the world from reality. We then live in darkness. This is emphasized by almost all spiritual traditions.

Conceptual Knowledge and the Disciplines of Consciousness

We also find that the spiritual traditions emphasize that our *knowledge about* ourselves, reality or God can stand in the way of our *acquaintance with* ourselves, reality or God. Stated in terms of contemplative psychology, our conceptual knowledge can block the development of perceptual knowledge. If we think we know who we are, what is real and what not, who or what God is, why should we attempt a closer look? Why should we then still want to cultivate our discernment? Especially in our culture, in which conceptual knowledge is considered to be almost the only valid knowledge, this danger of intellectual complacency exists. Our ideas and presumptions are enough for us: we no longer need to look closely at something, for we already *know* what we are supposed to see (see de Wit 1991, 90). The intellectual understanding of the spiritual way of life, then, is easily confused with the experience of the spiritual way of life. And that is, as we said, a form of *perceptual confusion*. It actually withers that way of life. Instead of a willingness to tame our mind and develop wisdom, an intellectual arrogance easily arises — the arrogance that we *know* the spiritual path without ever having led that life. We do indeed know it to a certain extent intellectually, but not with the heart. Nothing has happened to us yet. We might dabble in spiritual concepts, reflect on them and believe that this occupation in itself is already the whole of the spiritual path. We may even derive a feeling of superiority from it. We then easily look down upon those who actually practice a spiritual discipline or upon those who without much knowledge use a primitive prayer like "O God, be merciful to me, a sinner." We recognize this theme from the parable of the Pharisee and tax collector (Luke 18.9–14).

This, however, is not to say that the spiritual traditions do not consider conceptual knowledge to be worthwhile. But it does say that spiritual traditions hold conceptual knowledge to be a *means* rather than the end. Conceptual knowledge can *point* us in the direction of perceptual knowledge. If we understand conceptual knowledge as a pointer, it can help us on the spiritual path. It can be a clue. Or, as it is said in the Buddhist tradition, conceptual knowledge can be like a finger that points us to the moon. If a parent wants to teach a child the word "moon" and says "moon" while pointing to it, and the toddler gazes with fascination at the pointing finger, then the pointing does not fulfill its function. The child may even believe that a finger pointing upward is called "moon." The child thinks then that it, too, knows what the moon is, even though the child does not see the moon.

But if we look at the pointing of the finger as a metaphor for conceptual knowledge, it can help to bring the head and the heart, the intellect and intuition together. It is for this reason that the mental disciplines that we find in the spiritual traditions include disciplines both of the head and of the heart. We will look more closely at these disciplines in the second part of this book.

II

SPIRITUAL PRACTICE AND DEVELOPMENT

FIVE

On the Path

INTRODUCTION

The second section of this volume will focus on questions of a
more practical nature. We will examine questions such as
why and *how* people in all times and cultures do such peculiar things as meditating, contemplating, praying and many
other "strange" and "absurd" things like studying obscure,
inaccessible texts, complicated liturgies, living according to
unusual and supposedly edifying rules for behavior in almost
all areas of life. And, *last but not least*, we will look at how
and why these people allow themselves to be led or guided
by others in all these things. This is strange indeed from the
perspective of ego and its concept of humanity. Is life not difficult enough without saddling ourselves with even more
peculiar and demanding practices? But from the perspective
of the flourishing within, all of these practices, which together
shape the spiritual way of life, are not only not strange but
useful and a source of inspiration.

Since we have outlined a psychological framework in the

first section of this volume, it is less difficult for us to discuss progress along the Path — the *spiritual disciplines, development* and *guidance*. Allow me to summarize the main themes in the first section again. In the first chapter, we became acquainted with the first-person perspective of this psychology. We also outlined to some extent the sphere in which the spiritual traditions work. In the second chapter, we discussed the metaphor of the spiritual path or way, and its sphere of influence: our experience of reality, including our self-experience. In the third chapter, we looked more closely at the concept *ego*. We sharpened our psychological view of the origin of our dualistic, egocentric experience of reality and of the nature of a nondualistic experience that is free from ego. We also indicated that such a transformation is not simply a fantasy but a real possibility anchored in our being human. Finally, in the fourth chapter we looked at a number of psychological core concepts that all spiritual traditions use, yet refer to by various names: mind, thought, consciousness and forms of knowledge. We saw how our experience of reality with all its emotional coloring is formed by the interplay of experiencing, thinking and consciousness. And we saw that contemplative knowledge is involved in the elimination of confusion and ignorance. All of this laid a foundation for a psychological understanding of what will be discussed in this second section: entering on and proceeding on the Path.

First Steps Toward Conversion

Let us start at the beginning: why is it that people, sometimes consciously and willingly, sometimes unconsciously and even unwillingly, set off along a spiritual path? In the spiritual traditions this question is often answered in terms of conversion and renunciation. They may be old-fashioned words, but they are words with very important meanings that are not always easy to comprehend. We will examine them again here, not so much from the more usual theological point of view but from that of a contemplative psychological approach. In particular, we will discuss *gradual* conversion — in other words, the not so spectacular conversion that entails a *process* of *metanoia*, a change in attitude. For it is in the gradual conversion, such as those chronicled in the *hagiographies* (saints' lives) of Anthony, Pachomius and Benedict and also in the biographies of saints in the other great religions, that the dynamic of the contemplative psychology is very visible. The sudden conversion, which is also mentioned in many traditions, will not be discussed here.

The Christian monastic life is traditionally referred to by the Latin word for conversion, *conversio*, but we will use the term *conversion* with a much broader, contemplative-psychological meaning. In this broad sense, the term does not refer to *conversion to a religious tradition*. We are primarily concerned here with an internal and existential process, with a turning around of a way of life that up until this moment was assumed to be natural, with a fundamental revision of one's own experience of reality.

Openmindedness

As we indicated briefly in earlier chapters, the movement of the mind that consists of repeatedly building up and continually maintaining the fortifications of ego is not the entire story. There is yet another movement that we could, in terms of the Christian tradition, call the movement of *grace*. Hinduism and Buddhism use the term *adhishthana*, usually translated as *blessing*. It is a movement that disrupts *ego* — that which we *think* we are and to which we are attached. Let us take a look at this other movement of the mind.

In our lives there are always moments of openness occurring — moments which very clearly have their own character. As we discussed in chapter two, people rarely recognize them — certainly if we are dealing with the individual before his or her conversion. We are referring here to those moments when we are openminded and not preoccupied with strengthening the fortifications of our ego-city, moments that from ego's perspective are aimless and groundless, perhaps even frightening, but from their own perspective are also peaceful, clear, warm and joyful. Such moments can occur when we are waiting for the bus as well as when we are engaged in our spiritual practices. They simply occur and cannot be forced. We cannot evoke or manipulate them; in a certain sense they are moments that are not *ours*, occurring outside of the fortress of ego. At the same time, however, they are very common moments, too common; they are clear moments, but often too clear, peaceful, but often too peaceful. They are colored by a sense of reconciliation and union, but it is a reconciliation or union that is so complete that we cannot retreat and cannot find ourselves again, and that is what is both so unbearable and at times even so frightening about it.

All spiritual traditions have their own names for these moments. There are also many ways in which the traditions attempt to point these moments out to us. Allow me to give a few examples. A very ordinary and therefore striking example is the moment when we have to sneeze. Let us look at the movement of our mind at such a moment: we are occupied with something and then feel the prickling of a sneeze coming on. We try to concentrate on what we are doing for as long as possible but are finally forced to succumb, to surrender to the sneeze. At that moment the entire situation with which we were occupied is lost for an instant and there is complete openness and union with the occurrence of the sneeze. Afterwards, we get hold of ourselves (mentally) as quickly as possible and check to see that nothing serious has happened. . . . This is a seemingly trivial but also very classic example from the Buddhist contemplative tradition. No less classic is the designation of these moments by pointing out what happens to us mentally when we burst into laughter. At the moment that we laugh, the worrying, deadly serious monitoring of ourselves falls briefly away. At that moment we see "both poles of a situation as they are from an aerial point of view. Sense of humor seems to come from all-pervading joy, joy which has room to expand into a completely open situation because it is not involved with the battle between 'this' and 'that'. . . . This open situation has no hint of limitation, of imposed solemnity" (Trungpa 1973, 113–14). Precisely when we are very seriously and solemnly occupied with something we can suddenly surprise ourselves and burst into laughter. It is an absolute moment that in a sense stands on its own. The practice of spiritual disciplines is also concerned with the admission of such a sovereign space. Bataille, who also uses laughter as an example to indicate these absolute moments of total openness, also calls meditation a "opération souveraine" (Bataille 1981).

Being suddenly confronted with a great loss can also lead to such moments, moments that cut through our customary experience of reality. We are dazed in a positive sense. This is why it is said that our own final hour can be such a moment. We all know the peculiar atmosphere following a funeral. We have buried someone who has died and subsequently gather together. These moments often have a very special atmosphere: very subdued and open. We are briefly immersed in the situation, and all other concerns have fled our mind. Because of this, these moments are often very carefree — not because of a banal defensive measure but because of the tenderness of the moment. Not only moments of intense loss but also moments of great happiness can cause all previous

events to fade for a brief while. Such moments lift us out of
our daily routine just as sneezing or laughing do.

Cracks in the Walls of the Fortress of Ego

What is striking about such moments is that it is often
difficult to recognize them *for what they are*. Because these
moments exist *outside of our egocentric experience of reality*,
they cannot be interpreted or grasped from our usual perspective. But, precisely because they are *outside*, they are
also the basis for conversion. Viewed from the fortress or
shack of ego, they represent a crack in its structure. They
are not part of the fortification but an opening in its walls —
a crack that at the same time allows some light to fall within
the fortress. It is lit up briefly from the outside and from
within, allowing us for a moment to see very clearly the structure of the fortress. Let me repeat again that the metaphor
of a fortress does not refer to an object but a mental activity — the continual mental preoccupation with ourselves in
relationship to the other, with our place, position, our self-
importance, our ups and downs.

This light allows us to see even more clearly how ego is
continually lost in that which is temporary, in its own "world."
It allows us to see how ego "believes" that its glory or downfall is determined by its relationship with the temporal world.
This is why ego is so involved in it. But it is precisely this oper-
ation that is relativized by this light. Its triviality is lit up
and becomes thoroughly clear to us, at times as a shock and
at times as a liberation.

These moments of openness or openmindedness occur, so
the contemplative traditions maintain, in all people. They
are not reserved only for the happy few. They always occur
because it is simply impossible for the walls of the fortress of
ego to be 100 percent watertight, airtight and lightproof. We

need water, air and light within the fortress as well, and thus continue to be dependent on them. The theistic traditions express this by saying that God's love and light is greater than our egotism and conceit with all its hate and blindness with respect to God. The nontheistic tradition of Mahayana Buddhism states that we can never completely repress the clarity and warmth of own heart, our own Buddha nature. In this sense, the maintenance of ego is a losing battle, but it is nevertheless a battle that we can continue to wage throughout our whole life and one that is very difficult to yield.

Mental Responses to Openmindedness

The very first phase of conversion is that of breaking through to the awareness that the moments mentioned above are very essential — moments that we can trust and to which we can open ourselves. We can turn toward them rather than toward the direction of ego; we can learn to go along with them.

But that awareness is not something obvious, for from the perspective of ego's mentality these moments can very easily be misunderstood and in a certain sense abused. When we do *not recognize them for what they are*, we tend to make them something very special. We then want to pull this special moment in our experience toward ourselves and, as it were, *appropriate* it: "What I have experienced is something very special, possibly even a spiritual experience!" But because the mental movement of holding onto it is diametrically opposed to the movement of letting it go, which is the essence of these moments, it actually chokes these moments. We are left with only its memory, which we may still decide to drag within the walls of ego's fortification. This is one of the possible responses from the perspective of ego.

Another response, which we briefly touched upon, is that such moments are seen as distinctly threatening. After all, that is what they are when viewed from ego's perspective: they *are* cracks in the walls of our familiar, egocentric experience of reality. In this response, too, the openness of such moments is not recognized for what it is. When we see these moments of openness as threatening, we experience them as *horror vacui*, the fear of emptiness. This happens not because those moments are actually empty — far from it — but because from the perspective of ego they offer no support whatsoever. In this sense they are "empty." We tend to resist and fight against these empty moments, these moments of being "at a loss."

A third response that causes the true nature of these moments to be concealed from us is that of indifference — an attempt to ban these moments from our consciousness and from our memory so that we can get on with ego's business for the day. We had resolved not to fall apart and thus attempt to get beyond such moments. But we are not entirely at ease when we wave them aside as "having no meaning" for our lives or as irrelevant disturbances of our tranquillity of mind.

All of us are familiar with these three responses. In Christian terminology, we could call them the responses of the *hardened sinner* (see Louf 1992) — that is, the response of the individual who does not recognize or appreciate these moments for what they are. But, as we saw in the examples given above, it can also happen that these moments do not allow us the time or opportunity to react to them in these three ways. It is then possible that we do recognize these moments for what they are and learn to trust them. We are prepared to accept the fact that our egocentric experience of reality is, so to speak, up in the air. We accept that our egocentric attitude in life has been exposed. Then we are *sinners-in-the-process-of-conversion* (Louf 1992). We appreciate the beauty, tenderness and groundlessness of those open moments and, in conjunction with that, the agony of seeing our own ego fortifications exposed in precisely these moments.

It is in recognizing these moments, in these early stages of conversion, that guidance plays an important role by making clear that that open space, which from ego's perspective is groundless, is inhabitable even though it may not be so at this time. And yet, the more familiar we become with it the stronger our faith and trust become in its being inhabitable. We begin to develop genuine trust or faith. We will return to this in chapter ten.

When we begin to recognize that these moments are essential for our lives, an inspiration arises that is no longer constrained by ego: an egoless motivation. But, together with this, an ego-directed motivation plays a role for a very long time: the desire for self-improvement and self-elevation that prompts us to attempt to draw these moments toward us, to struggle with them or ignore them — in short, to manipulate them in one way or another for our own benefit. Within the contemplative life, the ego-directed motivation is also called *spiritual materialism* (Trungpa 1973). This motivation makes us practice spiritual disciplines externally but is based on the desire to gain or possess something that can strengthen and elevate our ego. If we practice with this motivation, we ultimately turn away from these moments of openness. All of us have experienced times when this occurs.

From a contemplative-psychological point of view, we can recognize the ego-directed motivation by the fact that it makes us very unstable. We become unstable because, on the one hand, there is a vast (albeit perverted) effort whereas, on the other, no actual spiritual growth occurs. We see ourselves (and others) wavering back and forth between an attitude of *nihilism* and one of *fundamentalism*. The basis of both attitudes is ambition in the sense of ego striving toward self-confirmation. The fundamentalist attitude is one of mentally *holding on to* that which is seen as unchanging, eternal and absolute. The latter can be certain experiences but also certain ideas or forms that one's religious tradition provides. Thus the value of one's spiritual tradition is measured by the degree to which it offers an unshakable *buttress*, a justification and prop for our experience of reality. As long as a spiritual tradition appears to offer this, the ambition of ego is satisfied. This materialistic approach also causes us to identify frantically with the tangible, external forms of the tradition, possibly with the proud feeling that we are sitting on the right side of the line. We think we can elevate ourselves by linking ourselves with and possessing something that in our eyes has been elevated to incontestable heights: our own religious tradition.

But if there are indications — perhaps from the tradition itself — that there is something fundamentally wrong with such an attitude, it is easy to veer in the opposite direction: toward an attitude of *nihilism*. If our egocentric spiritual ambition, our spiritual materialism cannot be satisfied, we are disappointed and reject the religious disciplines since, from ego's point of view, they have proven to be worthless. We thought we had found gold but it turned out to be lead, and so we are willing to discard the entire kit and caboodle of our spiritual experiences and our religious tradition (and often those of others). Because we value only that which we can possess and, upon closer examination, discover there is nothing in our tradition that we can possess, we no longer find anything valuable. This is the core of a nihilistic attitude —an attitude in which disappointment and contempt are conjoined. We reject and begin to despise that which disappoints us, thus avenging our disappointment until we once again find a new (spiritual) object that our ambition can offer to ego as a buttress. And so we continue to swing back and forth between fundamentalism and nihilism, between belief and unbelief in a spiritual buttress. In fact, belief and unbelief themselves serve as a spiritual buttress, paralysing the activity of our open intelligence, our clarity of mind.

The moments of openness, however, disrupt both of these two materialistic attitudes at the same time so that our clarity of mind can move freely. When, in spite of such moments, we hold on to our fundamentalist or nihilistic attitude in life (and often we cannot help ourselves), we see them as threatening. We then meet with what the theistic religions call the *wrath of the gods or God*. We no longer encounter the tenderness, warmth and freedom of such experiential moments but experience them as a *counterforce* that seems to turn against us (ego) and threatens to crush us. For ego there is, we could say, only a wrathful God or a hostile reality that threatens our possessions and buttresses and that perhaps or at best can be manipulated or pacified. Conversely, when these moments are recognized for what they are, they reveal their serene form and work as moments of conversion. Then the (partial) collapse or evaporation of the fortification of ego that occurs at such a time calls us to surrender, also giving us the courage to expose ourselves (our ego) and stand naked in the light of these moments. Then we become aware that we have always stood naked. Even when we believed we could hide ourselves, we were always seen by our Buddha-nature, by the gods or God.

From Openness to Doubt

Let us now take a more detailed look at what these moments initiate within us if we no long pursue, repel or ignore them, and how they are the first steps of conversion. These moments have two sides: what we see clearly and the fact that we see clearly. What we see clearly is our ego. The fact that we see clearly is characteristic of these moments themselves.

In religious terms, this clarity belongs to the Holy Spirit (being *moments of grace*), to the *Shekinah* (Hebrew for the presence of God) and to our Buddha-nature when it is given the chance to be at work within us. We are often struck by *that which* we see at first glance and the elating fact *that* we can see so clearly escapes us. In a certain sense, we do not yet fully recognize the nature of these moments but we are able to recognize it sufficiently to see the failure of ego by means of the light that these moments shed on ego. When we see that failure, we begin to doubt the possibility of cultivating insight and joy in life *within* the walls of our egocentric experience of reality.

Initially, this doubt often manifests itself as a distrusting, critical attitude toward ourselves. But this is a very positive development because this distrust is born out of the awareness and the insight that building up an egocentric and egotistical attitude brings only suffering and no joy in life. This insight comes with the moment of openness. And when that moment has passed, it leaves distrust and doubt behind as fruit in our mind. This wholesome but extremely uncomfortable doubt is often at its strongest before we take the first step along the spiritual path, which is why it is important (also in guiding people in this phase) not to gloss over or reason away this distrust but to make room for it, to respect it. For it is precisely when we have arrived at this uncomfortable point that it is very tempting to rid ourselves of this spiritual distrust by escaping into the materialist attitudes of nihilism and fundamentalism. By allowing room for this distrust, a renewed search for yet another buttress can be prevented. After all, this distrust is a first albeit rather one-sided manifestation of clarity of mind.

The distrust about which we speak here is usually quite all-embracing: it is not only distrust *with regard to ourselves* and the way in which we have attempted to build our lives around ego but also *with regard to our surroundings*, with regard to the demands, expectations and promises of the world. "If you do what is expected of you, if you have a good job, if you have a nice family, if you have nice friends, then you'll have made it. Just make sure that you accomplish *that* and you'll be happy." All these requirements and promises are usually presented in such a way that they suggest that they will lead to peace in life, if not inner peace. These promises are also disrupted by these moments. Thus the distrust not only affects our own attitude to life but it is also directed at the world around us and at the attitudes to life that are held and lived there. The world around us *also includes the religions*, which is why the distrust applies not only to the promises of the world but to the promises of the religions as well. There, too, the individual will look at them critically once again or for the first time.

When the failure of our egocentric experience of reality in these moments of openness have become visible and a fundamental, penetrating doubt has been raised, several questions arise. "Yes, but what now? Are there other people who have experienced this as well and survived, or am I the only one? Is it just me? Should I just find (a) different job/ friends/spouse? Is it a crisis that belongs to my puberty/ado-lescence/mid life/old age, or is it more fundamental than that? Are there people who talk about this and, if so, where can I find them?"

These questions make us look for possible contact with people who we think are engaged in "these kinds of things." Now, however, our purpose is not to seek out a buttress or a place to belong but to continue our basically lonely exploration of our experience of reality. We talk to them while maintain-ing a very critical attitude, which is very healthy. We often play the devil's advocate: we fire critical questions at the tra-dition and at those who express or embody the tradition's

point of view. There have been so many promises made, so
much has been suggested in so many shapes and forms from
our youth until now by our environment, by our culture, by
religions. And it is precisely our moments of openness that
allow us to see clearly that they were unrealistic promises.
While promises may sound very good, they themselves do
not have the power to transform our experience of reality.
This is the reason behind this critical attitude and with it
comes an urgent desire to assess what is real and authentic — also in those traditions that (appear to) discuss matters of reality and authenticity. Thus at the same time that
the distrust with regard to the promises of religions arises,
there also arises a need to become further acquainted with
and to explore that religion. We can learn much about this
from Augustine's *Confessions*.

THE FIRST STEPS ALONG THE PATH

When contact is first made between an authentic spiritual
tradition and this searching, critical individual, one of the first
pieces of advice given to the individual is to relax and take
the time to examine and get to know *himself* thoroughly.
For if we want to be able to justify our distrust and if we
want to investigate a tradition's authenticity, we must possess
discriminating awareness with regard to this point. One of
the first things that almost all spiritual traditions stress is
the fact that we must begin with ourselves, that is, our experience of reality, our thoughts and feelings as they manifest
themselves from moment to moment throughout the day.

This first contact may arise because we approach a spiritual community and are invited to taste their way of life:
"Come in and join us for a day in the daily spiritual life that
we lead in the community or congregation and be yourself:
look at yourself as you encounter yourself while following

the disciplines of work, study and contemplation." Or we may approach a spiritual teacher who advises us: "Make room in your daily schedule to explore your mind. Here is a discipline of meditation that will enable you to do this. Practice it. Take a break from all those books about psychology and spirituality and from those deep discussions on the philosophy of life. Study the movement of your own mind."

Self-Knowledge as Personal Reliability

By getting to know the movement of our own mind with the help of a contemplative method, we become acquainted with ourselves as well as with the value of the method. At the same time, we also sharpen our discernment, our discriminating awareness, and this ability becomes more reliable. I have used the term *personal reliability* for this elsewhere (de Wit 1991, 172ff.). This is the ability to distinguish our own spiritual materialism, our egocentric motivation from true inspiration. As our personal reliability develops, we begin to recognize our tendency to flee from reality and to preserve ourselves. We see that it is that tendency that makes it impossible to look realistically at ourselves and the tradition. Because of that tendency, we would not recognize the truth about ourselves or our spiritual tradition even if we were staring right at it.

The development of this type of self-knowledge is very important and needs to be fostered and fed. The more we learn to trust ourselves, that is, to trust our moments of openness or openmindedness, the better we can see when our mind makes that quick movement in the direction of the creation of ego. Through this we are better able to stop feeding that movement. In this way our inner discernment develops and, with it, the reliability of our judgment. What we are discussing here is often expressed in the theistic traditions as follows: getting to know oneself and getting to know God is one and the same movement. The unfolding of this learning process occurs simultaneously for both aspects.

Openness as Surrender

The development of this form of self-knowledge is not only necessary for a further step but also makes that step possible: we are now better able to listen and actually hear what the tradition has to offer. This is also the moment when more personal contact becomes possible and also necessary between the guide and the person being guided. During this contact the guide is also tested in various ways — sometimes openly but often more subtly. That is how trust in the guide (and thereby in the tradition) develops along with the growth of our trust in ourselves, this is, in our self-knowledge.

This development also contains the beginnings of a process of *surrender*: surrender both in the sense of surrender to openness and in the sense of the surrender of ego. We begin to suspect what the surrender of ego entails: the open, naked acknowledgment of the egocentric movement of our mind at every moment that this movement occurs, again and again, time after time. The moment we feel ourselves turning in the direction of ego's way of experiencing, we jerk ourselves back, as it were. That requires a certain amount of self-discipline. But it is also possible that the guide jerks us back. In this way, he or she teaches us how and when we can do this ourselves. Naturally, the guide can accomplish this only if we are prepared to reveal ourselves as we are, if we are prepared to expose ourselves completely. In an absolute or fundamental sense, this is baring ourselves to ourselves or to God. But in a relative or practical sense, this is baring ourselves completely to a fellow human being: baring ourselves and surrendering our ego in the concrete, actual interaction with the other, which is not easy to do. The first step toward this is to bare ourselves to that fellow human being whom we have come to trust: our guide along the spiritual path. In this sense there is also a surrender to the guide. And that trust is, in turn, again based on our growth in self-knowledge.

This surrender is very different in nature from the form of surrender based on the idea that "the tradition or the guide will surely know what is good, which is why I surrender myself, for I am not capable of that knowledge." For the latter form of surrender implies an abandonment of the development of our discriminating awareness. This is why this naive form of surrender is also called *blind surrender* (see also chapter ten). In fact, it shifts our responsibility for ourselves onto a higher authority that is viewed as more competent and is therefore a form of spiritual *escapism*. The basis of blind surrender is the motivation of *not* having to face who or what we are and what our existence is about and what can give it meaning. Blind surrender is ego's attempt to *imitate* actual surrender: "I surrender. Do what you want to me. I trust you." Ultimately, such a form of "surrender" is not strong enough and not good enough for something as fundamental as the total transformation of our attitude in life because it does not arise out of and is therefore not supported by a bond tested by experience. The development of such a bond includes, in its initial phase, doubt, sounding out and testing our connection with the tradition and guide. Genuine trust can develop out of this so that later, when we take steps that go deeper into uprooting the world of ego, there is someone who can stand by us at difficult moments — someone who encourages us to enter further into the moments of openness; someone who, through his or her own example, demonstrates that it is possible for people to live within those moments of openness, in this wasteland or desert that lies outside the territory of ego. The saints and great contemplatives of the traditions have preceded us, speaking to us from that very place. It is from that wasteland that they, with all the means available to them, have, so to speak, been calling to us all the time and beckoning: "Here, here. . . ."

In the next chapters, we will examine which means the spiritual traditions offer us for continuing in this direction. In the last chapter we will once again pick up the theme of spiritual development, the beginning of which we have discussed here.

SIX

The Disciplines
of Thought

INTRODUCTION TO THE SPIRITUAL DISCIPLINES

How do the spiritual traditions handle the first steps to conversion that are the beginning of the flourishing within? Do they have something to offer here that can support this process and take it further? If so, what is it?

The spiritual traditions have, in fact, quite a lot to offer: an enormous wealth of disciplines and methods. Human inventiveness has been richly manifested in this area as well. There is hardly any aspect of life that has not been addressed by one or more disciplines in the spiritual traditions. Naturally, the spiritual traditions differ in their emphasis on certain disciplines. The emphasis is sometimes unique to the tradition itself and sometimes has to do with the culture in which the tradition has taken root.

However, let me first say something about the term *discipline* itself, since for many people it has a somewhat strict, almost military ring to it and seems to lie close to the notion

171

of forcing ourselves and putting ourselves under pressure. But the spiritual understanding of *discipline* is much more neutral. It simply means *systematic and ongoing practice*. Characteristic of these disciplines is precisely that they must be carried out with a certain gentleness and flexibility rather than in a hard-handed way. We can characterize them as spiritual skills for handling our mind, our speech and our actions. These skills reflect the practical insight on the part of the tradition into what is humanly possible. This does not detract from the fact that we occasionally find people in spiritual traditions who practice all kinds of outlandish exercises. But when such exercises are prompted by self-aggression or spiritual ambition, they are certainly rejected by the traditions themselves. The Buddha, who himself experimented for years with extreme forms of asceticism, later warned his pupils of the two extremes of self-torture and indulgence. That is why Buddhism is known as the *Middle Way*. An often recurring metaphor for the correct use of the disciplines is that of the gardener's method of working: making a garden flourish through love and knowledge. Besides using fertilizer, the gardener also at times carries pruning shears. The gardener's love prunes the excessive growth of self-torture, and the gardener's knowledge prunes indulgence and indolence.

To speak of these disciplines in more general terms, we can draw on a very classic division employed by the spiritual traditions themselves, i.e., the division into three domains: that of the mind, of the word, and of the deed — or, as we have called them elsewhere (de Wit 1991), the mental domain, the domain of speech, and the domain of actions. For all three domains, there are specific spiritual disciplines or practices. We will refer to them respectively as the *mental disciplines*, the *disciplines of speech* and the *disciplines of action*.

The mental disciplines are naturally concerned with cultivating insight into the nature of our mind. They are *par excellence* directed at the cultivation of the flourishing within: at our dealing with ourselves, with our thoughts and our attitude toward life. We can therefore practice them by ourselves during an individual retreat in a situation in which we are alone with our own mind.

The disciplines of speech and action are directed at the cultivation of a decent, caring way of communicating and relating to our fellow human beings and our environment. Their function is to help us transcend the callous, egocentric emotionality with which we (out of *ego*) respond to our environment. Therefore, we practice these disciplines towards one another and with one another. Of course, those who live in a contemplative communal life — the Christian tradition calls them *cenobites* — place a great deal of emphasis upon these disciplines. These are disciplines that have an interactive and a communicative character. But these disciplines are, of course, of fundamental importance also for those of us who live in the so-called "world." We could also call them *social disciplines*, if not for the fact that this term does not do justice to the importance of a compassionate treatment of nature and the material world. We can therefore refer better to the disciplines of speech and action together — also because of their practical orientation to everyday life — by the term *practical disciplines*.

On the spiritual path, the mental and practical disciplines are not practiced in isolation from each other. This gives the traditions their power and makes them a whole that covers all aspects of our lives. We will discuss the mental disciplines in this and the following two chapters. The disciplines of speech and action, which are concerned with the cultivation of the visible fruits of this flourishing, are discussed in chapter nine.

THE MENTAL DISCIPLINES

The explanation of what contemplative psychology means by the word *mind* has provided us with a certain background for understanding the how and why of the mental disciplines. All great religious traditions possess a whole range of such disciplines which are directed at getting to know and cultivating our mind in one way or another. If we look at the range of *mental disciplines*, we come upon two main groups which we will call the *disciplines of consciousness* and the *disciplines of thought*. These two kinds of disciplines are in fact the contemplative forms of the two fundamental ways of acquiring knowledge that we discussed in chapter four. Elsewhere we have discussed their methodological background in terms of the so-called *conceptual strategies* and the *awareness strategies* (de Wit 1991, 102ff.).

The disciplines of consciousness are intended to provide and enhance our *perceptual knowledge*, which we also discussed in chapter four. They do this, on the one hand, by cultivating our mindfulness and, on the other, by sharpening our discriminating awareness. Within these disciplines of consciousness, we can again distinguish two kinds: we will call them the *disciplines of mindfulness* (or stability) and the *disciplines of insight* (or discriminating awareness). We will discuss them in chapters seven and eight, respectively.

The disciplines of thought work with the creation and use of *mental content*: with concepts, ideas, theories, representations, images and symbols. The term *thought* here thus has the broad meaning that we gave it in chapter four. Some of these disciplines are directed at enlarging our *conceptual knowledge* of the contemplative life, that is, our intellectual understanding of it. Others make use of our *power of imagination*. They offer us, as we will see below, mental representations and images that can help in changing our experience of reality in a direction that leads to clarity of mind and great-ness of heart. So, again we can distinguish two groups within the disciplines of thought as well: we will call them the *intel-lectual disciplines* and the *disciplines of the imagination*.

THE TWO DISCIPLINES OF THOUGHT

Let us first explore the area of the disciplines of thought, which includes both the intellectual disciplines as well as those that make use of our power of imagination. Precisely because they are concerned with mental content, we could also investigate the disciplines of thought from a religious or theological perspective. We would then ask: what is the place of the mental content which the disciplines use within the whole of the religious (and theological) content of the tradi-tion itself? Nonetheless, we will not take up that investi-gation — however interesting it may be. Rather, we will explore primarily the disciplines of thought from the angle of contemplative psychology. That means that our central ques-tion is: precisely how and what do these disciplines do with and to the mind and the experience of reality of those who practice them?

The systematic use of our intellect and of our power of imagination are, psychologically speaking, two very differ-ent disciplines. Of these two, the intellectual disciplines are the most well known. This is because we live in a culture that is strongly oriented toward the intellect. In everyday life as well, we make great use of our intellect, albeit mainly for purposes other than the furthering of our spiritual devel-opment. The disciplines of imagination are less familiar to us. Although we make representations of everything and any-thing in everyday life, our culture — with the exception of a few modern cognitive psychotherapies — hardly recognizes or values the systematic use of the power of imagination as a means of transforming our experience of reality. We will explore both disciplines more thoroughly in this chapter.

The Intellectual Disciplines

It is part of human nature to construct theories. We see it happen in all cultures and on all levels. We construct theories about all kinds of things: about the world of phenomena and how these phenomena cohere with one another, theories about ourselves and others, about the visible and the invisible. We also attempt to test these theories against experience. We adjust them as necessary on the basis of new data or results of (our own) research and attempt to avoid intellectual errors, testing the *consistency* of our theories, that is, making sure that they do not contain any internal contradictions. If we do this systematically, we are in fact practicing an intellectual discipline, one that has been primarily shaped and brought to great flourishing in our Western academic tradition.

Theories consist of a set of *concepts* that are related to one another in certain ways. They contain *knowledge about* a certain area of reality, which helps us to sharpen our thinking about our experience.

In the spiritual traditions as well, the intellectual disciplines have since ancient times been considered to be very important and have been used widely. They form the hard core of what we above called the *conceptual strategy* of the acquisition of knowledge. All religious traditions have a particular conceptual framework in the form of a more or less systematic doctrine or teaching, which is based on their holy writings: the *catechism* goes back to the Bible, the *aka'id* is based on the Koran, the *Talmud* goes back to the Torah of Judaism, the *abhidharma* of Buddhism is based on the *sutras* and the *Vedanta*, for example of Hinduism is based on the

Vedas. Here the practice of the intellectual disciplines thus entails studying as well as analyzing and reflecting on theories about the spiritual way of life.

In most traditions, this reflection continually gives rise to new and extensive commentaries in which the central concepts of their religion are clarified intellectually in terms that address the contemporary reader. It is here that the importance of such literature lies. This exegesis is never completed in a living religion. Christianity has its *theology*, Buddhism its *shastras* (commentaries), Judaism its *Talmud*, which includes commentaries on commentaries, and Islam its *Tafsier*. Hinduism also possesses a great variety of religio-philosophical commentaries. In some traditions, the study of commentaries has been greatly emphasized precisely because they are more contemporary and often contain an unfolding of insights that are present though still hidden in the original texts. In some Jewish Orthodox circles, the Talmud is studied almost exclusively. Many Buddhists study primarily the *shastras*.

The value of continued intellectual study is emphasized not only in the Jewish tradition, which is known for this; all traditions recognize its importance. The Buddhist and Hindu traditions speak in this context of the necessity of practicing the disciplines of study (Sanskrit: *sravana* — literally: hearing) and reflection (*manana*) alongside the other contemplative disciplines. *Svadhyaya* — the study of the Holy Books — is an essential discipline for Hindus.

That which is reflected on differs of course, from tradition to tradition but not so much that there are no common themes to which one can point. The traditions cannot, in any case, escape the existential themes of human existence, even though they may articulate their insights about them in their own way. H.M. Vroom gives the following summary of these themes: the finitude of human existence; human responsibility and human failing; the experience of the good, of happiness, peace, well-being, and meaning; the receiving of insight; evil and suffering (Vroom 1989, 330). All traditions have a conceptual framework for clarifying our thinking about these themes.

Thus the practice of the intellectual disciplines includes an intellectual training. If the training is successful, it clarifies both the conceptual framework itself and its application to our own concrete existence. It informs us and thus removes *conceptual ignorance* (see chapter four), and it also disciplines our thinking and thus removes *conceptual confusion* (see chapter four). The intellectual disciplines enable us to see the *how* and *why* of traveling the spiritual path. They can instruct and motivate us.

The strength of the intellectual disciplines is that they are very communicable, for they work with *language*. If we work with concepts, we also work with language. Various ways of using language are applied: descriptive, prescriptive and evocative (performative) linguistic uses. For the specific role of these linguistic uses in spiritual traditions, I refer to chapter four of de Wit (1991). By appropriating the religious concepts, the content of our stream of thoughts changes in a way that puts us — at least, that is the intention — in a somewhat better position to clarify and investigate intellectually our own world of experience.

The Disciplines of the Imagination

But there is yet another kind of discipline of thought, one which also employs mental content, but does not work with our intellectual and analytical abilities. Rather, it works with our power of imagination. This discipline does not work with concepts but with *mental representations* or images. We referred to them above as *disciplines of the imagination*.

There is an enormous variety — too many to mention — of mental images and representations that the spiritual traditions use. Making an arbitrary selection, we could list the following: images and representations of God; the image of one's own mentor, *guru* or person who is an example for us; stories from the tradition, images in the form of biographies of the prophets, of Jesus, Buddha, Mohammed, Arjuna; images that are associated with various kinds of prayers: prayers of aspiration, intercessory prayers, short prayers, prayers of thanksgiving and, of course, images in the form of sacred formulas, meaningful mantras, prayers of one word, and vows which people repeat to themselves; religious representations and visualizations; *koans* on which people brood mentally, reminders of mortality (*memento mori*), etc. There are also images or representations that do not have any formal place within a religious tradition but have spiritual value for us personally. They inspire us and lift us up: a precious memory or hopeful expectation, an image from a poem by Gerard Manley Hopkins or from a piano concerto by Mozart that we suddenly remember, a liberating thought that opens up new perspectives and which we keep with us. All of these mental images have a place in the practice of the disciplines of the imagination.

Allow me, in order to clarify the character of these disciplines themselves, to give a few examples. In Christianity, for instance, we know the discipline of entering into the suffering of Jesus Christ by pausing at the 14 stations of the cross and reflecting on the suffering of the Lord. Another, more general, example from this tradition is the *lectio divina*, also called the "spiritual" or "monastic reading." The practice of this discipline is not concerned with acquiring information, gaining *knowledge about* the text (i.e., *conceptual knowledge*, see chapter four) but with *becoming acquainted with*, gaining *perceptual knowledge* or developing familiarity with a text. The experiential value of the text can then reveal itself to us and transform us. Thijs Ketelaars (OSB) characterizes the *lectio divina* as follows:

> The monastic reading, in reading a text, does not aim primarily at the acquiring of information, even though that is also present, but at being born through a text in order to merge together with the text and its author, and by means of the word to come to a truly internal intimacy. In other words, it does not have to do with manipulating or transforming the other or the text but being transformed oneself in a true encounter. (Ketelaars 1986, 57)

In Mahayana Buddhism we find, for example, the discipline of *giving and taking* (Tibetan: *tonglen*) in which one imagines breathing in all the negativity of the world and breathing out all that which is positive within oneself over the world (see, e.g. Kongtrul 1987; Chödrön 1991, 56). In Vajrayana Buddhism, those who practice the disciplines of the imagination visualize an anthropomorphic representation of enlightenment (Tibetan: *yidam*). By identifying with this they bind their minds (*yid* = mind and *dam* = bond) to the qualities of enlightenment. In Hinduism as well we find mental exercises through which one identifies with a mental content, for example, the image of a divinity (*Istadevata*). And in all Buddhist schools we encounter a mental discipline which, by means of consciously invoked images of people we know, cultivates four specific mental attitudes toward those people. These four attitudes, which are called "immeasurable" (*apramana*) because of their effectiveness, are: friendliness (*maitri*), compassion (*karuna*), joy at another's prosperity (*mudita*) and impartiality (*upeksa*). Patanjali, the well-known Hindu master, also recommends this exercise.

In the Buddhist and Hindu traditions, the disciplines of the imagination are often called *meditation with form*. Here the term *form* refers to the mental content with which it works. In the Christian tradition, the spiritual disciplines that work with images are listed under the so-called *cataphatic spirituality* (*kata* means "according to" and *phatis* literally means "speech" or "word"). This has been defined as follows: "Cataphatic spirituality works with the content of consciousness, that is, with images, symbols and representations and concepts. It is oriented toward content and proceeds on the basis that human beings need images and concepts in order to come to God" (Jaeger 1992, 77).

The Purpose and Practice of the Disciplines of the Imagination

The disciplines of the imagination are directed at replacing the images and representations that prevent our fundamental humaneness from manifesting itself by a different mental content that causes our fundamental humaneness to develop and become visible. They therefore transform (even if only briefly) our experience of reality. Their efficacy rests on the fact that our dualistic experience of reality is also permeated by images. Alongside intellectual reasonings with all their concepts, images are always surfacing in our stream of thoughts in the form of memories, images of the future, metaphors, symbols, etc. And this stream of thoughts colors, as we have seen, our experience of reality. The images that we have either consciously or unconsciously appropriated in the course of our lives and which have become part of our stream of thoughts can advance or prevent the development of our fundamental humaneness. That fact is, of course, also recognized by the contemplative traditions and that is why they have developed the disciplines of the imagination. These disciplines amount simply to the replacement of unwholesome images by mental representations which have a beneficial *experiential value*. Our experience of reality can be influenced in this way. This is what these disciplines are concerned with: waking us up and causing us to identify with experiential qualities that are contained in a mental image. The mental image is a means of invoking in us a more spiritual way of experiencing.

In general terms, the traditions offer us representations or images that, as far as their experiential value is concerned, are at odds with our egocentric experience of reality. Because of this, ego gradually loses its grip and there is more room for openness. We could therefore characterize the disciplines of the imagination as a kind of surgery in our way of thinking: a mental transplant in which one image is removed and another, more beneficial image is implanted. In this process, *symptoms of rejection* can appear, because ego experiences these images initially as less real, less true than its own familiar images. Some spiritual traditions attempt to overcome these symptoms of rejection by choosing the images in such a way that we can *believe* in them, that is, that we believe them to be "true" or "real." Their truth lies in the fact that in some way they are a mental representation of our fundamental humaneness. They do not appeal to ego and its reality but to the open psychological space which is liberated from ego and awaken this space in us. They compete in a certain sense with our belief in the egocentric images of our own making and our experience of reality. If the "truth" of the former wins, as it were, over the "truth" of our egocentric representations, then our way of thinking undergoes a reversal.

Even though these mental images are nothing more than images in our stream of thought, nonetheless their experiential value can open our eyes to the qualities of our own fundamental humaneness, which itself lies *beyond* these images, in the sense that it is not dependent on these images themselves. It is rather the reverse: all the images with which the disciplines of the imagination work sprout from and derive their effectiveness from our fundamental humaneness. They are its expression in images, just as our profane, egocentric representations originate in the self-contained space of ego.

In every period, culture and religion we see how this fundamental humaneness looks for ways to make itself known and manifest in images as well. The disciplines of the imagination are a deliberate means for doing this in the most effective way: they are directed at the transformation of our egocentric images of ourselves, humanity, the world and God by substituting more contemplative images for them.

More specifically, over against an ego-centered *self-image* that portrays ourselves as the center of the world, the theistic traditions, for example, provide us with images of ourselves as servants, as subjects, as a bride, even as slaves of God. In nontheistic traditions, as in Mahayana Buddhism, an *egoless* self-image is presented to us in the following prayer:

> May I be a wishing jewel, the vase of plenty,
> A word of power and the supreme healing;
> May I be the tree of miracles,
> And for every being the abundant cow.
>
> Like the earth and the pervading elements,
> Enduring as the sky itself endures,
> For boundless multitudes of living beings,
> May I be their ground and sustenance.
>
> Thus for everything that lives,
> As far as the limits of the sky,
> May I provide their livelihood and nourishment
> Until they pass beyond the bonds of suffering.
>
> (Shantideva 1997, 50–51)

In Vajrayana Buddhism, the practitioner, as we saw above, often identifies herself with a *yidam*, an anthropomorphic visual representation of enlightened mind. The *yidam* functions as a self-image in which all emotional and intellectual qualities of the egoless state of mind are symbolically represented.

Over against an *image of humanity* that considers the human being to be fundamentally "beastly" and evil, the theistic traditions provide images of the human being as of divine origin, as created in God's image. Nontheistic traditions offer an image of humanity according to which all human beings, without exception, are *in essence* good, tender and clear of mind. These spiritual images of humanity go directly contrary to every form of misanthropy. And at the same time they convey the idea that misanthropy arises whenever we have lost contact with our fundamental humaneness.

Over against an *image of the world* that portrays it as a place to be rejected or as a place that should continually satisfy our needs but does not often do so or as a place where the hard realities of our human existence are seen as *errors* of the world by which we can justify our rancor and fear of life, the spiritual traditions offer an image of the world that emphasizes its sacredness. This is an image of the world in which misfortune and disappointment are seen as *challenges* for the development of our humanity. We have discussed these two images of the world and the mental attitude to which they give rise more extensively elsewhere in terms of the sacred and profane experience of reality (de Wit 1991, 192f.).

The mental attitude in which the world is seen as sacred is also expressed in the theistic traditions when they claim that human beings should be *grateful* to God for adversity. In the nontheistic tradition of Buddhism, one finds the proverb, "Be grateful to everyone" (Kongtrul 1987, 18). These are certainly bold statements, but we should understand that here gratitude does not mean that we have to resign ourselves to everything that happens. Rather, *gratitude* refers to a state of mind in which we are able to approach moments of adversity — as much as moments of prosperity — in a way that makes us and others grow in wisdom and loving kindness. This, of course, presupposes that we can handle adversity and that is again dependent on our mental maturity which grows rather than withers with every successful handling of adversity. Adversity thus places us spiritually at a crossroads: mentally withering by closing ourselves off or mentally growing by working with it. The recommended way here, as in all education, is to begin small. If we begin small (and what "small" means is different for everyone), then more intense adversity also gradually becomes more manageable. In that sense, we can be grateful for adversity. Adversity can be fertilizer for the flourishing within.

Finally, the theistic traditions offer an *image of God* that goes against all kinds of egocentric representations of God, images in which we have cut God down to human measurement: God as Big Brother who as an almighty ally is on our side when we want to have things our way, a God who protects our egocentrism and justifies it or who watches us like a kind of *super ego*, a God who threatens us (*ego*) with reward or punishment and whom we must keep as a friend, and so on. Over against these images the theistic spiritual traditions offer an image of God that, with respect to its experiential value, *does not fit* into our egocentric experience of reality. Whenever we transplant that image of God into our stream of thoughts, it changes our experience of reality as well.

In short, the disciplines of the imagination are directed at transforming our egocentric experience of reality by changing our world of thought and feeling. By providing nonegocentric images they remove the obstacles that our egocentric images produce.

The actual *practice* of the disciplines of the imagination

consists in continually internalizing these images, keeping
them in our mind until their experiential qualities unfold.
This presupposes that those images and representations have
meaning and experiential value for us and that we, if we
have not yet done so, can learn their significance. Whenever
that more intellectual preliminary work has been completed,
their experiential value can begin to make itself felt. Sometimes it is a process that takes place in a flash as soon as the
image is obtained. But most often it is necessary to keep the
image in our mind for a long period and to taste it again and
again before its experiential value can be felt. The latter
is characteristic for the *practice* of the disciplines of the
imagination.

The Disciplines of the Imagination and the Devotional Path

Our power of imagination is strong because its products
are not simply neutral mental pictures but are emotionally
charged images. This emotional charge can bind us both to
an egocentric perspective as well as an egoless perspective.
The efficacy of the disciplines of the imagination rests on that
fact: they work with images that not only conceptually but
also emotionally fly in the face of the imagined reality of ego.
They offer images that work as an emotional antidote. On
the basis of the desire to liberate ourselves from the preoccupation with ego, we master other images: images that with
respect to their experiential value evoke an egoless or theocentric experience of reality, such as images that express the
fundamental sacredness of reality (including our fellow
human beings) and the love and omnipresence of God — in
short, images that move us to *surrender* and *devotion*, that
is, to surrender of ego and to devotion to reality or God.

Which images are a good antidote for those practicing these
disciplines is an individual matter in which supervision by a

mentor is very important. In any case, the point is that one experiences these images to be at least as real as their egocentric image of reality. For this purpose, one needs to focus on these images with all the mental — and *emotional* — power at one's disposal, to surrender oneself to these images. For this reason, the cultivation of devotion is seen in many traditions as a path in itself. We find this very strongly emphasized within the Christian traditions in, for example, the Song of Songs, the spirituality of John of the Cross and Theresa of Avila and Christian bridal mysticism. But we also find it in the *bhakti yoga* of Hinduism, which is directed at the realization of the divine through devotion and love for a God who is conceived of as a personal lover. In Mahayana Buddhism and certainly in Vajrayana Buddhism, we also see this emphasis on devotion, which mobilizes human emotionality and directs it at a certain mental representation, an object or person who represents enlightenment.

Emotions have an object: they are always directed at something and the heart of the *devotional path* is that they are no longer directed at aspects of our egocentric experience of reality but at those that are manifested in an egoless or theocentric experience of reality. Discussing the path of devotion, Akhilananda formulates it as follows in his *Hindu Psychology*:

> The vast majority of the people in the world are predominantly emotional, so it is both convenient and necessary for them to use their emotions for higher spiritual development. We can hardly find a man or woman who has not strong emotional urges, and it is considered wise to express them instead of starving or discarding them. Emotions are great powers; a seeker after truth is, therefore, asked to direct them to an aspect of God which is suitable to his own temperament.
>
> That is the very reason the devotional mystics vary in their methods of approach to God. Some few may like to think of

Him as their child, while more prefer to look on Him as father or mother, and again others will love God as their friend
or beloved because this attitude is best suited to their individual temperaments and this relationship is natural and
spontaneous to them. (Akhilananda 1948, 178–79)

The devotional path thus uses the disciplines of the imagination intensively. The images used here are, by the way,
also used to guide action and speech and to cultivate them in
the direction of compassion. By practicing devotion and surrender — in our mind, action and speech — we give up more
and more of our preoccupation with ego. In other words, our
"preoccupation" with images that arouse a theocentric or
egoless experience of reality enables us to leave the preoccupation with ego behind. Thus there is continually more room
for an egoless or theocentric experience of reality, which itself transcends the images that aroused it.

The Limitations of the Disciplines of Thought

Western logic, the philosophy of science and the contemplative traditions regularly point to the limitations of the
intellectual disciplines. For centuries, people within the theistic traditions have sought in vain for logical proofs of God's
existence. In our culture, Immanuel Kant exposed the limitations of reason. Nagarjuna, the philosopher of Mahayana
Buddhism, has systematically shown the limitations of every
conceptual framework — including that of Buddhism (see,
for example, Inada 1970). We have already pointed out that
intellectual study and learning to understand a religious conceptual framework is not the same as following a spiritual
path. It is certainly part of it, but if we think that our practice need only go as far as an intellectual discipline, it is as if
we see the movement of our finger on a map as the journey
itself.

The limitations of the disciplines of the imagination are perhaps somewhat less well known. Particularly in Judaism and Islam we find an emphatic reservation with regard to making images of God. This reservation is present in other traditions as well, for it is generally recognized that the disciplines of the imagination also display a number of limitations.

The first limitation is that mental images and representations are also no more than images. The images that the spiritual traditions offer may well be better representations of ultimate reality than our ego-centered images. But even these images are not the original — they are and remain representations. When their experiential value has been appropriated we will have to leave them behind.

A second limitation is that these disciplines make use of our mental inclination to become *captivated* by images and representations and to view them as reality. Because of this inclination we live in and with an imaginary world that has its own deep valleys and high mountains. Seemingly, we go through a great deal in this reality as we *think* it to be. The disciplines of the imagination, however, do not oppose this inclination to become captivated. They do not liberate us from this inclination but make use of it. In a certain sense, they make a virtue of necessity by moving this inclination in a certain direction. As long as we still tend to be captivated by our own images and representations, it makes spiritual sense to replace our egocentric images with egoless or theocentric ones and thus change our experience of reality.

This is why the practice of the disciplines of the imagination is also compared with the administering of an *antidote*. The antidote administered by the spiritual traditions neutralizes the poison of our egocentric images. But an antidote itself is and remains poison. The user of this antidote is not yet immune to perceptual confusion, that is, not immune to the inclination to confuse representations with that which is represented. The disciplines of the imagination derive their efficacy from this. Precisely because and as long as we live in reality as we *think* it to be, the disciplines of the imagination are effective. We will see that the disciplines of conscious- ness are specifically directed at liberating us from being domi- nated and seized by the products — the harmful as well as the helpful — of our power of imagination.

Because the disciplines of the imagination have their limi- tations, it is dangerous if the tradition uses *only* these disci- plines. For, although the disciplines of the imagination lead us in a certain direction, that is, that of our fundamental humaneness, we have not yet uncovered its true nature. Holding a vivid and moving representation of Christ or Bud- dha is not the same as the discovery of Christ or Buddha within us. In that discovery, images are no longer necessary; it goes beyond every representation and is the fruit of a di- rect *vision*, just as we do not need any images of our hands because we can in fact see our hands. But this uncovering occurs through the disciplines of insight that will be discussed in chapter eight.

The disciplines of the imagination lie, as stated above, within *cataphatic spirituality*. In the Christian tradition, this form of spirituality is very much in the foreground. It is cen- tral in the tradition of Ignatius of Loyala's *Spiritual Exer- cises*. Because of this, for many contemporary Christians prayer has been virtually identified with the mental disci- plines that work with the content of thought.

But from the perspective of the spiritual traditions them- selves, this identification is not historically justified. "Chris- tianity has become trapped at some point by thinking that prayer is verbalization and asking. That's a wrong under- standing of prayer. The Greek word *proseukomai* means to move in a condition or state of being in which there is no thought, no imaging, no desiring" (Timko in Walker 1987, 216).

In the traditional Christian terminology of a few centuries ago, the term *meditation* was used to refer to the mental disciplines of thought, which are central to cataphatic spirituality. The term *contemplation* was used for the disciplines of consciousness that are emphasized in apophatic spirituality in particular (see chapter seven). Because apophatic spirituality, which held contemplation to be a central discipline, is almost forgotten, the meaning of *contemplation* has shifted to "thinking about something." With this the disciplines of consciousness have also disappeared from much of Christianity. In the original meaning of the word, however, meditation was seen as the preparatory phase for contemplation. In this, Christianity followed the same line as the Buddhist and Hindu traditions. Within Vajrayana Buddhism meditation, the use of mental representations (in the form of visualizations) is a preparatory developmental phase (*utpattikrama*) for the resultant phase (*sampannakrama*) in which representations are no longer used. In this tradition both are described as *meditation with form* and *formless meditation* respectively. The first is a discipline of the imagination, the second a discipline of consciousness. In Hinduism as well, the mental practices by which one identifies with mental content constitute a step toward the imageless experience of the transcendent reality itself (*para vasudeva*). In this tradition the mind is cultivated first by means of the mental disciplines which lead to a meditative state (*savitarka samadhi*) in which we gain conceptual knowledge. But the intention of such knowledge is that it points us in a direction that transcends all conceptual and articulable knowledge. It leads to a meditative state (*nirvicara samadhi*) in which a nonconceptual knowledge breaks through.

The Carmelite Tessa Bielecki outlines this development as follows:

In fact, as we advance and grow more intimately into union with Christ, we may not need the preliminary step of meditation at all. John of the Cross teaches us in the *Ascent of Mount Carmel* how to discern whether it really is time to stop meditating and to move into contemplation, or whether we are simply lazy and don't want to bother meditating anymore. He also describes the necessity of letting go of meditation when it is time to do so. His instruction is, "If you find the orange peeled, eat it." You don't have to peel it again. It is unfortunate that Christianity has a reputation for being word- and activity-oriented, because contemplation is actually at the center of the tradition. (Bielecki in Walker 1987, 208)

For the most part, we no longer use the terms *contemplation* and *meditation* today as Bielecki and others do in line with their original Christian meanings. In our time, the meaning of the term *meditation* has shifted to what the Christian tradition earlier called *contemplatio*, whereas *meditation* usually refers to a discipline of consciousness. This is also how we will use this term in this book.

IMAGINATION AND INTELLECT IN PSYCHOTHERAPY

Finally, let us look briefly at the relation between the disciplines of thought and a discipline that has become very important in our time: psychotherapy. In everyday life we are sometimes inclined to denigrate the human power of imagination. What we imagine does not have to be taken seriously: "Oh, you're only imagining that — it's not really true." Because of this, we may also be inclined to think that working with a mental representation is a relatively innocent, if not superficial, activity. It is outside the reality of everyday life and perhaps a form of self-hypnosis.

The spiritual traditions certainly do not share this flippant view of imagination. In chapter two we saw why: our entire experience of everyday reality is permeated and thereby shaped by our power of imagination. We live in an imagined reality. Intervening in our formation of mental images with the help of the spiritual disciplines thus also means a direct intervention in our experience of reality. And that is not at all a minor or innocent affair. These disciplines do something with our minds in a systematic, conscious and beneficial way — something we were already doing in a nonsystematic, unconscious and often harmful way.

It is interesting that the insights on which the efficacy of the disciplines of the imagination are based are not only commonly held by many spiritual traditions but are also recognized within psychotherapy. The latter also acknowledges that the images that people form also determine their experience of reality. They can lead to neurosis and even to psychosis.

Allow me to add here a brief remark about psychosis so as to clarify the enormous power of our imagination. A psychotic condition is one of extreme *perceptual ignorance* (see chapter four) with respect to our surroundings; our mindfulness and awareness no longer function properly. Because our surroundings are no longer adequately registered, they no longer serve as an anchor and we give ourselves over to the dynamic of our imagination which has free play. And whatever penetrates to us from our surroundings is adapted to fit into our imaginary world in the same way as an external sound merges into our dreams while we sleep. Our then unbridled and unrecognized power of imagination thus leads to extreme forms of *perceptual confusion* and our discernment is also paralyzed.

We can view our experience of reality as a tapestry that has been woven by our mind. The spiritual disciplines are directed at making that tapestry transparent, so that we no longer see the tapestry but the threads and the spaces in between. It can, however, also happen that this tapestry disappears completely from sight, namely when it tears or is torn. We then lose our familiar egocentric experience of reality and our power of imagination may, if it can no longer find any point of orientation, attempt to mend the tear in any way it can find: it produces illusions and hallucinations to create a hold. We are then psychotic. At the same time, in (the initial phase of) psychosis we are liberated from our conventional, egocentric everyday reality, and that can be experienced as a liberation from ego. It is in this that the "seduction of madness" (Podvoll 1990) lies. In this book, which is of interest for many other reasons, Podvoll shows why spiritual and religious themes and imagery so often come to the fore in psychotic episodes.

If we look at the way in which psychotherapy deals with psychological problems and neuroses, we can see that the approach is based partly on the same principles as those of the mental disciplines of the spiritual traditions. The power of the imagination, for example, is deliberately used to a great extent in the first phase of the treatment of phobias in *behavioral therapy*. The patient is instructed to form an image that has a calming effect and when that image has done its work, the patient is asked to form gradually an image of the situation that tends to trigger the phobia. If the patient becomes too frightened, he is then told to let go of the frightening representation and to return to the calming representation. The frightening representation is subsequently invoked again until the experiential value of the calming representation more or less remains intact during the representation previously experienced as frightening. After that one begins with exercises in practical situations.

Modern *cognitive psychotherapy* makes much use of the intellectual disciplines as well. The therapy here consists in acquiring other, healthier reasonings and interpretations by showing the inconsistency of the neurotic ones. Cognitive and behavioral psychotherapies are thus in a certain sense the therapeutic counterpart of the spiritual disciplines of thought. And, finally, it is remarkable that psychoanalysis and related forms of psychotherapy work with methods that are based partly on the same premises as those of the *disciplines of consciousness* (see chapter eight).

In spite of this similarity in underlying premises, however, there is, of course, a great difference between both traditions, and we must not lose sight of this. The difference lies in that their purpose and means are, in a certain sense, the reverse of each other: within the psychotherapeutic tradition insight and loving kindness are the means for solving problems (cf., e.g., Claxton 1986; Kwee and Holdstock 1996; de Wit 1990), whereas in the spiritual traditions problems are means for cultivating insight and loving kindness. An anecdote that illustrates this reversed approach to psychotherapy is as follows. When Buddhism was spreading to Tibet many Indian gurus were invited to teach the *dharma*. Not much was known about the Tibetans. One guru who had received an invitation heard that they were extraordinarily kind, helpful and always friendly people. This presented the guru with a problem: how could he practice the great spiritual discipline of patience if there was no one around to irritate him and challenge his patience? He therefore decided to take an assistant, a Bengalese, with him to Tibet. This was a man who was known to be extremely irritating because of his rudeness, obstinacy and temper. Grateful that the man wanted to be his assistant, he went to Tibet. Of course, once they arrived, it became obvious that this measure was superfluous: the Tibetans proved to be no different from other people.

THE NECESSITY OF GUIDANCE

Precisely because our imagination has such great power, the practice of the disciplines of the imagination is not without risk. Therefore, authentic spiritual guidance is an absolute necessity in these disciplines. The guide must not only know what the intended experiential value is of the mental images that the traditions contain but must also sufficiently know the pupil in order to know which images are suitable at a specific moment and which are not. Without guidance, there is the chance that we will wander around in fantasy worlds in which holding on to religious representations are mistaken for experiences. The consequence of this is not only a certain measure of alienation from the world — and, in extreme cases, religious delusions — but also an endless movement from image to image. We try one image and then another. There are always new religious images and spiritual maps that can enthrall our minds. After years of great effort, then, we may still have to confess that we have not grown in wisdom and loving kindness. We have devoted our time to the study of the map and have mistaken that for the exploration of the landscape.

Another reason for personal guidance is that the images and representations of the tradition itself are not immune to the march of time. They can lose their experiential value and thus also their effectiveness. After all, spiritual traditions are practiced and passed on by people. The experiential value of images are not inextricably bound to the images themselves but lie within the minds of people. If the people change, if their culture and mentality change, it can be that the originally intended experiential value of the images is no longer evoked. It is even possible that their experiential value shifts in such a way that the images themselves become obstacles. Their use can then even be destructive.

This can happen not only because people change but also because the tradition itself has changed. If the tradition, for example, loses its view of the Way, of the spiritual path, as a way of development, it is often no longer clear which image is helpful in specific developmental phases. Images that are effective in different phases for different people then become incorrectly connected, as if they all pertain to the same phase. It can then be that these images come into conflict with one another and in that way choke the seed of spiritual growth. This phenomenon is universal. We find it at times in all world religions. Because the effectiveness of the images is also dependent upon the local culture and mentality, a cultural and psychological regauging of the disciplines of the imagination in particular is thus continually unavoidable and necessary. For only then can the tradition survive. And that process of regauging occurs, in fact, within the concrete situation of personal guidance, which is why this guidance is also necessary for the transmission of the tradition from one generation to the next (see de Wit 1991, 152).

SEVEN

The Disciplines of Mindfulness

INTRODUCTION TO THE DISCIPLINES OF CONSCIOUSNESS

It is a striking psychological fact that the disciplines of consciousness are found in almost all spiritual traditions. These disciplines are intended to cultivate two aspects of consciousness: mindfulness and discernment. Whether or not we consider ourselves to be religious, this fact tells us something about the human mind: people in all cultures have discovered that they can cultivate their consciousness by means of certain practices or disciplines. The reasons given for practicing such disciplines are also almost identical across the board.

First of all, what is often cited as a reason is that our mind is scattered or fragmented. Continually carried along by the stream of our thoughts — thoughts about ourselves and our world — our mind has no rest and no stability. This becomes manifest in a continual mental agitation and lack of mindfulness, which denies us the opportunity to pause and look at the movement of our mind, to realize where, who and what we actually are.

A second important reason for the practice of the disciplines of consciousness is the phenomenon that we already touched upon above briefly in connection with the limitations of the disciplines of imagination — our mind has the tendency to *lose itself* in a self-created and egocentric mental world that obscures our vision and hangs in front of the world of phenomena like a veil (of projections). It prevents us from seeing phenomena (including those that appear in our stream of thoughts) as they actually are. We have become caught up in a consciousness that can no longer distinguish completely between imagination and illusion on the one hand and reality on the other. Within this perverted form of consciousness, we lack the mental discernment that enables us to recognize the range and depth of this captivity. Because of this we do not know ourselves, our mind, and thus live in an imaginary reality.

The disciplines of consciousness are directed in the first instance at overcoming this agitation and captivity and, in the second, at making direct *perceptual knowledge* possible (see chapter four). This double purpose allows us to divide these disciplines into two categories: the *disciplines of mindfulness* and the *disciplines of insight* respectively. We will see below that the disciplines of mindfulness are mainly preparatory exercises for the practice of the disciplines of insight. In terms of what we discussed in chapter four, we can say that the disciplines of mindfulness are helpful in removing *perceptual ignorance*. These disciplines make us more conscious of what is happening around us; we become more mindful or attentive. Subsequently, the disciplines of insight help us to clarify *perceptual confusion*.

That the spiritual traditions teach these disciplines is not only important for religious people. These disciplines are of general psychological importance because they supply us with the means to develop insight into our minds and to encourage our humaneness to flourish. They offer us a very practical way of handling and rising above our agitation and psychological blindness. Precisely because they do not work with mental images and concepts (religious or otherwise), these disciplines are less bound to a particular culture or religion than the disciplines of thinking discussed in the previous chapter. The disciplines of consciousness, which include both the disciplines of mindfulness and those of insight, cultivate the human mind itself in a very direct way, which is why they are so universal. In this chapter, we will explore the disciplines of mindfulness to some extent, and in the next, the disciplines of insight.

THE DISCIPLINES OF MINDFULNESS

A familiar metaphor for the agitation of our mind is that of a wild horse — a horse that seems free to come and go as it pleases. But, in fact, precisely because it is wild, it is extraordinarily skittish: it takes only the flutter of one leaf on a tree to send it rushing off. It is too high-strung, too vulnerable to unrest to give itself the time to take a good look around. This is also the way our mind is when it is captured by the egocentric experience of reality: only one ego-threatening thought needs to arise to make it skittish and bolt. We only have to think of one idea and the mind rushes off with it. Zen Buddhism relates the story of a man on a horse dashing by at a wild gallop. A man on foot sees him go rushing past and calls out, "Where are you going?" The man shouts back over his shoulder, "I don't know! Ask the horse!" Carried along by our passions, our hopes and fears, desires and aversions, honor and blame, profit and loss, we lack a kind of steadfastness and overview of our (mental) situation.

Another way to characterize this absentmindedness is to point to the lack of synchronization between our body and our mind: when lost in our thoughts, our mind can be in a very different place than our body. And if we then experience our world of thoughts as reality, our body and the situation in which we find ourselves count for little. Where our mind is and the actual place where we are physically are then not one and the same. *Apparently*, then, we live in two realities. This, too, is a form of brokenness, of rupture. Because of this, it is possible that we will not be mindful and aware of our concrete situation, that various matters may escape us and that we will therefore make a mess of things. When we live mentally in the situation that we expect or remember — in what we tend to call the future and the past — we are not as conscious of our actual situation, either. In both cases we are not synchronized: we are *absent*, not completely there or, as many traditions put it, we are *asleep*, not awake, not alert.

The Practice of the Disciplines of Mindfulness

The purpose of the disciplines of mindfulness is to do something about this absentmindedness. Although these disciplines have, of course, developed in somewhat different forms in the various traditions (because their religious embedment differs), all are concerned with cultivating mindfulness, with rising above the captivity that becomes manifest as disunity or absentmindedness. To this end, we practice focusing our attention, alertness, vigilance, concentration or whatever we wish to call it on one point. This *focal point* can be a certain object or a certain representation, but it can also be a process such as, for example, breathing or a certain action. All disciplines of mindfulness rest on the same basic instruction: as soon as one notices that one has been caught up in thoughts, one redirects one's attention back to the focal point prescribed by the discipline.

The disciplines of mindfulness offer us a technique for doing this systematically. In many traditions, the technique takes the form of *sitting meditation*: we sit erect in quiet surroundings on a chair or a meditation cushion and focus our attention on, for example, our breathing. While sitting in this position, we notice that our attention becomes constantly caught up in the content of our stream of thoughts. When we notice this, we turn our attention again to our *breathing*, which in this technique is the *focal point* for our mindfulness. A very simple yet effective instruction for training our attention. Initially, it takes a certain amount of effort, of discipline to do this. After all, we are used to allowing ourselves to drift along with the stream of our thoughts. It is against this habit that the practice of these disciplines is directed.

We could compare this practice to continually grabbing a stick drifting along in a river and planting it in the river bottom. Stabilizing the attention is like planting a stick in the stream of our thoughts. When we practice this discipline, the stick continually comes loose and once again drifts for a short distance: our attention keeps getting caught up in our streams of thoughts. But the discipline consists of grabbing the stick and once again planting it in the river bottom, creating a fixed point. It comes down to *letting go* of our stream of thoughts time and again. We thus practice waking up from being submerged in our stream of thoughts and thereby from being captive to our own experience of reality, which is also permeated by this stream. Our mindfulness becomes a rock in the surf of our mind.

How is it that we are able to bring our mindfulness back to its focal point at all? Apparently, the human mind is shaped so that moments naturally occur when we notice that we have again been caught. These are crucial moments in the practice of the disciplines of mindfulness. For at such moments we can choose either to return to our stream of thoughts and lose ourselves in that, or to direct our mindfulness once more to the focal point. Each discipline of mindfulness makes use of this natural ability. When practicing this discipline, we choose to return to the focal point again and again. In this way, we cultivate our mindfulness, and this leads to the freedom that is the fruit of this discipline.

The Focal Point of Meditation: An Anchor for our Mindfulness

As we indicated above, the focal point of our mindfulness during the practice of meditation can be anything, which is why the disciplines of mindfulness have taken so many different forms. The focal point of meditation need not be a religious object like a candle, an icon or a stick of incense. It need not even be a thing; it can, as we have seen, also be a more or less continual process of movement like our breathing. Even a mental object — a representation or an image — can be used as an anchor for mindfulness. But within the disciplines of mindfulness, such a mental object has a very different function than in the disciplines of the imagination discussed earlier. The disciplines of mindfulness do not aim at evoking the experiential value of the mental object but only use the object as an anchor for mindfulness. Even if we use an action as an anchor for our mindfulness, that does not, as we shall see below, make this discipline a discipline of action (see chapter nine). Even so, it is striking that breathing is so popular as an anchor in many traditions where the discipline of mindfulness is practiced in the form of sitting still. There are a number of practical and psychological reasons for this. A practical reason is that we are always breathing, so our breathing is always available as an anchor for our mindfulness. Psychological reasons include the fact that breathing is a very simple and monotonous process and, nevertheless, at the same time involves movement. It is a well-known psychological fact that it is easier to keep our attention focused on something that moves than on something that does not. Moreover, there is a close psychological relationship between breathing and our consciousness (see Nyima 1989, 165).

Most traditions also have forms of the discipline of mindfulness in which an elementary manual task serves as an anchor. This may be a task that one performs within the contemplative community such as gardening, sweeping floors, washing up, etc. The Buddhist tradition relates a well-known story of a woman with 12 children who had to walk a couple of miles every day to get water from the nearest well. She longed to practice meditation, and so one day she approached the Buddha with the request that he instruct her in this. She added that she had no time to sit for a little while — let alone to do so undisturbed — each day and train her attention by observing her breathing. When the Buddha heard that she had to walk to a well every day, he told her to use that activity as an anchor: during her walk, whenever she noticed that she had become caught up in her (undoubtedly worrisome) thoughts, she was to focus her attention again on the movement of her body, to the act of walking itself. This is how she disciplined her mind and achieved enlightenment.

In these practices, whether one's mindfulness is focused on breathing or another fixed point such as an image or the repetition of a word or a single action, all such focal points serve as a kind of anchor for our mindfulness, a resting place for our mind. The presence of such an anchor is characteristic for the disciplines of mindfulness. In this context, the Buddhist traditions do speak of *meditation with an object* (see, for example, Dorje 1978, 43). That on which we focus our attention during the practice of the discipline is called the *object of meditation*. Thus the object is *not* something about which we *think* but something on which we *focus our mindfulness* during the practice, something to which we continually return.

Finally, the object of meditation need not be something small, but it must be something that is constantly present and that we can handle, psychologically speaking. In principle, therefore, it can be the entire situation of this moment — the here and now itself — if we can handle it, since it is not the easiest choice for a object of meditation. It is certainly not to be recommended for a beginner in the discipline of mindfulness — it is too easy to become trapped, to confuse our absentmindedness with alertness. A relevant, well-known story can be found in the Zen tradition. A *roshi* (Zen master) instructed his students in the discipline of mindfulness as follows: "When you eat, eat. When you read, only read." In this way he indicated that our attention must be directed exclusively or "one-pointedly" at that which one is doing rather than wandering off on other matters. One day one of his students came into his office and found the *roshi* reading a newspaper while eating a sandwich. Surprised, the student exclaimed, "But master, you taught us: 'When you eat, eat. When you read, only read.'" To which the *roshi* replied: "When I *eat and read*, then all I do is *eat and read*."

The Disciplines of Mindfulness in the Various Traditions

In the Buddhist tradition, the discipline of mindfulness is called *shamatha*, which is usually translated as "peace" or "stability." *Shamatha* is directed at disciplining mindfulness in the sense of stabilizing it. In this discipline, the attention is directed again and again at the movement of one's breathing. It is also called *anapanasati* — *anapana*, that is, "breathing in and breathing out" and *sati* is often translated as "peaceful concentration."

In the Hindu tradition, the disciplines of mindfulness are called *dharana*. "Through *dharana*, our consciousness is kept in a state of attentiveness. To this end, one's attention is fixed on an object and, as soon as other thoughts arise, is redirected toward that same object" (Giri 1992, 63). In both the Buddhist and Hindu traditions, the term *one-pointedness* (*ekagrata*) is used to characterize the nature of the disciplines of mindfulness.

In the Jewish tradition, the discipline of mindfulness is called *kavana*. Here, the discipline involves paying attention to what we are doing when we are doing it rather than allowing our minds to wander through all possible thought-worlds. The mystical schools of Islam also stress the disciplines of mindfulness (see, for example, Naranjo and Ornstein 1972). Within the Christian traditions, particularly within the so-called *apophatic spirituality* (for this term see the following chapter), a great deal of importance is attached to the disciplines of mindfulness. In the *Philokalia*, the source book of the spiritual disciplines of the Orthodox Christian traditions, one can find many passages on this: "After sunset, having asked the help of the all-merciful and all-powerful Lord Jesus Christ, sit you down on a low stool in your quiet and dimly lit cell, collect your mind from its customary circling and wandering outside, and quietly lead it into the heart by way of breathing." (*Writings from the Philokalia* 1972, 195). But one can also use a word instead of breathing to redirect one's mindfulness: "[T]ake but one short word of a single syllable. This is better than two, for the shorter it is the better it accords with the work of the spirit. . . . [I]f any thought should press upon you to ask you what you are seeking, answer him with this word only and with no other words."

(*The Cloud of Unknowing* 1957, 76–77). Evagrius Ponticus, one of the desert fathers, stressed the value of "one-pointed" attention during prayer: "Pray with fire and dispel the cares and doubts that arise. They confuse you and deafen you with their noise, so that they may paralyse your efforts" (Evagrius Ponticus 1987, 1:115). A certain amount of concentration or mindfulness is needed to rise above this absentmindedness. Otherwise, we will find ourselves in the situation Evagrius describes: "If the evil spirits see that you are fervently doing your best to pray, they will put thoughts in your mind about so-called 'pressing matters' and somewhat later they once again arouse your memory of them. In this way they incite the mind to look for them again . . . so that it becomes expressed in it and thus cause the fruitful prayer to fail" (1:115).

Three Aspects of the Discipline of Mindfulness

There are many contemplative psychological aspects and effects linked to the cultivation of mindfulness (see, for example, Naranjo and Ornstein 1972; Namgyal 1986) and, since the seventies, it has also been the object of investigation in academic psychology (for a survey of this, see Shapiro and Walsh 1984). We cannot discuss them all here, but some of these aspects are so typical of the disciplines of mindfulness that the latter often take their names from them. Thus these disciplines are also called the practice of *peace, simplicity* and *purity*. We will look at these aspects briefly below.

The first aspect, which we already touched upon briefly above, is the quality of *peace* or *stabilitas*: the ability to keep our attention on one thing, a mental steadfastness. This prevents us from being dragged along and drowned in the turbulent stream of our thoughts and experience. The disciplines of mindfulness are said to calm the agitation of our mind by continually returning to the focal point or anchor of our mindfulness. This also contributes to the calming of our stream of thoughts. The Buddhist meditation master Chokyi Nyima (1989, 153–54) states:

> "Water clears when undisturbed" it is said. If water in a pond is disturbed, it becomes murky. But if left alone, it naturally remains clear. Likewise, when your mind remains focussed on a single object, whatever it might be, and doesn't follow after gross or even subtle thought of the past, the present, or the future, it automatically relaxes and remains still, calm, and peaceful. This properly laid foundation is of great benefit for training in the more advanced practices.

A second aspect that is closely related psychologically to the cultivation of mindfulness is the development of *simplicity (simplicitas)*. Simplicity is, again, such a typically contemplative concept that we find it in almost all traditions. This aspect stresses that the practice of the discipline of mindfulness can disentangle the complicated, intricate jumble of our mind. After all, what else but simplicity could penetrate complexity?

By *complexity* we do not mean here the sophistication that arises when we think about an intellectually difficult subject. In itself, there is nothing wrong with that. But here we mean the endless complexity that arises from having thoughts about thoughts, emotions about emotions, fantasies about fantasies and thoughts about emotions about fantasies, which then become inextricably mixed up with our sensual experience. This mental movement complicates our experience and clouds our clarity of mind. We wander around in our thoughts as in a castle in the air. We know that the castle is connected somehow with reality but do not see how or where. We have, as stated earlier, lost our way in this psychological labyrinth of our own creation. And whatever means we devise to escape it are actually only further extensions of this labyrinth. The complexity of which we are speaking here is the result of the continually repeated mental movement of the dualistic split (see chapter three).

The simplicity of the discipline of mindfulness does not nourish this complicating mental movement. Why not? It continually brings our attention, when lost in our mental labyrinth, back to that which is the focal point of our practice of mindfulness. We do not add any more energy in the form of various thought contents but leave the labyrinth be for what it is. We stop where we are. And because the egocentric labyrinth requires thought contents for its sustenance, it slowly begins to decay, thereby losing its complexity. Because of this, our mind and experience of reality itself begins to show a greater simplicity and clarity. We become "poor in spirit" (Matthew 5.3). In this way, we also actually simplify our lives:

> Every situation in our lives becomes a simple relationship — a simple relationship with the kitchen sink, a simple relationship with your car, a simple relationship with your father, mother, children. Of course, this is not to say that a person suddenly is transformed into a saint. Familiar irritations are still there of course, but they are simple irritations, transparent irritations. (Trungpa 1976, 47)

This simplicity also applies to our attitude toward the technique of the discipline of mindfulness itself:

> You do not try to separate yourself from the technique, but you try to become the technique so that there is a sense of nonduality . . . [A]nd the proper attitude toward technique is not to regard it as magical, a miracle or profound ceremony of some kind, but to see it as a simple process, extremely simple. The simpler the technique the less danger of sidetracks because you are not feeding yourself with all sorts of fascinating, seductive hopes and fears. (Trungpa 1976, 45–46)

A third psychological aspect that is also characteristic of

the disciplines of mindfulness is *purity*. In a certain sense, this aspect is an extension of simplicity. The Christian tradition often uses the term *purificatio* (cleansing or purification) for this. The term is related to breaking free of our egocentric emotions, our passions. By cultivating mindfulness our mind is deprived of space to form more egocentric depositions and to stir up the waves of our passions. Cleansing or purification, therefore, entails here a *letting go* of our world of thoughts and thus the cultivation of *openmindedness* or *nonfixation*. Being caught up in our egocentric emotions is the source of continual restlessness which not only can destroy our stability but can also obstruct our clear view.

Purity in the sense of not being caught up in our egocentric emotions is very important. Evagrius Ponticus uses the term *apatheia*, which can be translated as "free from emotional turbulence." The desert father Cassian uses the term *puritas cordis*, "purity of heart," to characterize this aspect of mindfulness. The word *heart* already indicates that mindfulness is also a matter of the heart. For mindfulness is a purity that is free from captivity by egocentric emotions. Cassian says the practitioner's first goal is to strive to return continually to this purity of heart: For "[u]nless the mind has some fixed point to which it can keep coming back and to which it tries to fasten itself, it will flutter hither and thither according to the whim of the passing moment and follow whatever immediate and external impression is presented to it" (Cassian in Chadwick 1958, 198). As long as we are tossed back and forth by our egocentric emotions, we lack a purity of heart that can give us sight.

> But we would misunderstand "purity of heart" if we were to view it as sinlessness in a moral sense of the word. Rather, it is a spiritual condition that is pure in the sense of being free from preoccupation, from confusion and excitement. It is a serenity that has let go of everything in order to be free and open to God. (Jaeger 1992, 84)

By practicing the discipline of mindfulness, by continually letting go when we notice that we have again become captivated by our stream of thoughts with all its emotional turbulence and by refocusing our mindfulness on the focal point of our mindfulness meditation, we cleanse our mind of preoccupation and become "pure in heart" (Matthew 5.8). In this sense, our experience of reality becomes increasingly pure.

In sum, the three aspects of the disciplines of mindfulness, *stability* (peace), *simplicity* and *purity* (openmindedness) belong together and develop together. They lay the foundation for the practice of the disciplines of insight (see chapter eight).

THE DEVELOPMENT OF MINDFULNESS

How does mindfulness develop concretely within the practice of this discipline? Its development is marked by all kinds of discoveries. We will mention a few of them here because they give a somewhat more concrete idea of the nature of this discipline. Although we do not claim that the order in which we present them is the only one, these discoveries do tend to occur in that order.

When we begin practicing the discipline of mindfulness, it soon becomes apparent that it is difficult. The instructions are easy enough: keep your attention on the focal point of meditation. When you notice that your attention is getting lost in your thoughts, bring it back to the focal point. They are so simple that we tend to think: what can we learn from this? But the first and most valuable discovery occurs relatively quickly: our stream of thoughts has a very compelling nature. It is so compelling, in fact, that it is difficult to keep our attention on the focal point of meditation. Before we know it, we have already become lost in our thoughts. For many people it is surprising and often shocking to discover how

easy it is to be caught up in one's thoughts. They need not
even be important or very emotionally charged thoughts
that captivate us. The most trivial thoughts distract us. We
thought we were in charge of our own minds, but it becomes
evident that that is not the case at all: apparently, we do not
have the choice of thinking or not thinking. By practicing
the disciplines of mindfulness, we begin to see this.

A subsequent discovery about our minds — one that is
closely related to the first — is that thoughts not only go
through our heads involuntarily but also *almost continuously*.
At the same time, we are scarcely able to remember what we
were thinking about a few minutes ago, let alone throughout
the entire day. A few things may have stuck in our minds, a
fraction of all that we have thought. But whether we have
forgotten them or not, these thoughts have still formed and
colored our experience of reality almost continuously throughout the entire day.

Another discovery that is soon made is that the *content*
of our stream of thoughts is hardly controlled by our will.
Thought after thought occurs, sometimes with a certain co-
hesion, but they can also be interrupted and broken off by
the sudden recollection: "Oh! I still have to buy some milk.
What time is it? Are the stores still open?" Sometimes we are
able pick up the thread of thought again; at other times, we
have lost it completely. And so we drift along in a stream of
thoughts — meaningful thoughts, inane thoughts, beautiful
thoughts, ugly thoughts — all without having much control
over the direction in which these thoughts go. Even when we
seriously decide to think about something specific systematically — even then we notice that our thoughts wander
regularly and we must continually bring ourselves (our attention) back to the topic of our thinking. If we manage to
keep our attention focussed and not get caught up in other
thoughts, we experience that as a strain and quickly become

tired and give up. But then, strangely enough, there is no pause in our thoughts. Our thoughts simply continue to coast along.

It is as if our thoughts have a certain absorptive power, which is why it takes so much energy to channel our stream of thoughts for a short time. We begin to see the enormous power our stream of thoughts has and just how much we are subject to it. Perhaps we have always considered an individual's freedom to think as he likes to be of paramount importance: "freedom of thought," we say. But our practice of the disciplines of mindfulness leads us to discover that we are not free to think what we want: our thoughts have a stronger grip on us than we do on our thoughts. Our "freedom" is apparently not *our* freedom but the freedom of *our thoughts* to enclose us in a world of thought that also colors our experience. We have such a poor grasp of the content of this stream that we do not know what we will think in a few minutes from now.

A further discovery that we could stumble across is one that causes us to understand *why* our thoughts absorb our mindfulness so easily: we take the contents of our thoughts very seriously. Actually, we are especially interested in our *own commentary* which we give to the stream of our experience. We behave somewhat like a child who, while reading a comic book, reads only the written commentary or the text in the balloons. We become conscious of the fact that taking the commentary produced by ourselves so seriously causes us to live in a self-created reality and of the extent to which it does so.

As we mentioned above, when we begin to cultivate our mindfulness, our mind is like a wild horse that needs to be tamed. The disciplines of mindfulness first "tame" our mind. We train ourselves, i.e. our attention, in this initially by means of the discipline of mindfulness. This taming is a very gradual process that cannot be completed abruptly or with impatience. A classic Buddhist metaphor expresses it as follows. When we want to tame a wild horse so that we can ride it later, we tie a rope around its neck and hold on to the other end. Then we shorten that rope a little, but not entirely — the animal is much too skittish for that. When the horse has settled down again, we shorten the rope somewhat more until the tension becomes too much for the horse and it becomes skittish again, forcing us to slacken the rope. In this way, ever so slowly, bit by bit, with patience and perseverance, we pull the horse closer and closer until it is so close that it can smell us, which is a new phase, a new moment of tension. When it becomes accustomed to our smell, we continue to shorten the rope until we can touch him. The distance between ourselves and the horse is thus decreased. This cannot be done abruptly but only with great skill, by a gentle method of give and take.

This is also how we proceed in taming our agitated mind, which is thrown back and forth on the waves of our egocentric mental movements. The object of meditation is the point to which we direct our mind again and again and the discipline of mindfulness is the rope. We continually return our attention, which was lost in our stream of thoughts, to the focal point of meditation. We do so with great patience and without aggression. When our mind is wild, we do not shorten the rope but give our mind space. When it calms down, we tighten our discipline somewhat. We thus develop our mindfulness.

By developing our ability to pay attention, we gradually become conscious that we need not surrender to the content of our stream of thoughts. Although we must acknowledge it and not deny its existence, we need not yield to it and lose ourselves in it as if that is where we find our soul and salvation. Nor must we repress our stream of thoughts and fight it as though it were the source of hell and damnation. For our mindfulness is destroyed not by our stream of thoughts, but by our being caught by and submerged in it. There is more to our life than living in our stream of thoughts.

By practicing the disciplines of mindfulness, we also begin to discover that the moments when we wake up from our thoughts and notice them also show us that our stream of thoughts does not go on ceaselessly. There are openings: the moments when we wake up from our thoughts *are* those openings. These moments actually make it possible for us to focus our attention on the focal point of meditation once again. Sooner or later, these moments always reappear spontaneously. We cannot summon them or control them but, at most, can only give them space, which is what the practice of the disciplines of mindfulness helps us to do. We taste briefly what it means to be free, to find ourselves in moments of wakeful stillness — a refreshing mental pause. At these moments of wakefulness, our bodies and our minds are synchronized: we are present mentally where we are physically, in the here and now.

We often experience the transition from captivity to freedom as if something opens up. It is as though our wakefulness or the situation in which we find ourselves suddenly unfolds again. Our worries recede to the background and we are briefly liberated from the play of hopes and fears, from our usual preoccupation with the future and the past: the way things were, the way they should have been or should be — all of this has evaporated for a moment. We discover that wakefulness is an aspect of our mind and that we can cultivate it.

We then begin to value our practice of the discipline of mindfulness because we begin to experience in a very concrete way that it is an effective instrument with which we can tame and free our mind. We increasingly appreciate the openmindedness, simplicity and stability that appear at the moments we wake from our thoughts. Thus we gradually develop a certain *feeling* for the contrast between being lost in our thoughts and seeing our thoughts.

Initially, we experience this freedom at moments of *wakeful thoughtlessness*, moments during which we have no thoughts and are aware of this. At these moments we are obviously free from being caught, as there is nothing to be caught up in. Because of the pleasant feeling of space that we often experience at such moments, we are easily tempted to want to hold on to them and see thoughts as the enemy. But this is a mistake that impedes the further development of openmindedness.

This further development allows us to recognize the moment when a thought goes through our mind for what it is: a thought. At that moment of recognition we are also free. In this phase, we begin to discover that openmindedness does not depend on the *absence of thoughts*, on thoughtlessness, but on the *absence of captivity* by our thoughts. This is a key point. We gradually understand that both resisting thoughts and losing ourselves in thoughts are equally forms of captivity. Initially, thoughts have such a strong grip on us that having a thought almost always goes hand in hand with captivity. In that phase, thoughts were indeed obstacles to openmindedness. But the more we cultivate our mindfulness the stronger it becomes. Finally, not only do we not lose our mindfulness when a thought occurs but the occurrence of a thought even becomes a signal that redirects us to openmindedness, to the absence of captivity. Our openmindedness acquires increasing continuity: whether our mind moves or rests, it continues to endure, laying the foundation for further disciplines — the disciplines of insight.

EIGHT

The Disciplines of Insight

INTRODUCTION

In the previous chapters, we discussed the mental disciplines. First, in chapter six, we discussed the two disciplines of thinking: the intellectual disciplines and the disciplines of the imagination. In chapter seven, we explored the first of the two disciplines of consciousness: the discipline of mindfulness. Now we will look more closely as the second discipline of consciousness: the discipline of insight. Because this is the last of the mental disciplines that we will explore in this book, we will close this chapter with a section on the combined action of these four disciplines.

As stated above, the Christian tradition originally referred to the discipline of insight by the term *contemplatio*. Together, the disciplines of insight form the core of what in this tradition is called *apophatic spirituality* (here *apo* means "separate from," so we could translate apophatic as: separate from words, concepts).

217

> Apophatic spirituality is directed at being conscious in a pure,
> empty way so that the divine can manifest itself. Contents
> are viewed as obstacles. As long as the consciousness [i.e.,
> mind] holds on to images or concepts, it has not yet arrived at
> that point where the particular experience of God occurs.
> Images and contents cloud the divine rather than clarify it.
> (Jaeger 1992, 72)

In some Buddhist traditions, the disciplines of insight are
called *formless meditation*. Here *formless* means that these
disciplines do not make use of those mental forms (concepts
and images) which are used by the disciplines of the imagination discussed earlier. Thus the disciplines of insight are
not concerned with arousing a certain experiential value by
means of an image or representation. Rather, practicing these
disciplines consist of a direct, *open* look at our mind and experience of reality. Openmindedness is crucial, because at
moments of openmindedness we can see the stream of our
experience without distortion, and this leads to insight and
knowledge. This knowledge is a nonconceptual form of knowledge (see chapter four); it is *perceptual* knowledge.

The practice of the disciplines of mindfulness, which frees
our consciousness from being caught up in our egocentric
experience of reality, constitutes the preparation for the possibility of such knowledge. The most common Sanskrit term
for the discipline of insight in the Buddhist tradition is
vipashyana (Pali: *vipassana*) or insight meditation, which is
practiced on the basis of *shamatha*, the discipline of mindfulness. In Hinduism, the term *dhyana* is used to refer generally to this discipline, the practice of which is supported by
dharana, the discipline of mindfulness.

In the Western Christian tradition, the disciplines of insight have faded from sight in the last few centuries, as far
as the average churchgoer is concerned, and thereby from
our culture as well. This is why people now often think that

these disciplines are typical of "Eastern" traditions. It is often not understood that "the East" is a Western concept that does not correspond in any way to a cultural or spiritual unity. The Indian culture, for example, is much closer to our Western culture than to the Chinese or Japanese cultures, not only with respect to language but also with respect to its way of thinking.

Within the traditions of Eastern Christianity, apophatic spirituality with its disciplines of insight has always persisted. Today these disciplines have once again been brought to the attention of the practitioners of the Western Christian contemplative life. Interreligious dialogue has greatly contributed to this, for right up to the present it has been the other world religions in which these disciplines have played a major role. In those traditions, they are taken up when the disciplines of mindfulness and of the imagination have reached a certain maturity.

THE PRACTICE OF THE DISCIPLINES OF INSIGHT

How do we practice the disciplines of insight? Is there a certain spiritual technique for training our discernment, our discriminating awareness, just as we have trained our attention with the help of a focal point? The answer is typical for the disciplines of insight: the practice of these disciplines goes beyond every technique. Nonetheless, it is a very disciplined practice. How are we to conceive of this? The practice of the disciplines of insight is the *disciplined practice of openmindedness itself.* By openmindedness we mean a mind or consciousness that is *free from being fixated* on or lost in the contents of thought.

Openmindedness, which is the fruit of the discipline of mindfulness, forms the basis for the practice of these disciplines. We cultivate this openmindedness further in the disciplines of insight so that it becomes *unconditional openmindedness*, which in no way allows itself to be driven off or fenced in by any internal or external experience. In turn, this openmindedness creates the space in which our *discernment* can be active. And it is this discernment that leads to the insight that these disciplines seek to cultivate. It is insight that gives us a concrete answer to the question of (or causes us to experience) how the world of phenomena looks if it is viewed from the perspective of unconditional openmindedness or egolessness.

We could say that this discernment is grafted onto, and blossoms on one and the same branch with, the discipline of mindfulness. From that perspective we could say that — if we want to speak of a "technique" with regard to the disciplines of insight — it is *the same* as that of the disciplines of mindfulness. But the place that openmindedness occupies has shifted: it is no longer a goal as is the case in the practice of mindfulness, but it is a means for rousing the mental discernment that allows us to distinguish between illusion and reality. It differs from the disciplines of mindfulness on this score.

A second difference is that cultivating openmindedness within the disciplines of mindfulness comes down to developing a certain distance toward our stream of thoughts, a certain *Abgeschiedenheit*, "separateness," as Meister Eckhart calls it. But in the disciplines of insight, this openmindedness is like that of a child who, with unfettered curiosity, stands *as close as possible* to everything to get a good look. For the more we develop our ability to pay attention, the less absorbing is our stream of thoughts, and thus we practitioners can see our stream of thoughts from a continually closer perspective without losing our openmindedness.

A third difference is that the disciplines of mindfulness initially require a certain effort and manipulation of mindfulness, whereas the disciplines of insight are based on mental relaxation. We realize that openmindedness is a very natural aspect of our mind and that we can relax in it. The only reason that it has so few opportunities to manifest itself is that we continually try energetically to hold on to our egocentric experience of reality so as to be able to find refuge in it. Ego fears our natural openmindedness because it does not buttress ego in any way.

But we have learned to appreciate our natural moments of openmindedness through our previous practice of the discipline of mindfulness. And now we discover that these moments are not something that we must produce through much effort but that they occur when we cease to manipulate ourselves, our mind, our experience of reality, when we relax in our practice. Then our natural alertness is given the chance to clarify our experience of reality.

Why is it that the practice of the disciplines of insight can lead to direct perceptual knowledge of ego and egolessness? To be able to understand this, let us return to the metaphor of planting the stick in the stream. If we have developed the ability to plant the stick somewhat firmly in the river bottom — that is, if we have developed our discipline of mindfulness to such a degree that it offers a certain stability — then, for the first time, we may also be able to observe the qualities of the water that flows *past* the stick. We notice the varying temperatures and speeds of the water as well as all its other empirical qualities.

At the moment that the stick is worked loose again and is swept along with the stream, we no longer observe any of this. The stick moves along as quickly as the water does. With respect to the water around it, it appears to be lying still and it seems that nothing happens. Our mindfulness as well as our discernment has once again vanished. We have submerged once again and are caught up in the stream of our thoughts. The moment we awaken from our captivity, the stick stands straight up in the stream and once again we notice its empirical qualities.

During these moments of stability, our discernment once again begins to operate. It offers us the ability to view our stream of thoughts openly and recognize it for what it is. And because this stream permeates our total field of experience, our discernment penetrates and clarifies our egocentric experience of reality as well.

Openmindedness as Surrender

Cultivating openmindedness, which is the basis for the development of the kind of insight with which this discipline is concerned, also means that we cannot afford to cling to the fruits of this discipline and other disciplines practiced earlier. With regard to the discipline of mindfulness, this means that the practitioner does not cling mentally to the calm and openmindedness to which it leads. After all, clinging and openmindedness are incompatible. With regard to the discipline of imagination, this means that the practitioner does not cling to the experiential value that is the fruit of these disciplines. This "not clinging" obtains *a fortiori* for the practice of the discipline of insight itself: no matter which particular fruits of insight appear, we must not attempt to cling to them and become fixated on them. If we do, we will again be captivated in a very subtle way and our discernment cannot develop and have its proper effect. When this capacity becomes stuck, it loses its quality of panoramic awareness; it can no longer fly around freely and look around. John of the Cross expresses it this way:

> For it comes to the same thing whether a bird be held by a slender cord or by a stout one; since, even if it be slender, the bird will be well held as though it were stout, for so long as it

breaks it not and flies not away. It is true that the slender one is the easier to break; still, easy though it be, the bird will not fly away if it be not broken. And thus the soul that has attachment to anything, however much virtue it possess, will not attain to the liberty of Divine union. (John of the Cross 1963, 180)

In practical terms, therefore, cultivating discernment means continually letting go of the fruit that it produces — including *the idea* that we should cling to the fruits of contemplative flourishing in order to preserve them. Concretely, this means letting go of our fear of losing them. The insight that we cannot possess these fruits *at all*, that we never have and never will possess them, frees us from this fear. This is a very subtle affair, for already the fact that we cling to that insight breaks our discipline.

In practicing the disciplines of insight, therefore, there is no room left to count our blessings and attempt to hold on to our spiritual achievements of insight. There is no longer any room left for spiritual strategies and manipulation nor is there any room left to monitor oneself in an anxious and strenuous way. There is not even any room left to hold on to the framework of one's own tradition. It goes beyond every hope of achieving and fear of not achieving. In this sense, the practice of this discipline is without hope and without fear: it is *free of* hope and fear. It goes beyond every goal that has been previously established. It is, in this sense, also without a goal.

The discipline thus consists of cultivating *unconditional openmindedness*, not as a goal but as a means, so that our discernment can move freely and lead to insight. The practice of openmindedness comes down to continually undoing the mental movement that leads to ego: the undoing of the dualistic split which we discussed in chapter three — the constantly recurring dualistic split that causes us to see the world of phenomena in a distorted way by splitting it into *my* surroundings, *my* wife, *my* husband, *my* child, *my* body, *my* thoughts, *my* mind and that which is not *mine*. By undoing this distorting mental captivity, we begin to see how (internal and external) phenomena relate to each other rather than how they relate to the phantom of ego. Stated in theistic terms, we are now open to see the world of phenomena as God's world or as God's creation instead of a world that is for (or against) *me*. Stated in nontheistic terms, we begin to find that uncovering our humaneness and manifesting it in the world is more valuable and more interesting than cultivating our being John or Mary or whoever we think we are.

This is why we could also characterize this discipline as cultivating *mental surrender*; a gradual process of mentally letting go of who we think we are, a letting go of the dualistic mentality in which ego sees aspects of its experience as possessions, as *mine* as opposed to not mine. Thus, complete surrender is the mental attitude that no longer possesses (anything): the mind has returned to its nakedness and also sees the world of phenomena in its nakedness. Through this surrender, this mental nakedness, *joy in life, tenderness* and *insight* are no longer bound to what we hope to gain or attain nor fear to lose or not attain. But they continue to flourish through this unconditional openmindedness itself. In the Heart Sutra, one of the most well-known texts in Mahayana Buddhism, those who have achieved this open insight or perfection of wisdom (Sanskrit: *prajnaparamita*) are called *bodhisattvas*. It is said of them: "Because *bodhisattvas* have no attainment, they rely on and abide in the perfection of wisdom; because their minds are without obstruction, they have no fear" (Lopez 1997, 520).

The spiritual traditions call this naked mind by many different names, although it cannot be known conceptually but only perceptually: it is the *Shekinah* in the Jewish Chassidic tradition, the *Holy Spirit* in the Christian tradition. It is inspiration, enthusiasm. A famous passage in a Buddhist *terma* text includes the following:

> With respect to its having a name, the various names that are applied to it are inconceivable (in their numbers). Some call it "the nature of the mind" or "mind itself". Some Tirthikas [non-Buddhist] call it by the name Atman or "the Self". The 'Sravakas call it the doctrine of Anatman or "the absence of a self".... Some call it the Prajnaparamita or "the perfection of wisdom." Some call it the name Tathagatogarbha or "embryo of Bhuddahood...." Some call it by the name Alaya or "the basis of everything". And some simply call it by the name "ordinary awareness." (Reynolds 1989, 12)

Whatever we call the mind in which a completely open discernment is active, it is both the invisible ground and the hidden fruit of the disciplines of insight.

The Double-Sided Function of the Disciplines of Insight

Formulated in the somewhat more prosaic terms of contemplative psychology, the disciplines of insight offer the opportunity to observe and study our stream of experience without fitting it into (religious or egocentric) concepts and representations. This distinguishes these disciplines from our customary mode of observation because, as we discussed earlier, our experience is usually already adjusted to fit into certain concepts: our experience is usually given to us as *conceptualized experience* (de Wit 1991, 67) without our being aware of it.

Usually, when we want to study something, we also assume a specific conceptual framework and formulation that determines and limits our experience. But in practicing the disciplines of insight, we free ourselves from every formulation and every conceptual framework, thus creating room for an unlimited view which offers a direct, nonconceptual form of knowledge and which destroys our *perceptual confusion* (see chapter four).

In chapter two, we discussed our personal experience of reality and how it arises: at every moment of experience we *dress our experience up* in our concepts without being aware of this process and, as a result, we experience it simply as reality. In chapter three, we spoke of how the concept of ego structures our experience of reality, and in chapter four, we saw how perceptual confusion arises when our discernment does not function and what its nature is:

> When the deluded in a mirror look
> They see a face, not a reflection.
> So the mind that has truth denied
> Relies on that which is not true.
>
> (Guenther 1973, 66)

This is how *Saraha*, the great Buddhist tantric master, formulated it in a famous verse. The disciplines of insight are directed at developing that discernment, which allows us to see a face as a face and a reflection as a reflection. It allows us to see things, to know things as they are.

With regard to our self-created egocentric experience of reality, we begin to recognize it for what it is: a fiction. Our discernment therefore begins to remove the blindness that causes us to experience this fiction as reality. It thus makes us aware not only of the fact that (and when) we dream but also of what we dream.

In practicing these disciplines, therefore, the presence of thoughts does not necessarily also mean that we are caught up in them. How does this situation develop? In the previous chapter, we spoke briefly about two kinds of openmindedness: the first kind was the openmindedness that occurs at moments of wakeful *thoughtlessness*. Our discernment is then active in that it allows us to distinguish between being in thought and not being in thought. The second kind of openmindedness is one that is not lost when a thought arises. It develops from the first through practice. Our openmindedness gradually acquires a greater continuity: whether our mind is moving or at rest, this openmindedness can endure.

Thus the second kind of openmindedness or unfetteredness does not depend on the absence of thoughts. It is thus also the foundation of the disciplines of insight, for it opens the possibility of clear sight with regard to our stream of thoughts precisely because it *is free from* every fixation on the world of phenomena, including our world of thought. The discernment that functions in this second kind of openmindedness enables us to *see* the movement of our mind, to study it without being caught up in it. Then thoughts no longer threaten our practice. To the contrary, their occurrence allows our unfettered discernment to explore our egocentric experience of reality freely. That this discipline of seeing our stream of thoughts is very different than *reflecting upon* the thoughts that cross our mind should be clear from what we have said previously about the disciplines of thinking.

In this way, the discipline of insight leads in the first place to our being less and less of a mystery to ourselves. That which is internal — our mental life in the form of our stream of thoughts — becomes less of a frightening, unknown area for us, not because we know (intellectually) so much about it but because we know it so well (experientially). Of course, this mental life continues to be unpredictable and uncontrollable, but this is something with which we become more and more familiar. We develop a certain adeptness in dealing with our mind, just as good tennis players are good precisely because of their knowledge and skill in dealing with their opponents' unpredictable shots. In this way, we acquire a very direct form of self-knowledge: firsthand self-knowledge. It is not self-knowledge in the form of a narrative or theory about ourselves, which we have stored somewhere in our mental administration, but a nonconceptual self-knowledge in the form of being acquainted with ourselves, with the qualities of our stream of thoughts. This is the *first function* of the discipline of insight: it leads to *perceptual self-knowledge*, teaching us to know our ego and its experience of reality and to realize its illusory nature.

But these disciplines have yet a second function and fruition, which in a certain sense is the flipside of the first: they also open up another perspective, one that gives us insight into reality, such as that which appears when we are free from ego, free from illusion. They reveal an experience of reality that transcends ego. So, finally, our discernment enables us to explore the egoless state of openmindedness itself and to taste of its qualities — qualities that are none other than those of our fundamental humaneness. The discernment that is now operative here penetrates our entire experiential space or, better yet, it is the intelligent clarity of the space itself that places everything — the worlds of ego and of egolessness — in the light.

We gradually discover that this open space is inhabitable, real and joyous and not a religious fabrication. At the same time, we do not need to look up to it nor wrap ourselves in mystery about it. We simply observe that it is possible to live outside the stream of our egocentric reality — that we do not have to be caught up in the stream and that we can rest in that space. And this gives rise to an enormous inspiration that is based not on hope but on experience. For from the perspective of ego, this space may appear groundless, deadly and lonely, but when seen from its own perspective it is alive, clear and warm. It is the space in which our fundamental humanity is rooted groundlessly and from which it sprouts and flourishes constantly in our own lives and in that of others, in our own culture and age and in all cultures and ages. It gives us sight of the human existence with all its shortcomings and suffering and places it in a perspective that makes us milder, wiser and more caring. This is why the discovery of this space and allowing it to expand and permeate our experience is nothing other than cultivation of the flourishing within.

Expressed in theistic terms, the second function of the disciplines of insight is that they lead to *knowledge of God*: not conceptual but perceptual knowledge of God. These disciplines finally reveal a divine reality and induce us to turn toward it, which is why the disciplines of insight are also classified in theistic traditions as *directing oneself towards God*. Within the Islam Sufi tradition, this discipline is call *muraqabah*, about which Nurbaksh says that they "are reserved for God's saints, who see Him internally and externally, in solitude and in communion, and say: I see nothing if I have not first seen God" (cited in Naranjo 1992, 25).

We could again illustrate this second function in terms of the metaphor of the stick in the river. We could say that when the stick is planted in the river bottom, it projects out of the water to a certain extent. The stick appears to be standing in a bigger space than the space of the stream. A vast landscape is visible — at least, if we do not continue to be fascinated by all that we see in the stream. When we leave this fascination behind us, we slowly acquire a view of this space itself. In terms of Saraha's metaphor of the mirror, we could say that not only do we recognize that which appears in the mirror as a reflection but also that we become aware of the mirror itself. The discernment that sees ego is nothing other than the discernment that sees egolessness. In the Shambhala teachings, this discernment is called the wisdom of the *cosmic mirror*, which is a metaphor for the

unconditioned, vast open space. It is an eternal and completely
open space, space beyond question. In the realm of the cosmic
mirror, your mind extends its vision completely, beyond doubt.
Before thoughts, before the thinking process takes place, there
is the accommodation of the cosmic mirror, which has no
boundary — no center and no fringe. (Trungpa 1984, 174)

Perhaps we do not even have a conceptual framework and
terminology at hand to express more precisely the kind of
knowledge that is awakened by the disciplines of insight.
But that does not detract from its value and usefulness. We
gave an example of this earlier: we know hundreds of people
by their faces, but our vocabulary is not rich enough to describe the different outward appearances of all these people.
And yet that does not detract from the usefulness of our
knowledge. This is also the case with our knowledge of the
world that we acquire by means of the discernment that is
cultivated by the disciplines of insight.

Of course, every spiritual tradition speaks of this discernment in its own terms. Stated in Christian terms, this discernment (*diakrisis*) leads us in the first instance to see our
pettiness and sinfulness/sin in the light of the Holy Spirit,
and in the second instance it shows (and is) the activity of
the Holy Spirit. Stated in Buddhist terms, the discernment
(*prajna*) which is cultivated by the disciplines of insight
causes us to recognize *samsara* (the egocentric experience of
reality) as the greatest and most powerful illusion there is.
And at the same time it reveals *nirvana* (egoless experience
of reality) and the true nature of our mind, our Buddha nature. Why? Because this discernment itself is free of ego and
an aspect of our Buddha nature. The world of the phenomena that we first experienced as *samsara* is, because of the
development of our discernment, now experienced as *nirvana*.

The two functions of the disciplines of insight show that
nonconceptual self-knowledge and knowledge of God are

closely related. This is because the discernment that is developed in these disciplines functions in two directions. The first is that it *unmasks unreality*, that is, unmasks ego, and in this sense it generates self-knowledge. The second function is that it *reveals reality*, that is, reveals a reality that is egoless or created by God. We need to understand, however, that the moment when unreality is unmasked is the same moment that reality is revealed. This not because reality has somehow been lurking *behind* unreality but because seeing through the world of illusion *is* seeing reality. There is no reality hidden behind unreality. In short, the world of illusion — when one sees through it — is reality. That is why it is often said in Buddhism that, in the egoless perspective, *samsara* is not separate from *nirvana*, and why it is said in the Christian traditions that we are not far from the Kingdom of God (Mark 12.34) and even that the Kingdom is within us (Luke 17.21). From the perspective of ego, however, they are worlds apart.

Simply put, the disciplines of insight therefore not only teach us to recognize and acknowledge our blindness but also open our eyes. They help us to see the nature and causes of ego and our egocentric experience of reality clearly by placing us in the reality of an egoless experience of reality. We can agree with Rabbi Baruch in saying, "What a good and clear world it is when one does not become lost in it, and what a dark world it is when one does become lost in it" (Buber 1967, 133).

THE INTERPLAY BETWEEN THE MENTAL DISCIPLINES

In the previous chapters, we classified the mental disciplines into a number of types based on various mental functions that have a central place in contemplative psychologies. We discussed those functions in chapter four on the human mind: thinking, imagining, consciousness, experiencing, knowing, etc. In the daily practice of the spiritual way of life, however, the mental disciplines that we have described are used in various combinations and often in a certain order, about which we will now make a few comments.

Combined Disciplines

First of all, I would like to comment on the way in which certain mental disciplines are combined. In our discussion of the disciplines of mindfulness, we mentioned that these disciplines make use of an *object of meditation* or *focal point* that functions as an anchor for our mindfulness. Thus the intention here is not to think about or contemplate *on* that object but simply to pay attention to it and in that way discipline our mindfulness. And we have seen that, in principle, every aspect of our experiential world can be used for this purpose: we could therefore also use a mental object, such as a representation, word or sentence that we repeat silently.

The disciplines of the imagination, as we know, also make use of representations — not to use them as anchors but to evoke a specific experiential value. This naturally opens up the possibility of combining our mindfulness and the evocation of a specific experiential value in one mental discipline. Such "combined" disciplines therefore also exist in many traditions. A very central discipline in Islam is the practice of *dhikr*, which is a verbal formulation with a specific and deep meaning, such as *la ilaha illa 'llah* — "There is no (other) god than God." The practitioner keeps it in mind and repeats it silently. Some Christian traditions repeat the prayer, "Lord, have mercy upon me, a sinner," continuously. Hinduism makes use of the continual repetition of, for example, the divine name *Ram*, and (Vajrayana) Buddhists also often recite meaningful mantras, such as *om mani padme hum* while visualizing an anthropomorphic representation of compassion in the form of Avalokiteshvara sitting on a lotus in one's own heart.

What we observe in the actual practice of such "combined" disciplines is that initially they serve to cultivate mindfulness. When the practitioner becomes skilled in that, then the experiential value of the mental object becomes more important. When this experiential value unfolds, it can clarify our experience of reality (including our experience of ourselves and God). This is a logical development, because as long as we have not disciplined our mindfulness we are not capable of allowing it to rest upon a mental content nor can its experiential value be revealed. Many theistic traditions use the term *prayer* for this "combined" discipline. The description of prayer by the Benedictine monk André Zegveld beautifully blends all the mental disciplines that we discussed:

> Prayer is primary: express *everything* and hold nothing back, for that is what pleases God, the creature that He has created in his image and not in the image that the individual has of himself. Prayer is expressing oneself, maybe not in so many words but *by looking honestly into one's own heart* [italics mine]. This is how one travels along the way. Whoever has begun to travel can never say that he has achieved his goal or that he has definitively found his true self. One's proper name is always further along, and will be lost in the proper Name of God, which no human has ever been able to express adequately. This is why travelling along this way is a form of continual reorientation, of asceticism, and of *poverty of mind* as well. Slowly and painfully it will become clear that we want to hold on so frantically to our values and ideals, our longing for justice, our love, our religiosity and even our faith that it keeps us removed from our own name and from that of God Himself. They tell us more about our "I" than about *ourselves*, more about the roles that we (want to) play than about God. Travelling along this way therefore also means a *purification*,

a way of growing toward being a true *self*. Thus it is a way toward *undivided* attention so that we, looking beyond the coloring that is peculiar to each mirror, can see the name of God appear in the mirror of our own soul. It is a way in and at the same time a way out — an undivided attention to within and without characterized by both *compassion* (a mindfulness of gentle mercy and compassion) and *universality* (a mindfulness that encompasses everything). (Zegveld 1991, 107f.)

The Order of Application of the Mental Disciplines

The above already suggests that there is a certain order in the application of the four mental disciplines discussed — an order that corresponds to the contemplative development of the practitioner. Let us look more closely at this aspect.

With regard to the intellectual disciplines that we discussed first, they are actually practiced throughout the entire contemplative life. At the start they have the function of purifying our motivation and sharpening our insight into the how and why of the contemplative way. Later they also furnish us with the framework for formulating and communicating clearly the shifts in our experience of reality. As we stated, intellectual understanding is a means and not a goal of the contemplative life. It offers us an intellectual orientation and directions along the Path, but it does not provide us with the experience itself indicated by the Path. This also means that the intellectual disciplines must ultimately clear the field to make room for direct experiential and nonconceptual knowledge, for what we have called (in chapter four) *perceptual knowledge* and for those mental disciplines that provide such knowledge.

In addition to study, which from the start must be practiced as well as pursued while traveling along the spiritual pathway, the first discipline that the traditions usually offer is the discipline of mindfulness. This helps us to curb our restlessness and absentmindedness. Through this arises, as we discussed, room for the disciplines of insight. In the first place, the disciplines of insight are directed particularly at developing insight into ego, into who and what we are now, into how our mental patterns and our ways of acting and speaking create and maintain our egocentric experience of reality. This is the first function of these disciplines, the fruit of which is that we gradually see the illusory character of this experience of reality.

But seeing this is not always enough to cause us to let go of this pattern. After all, even if we do see that our preoccupation with ego and with our egocentric representations concern an imaginary world, we are not necessarily freed from this preoccupation. Our firm belief in the reality of our egocentric representation may be undermined to some extent, but this does not always conquer our constant tendency (habit) to become lost in this representation. We are like children who no longer believe in Santa Claus but are nonetheless spellbound if the jolly old man himself stands before them. We may be capable of recognizing these representations and the mental patterns that are connected with them, but letting go requires something more.

We have already discussed the fact that we can use the disciplines of mindfulness for this purpose since they are an exercise in letting go mentally: every time we notice that we were caught up in our stream of thoughts, we let go and direct our mindfulness again on the object of meditation. But within the mental disciplines there is yet another, quite powerful way of letting go of our preoccupation with our egocentric experience of reality: the disciplines of the imagination. In chapter six we stated that the products of our imagination are not simply neutral mental pictures for us but have an emotional charge — a charge that can link us to an egocentric perspective as well as to an egoless perspective. Precisely because our experience of reality is no longer experienced as absolute as a result of the use of the previous discipline of insight, it becomes possible to change our experience intentionally by means of mastering images, which in their experiential value awaken an egoless or theocentric experience of reality. The fruit of this is, once again, that this experiential value places us in egoless or theocentric reality itself — a reality that exceeds the images that have roused it. The familiar metaphor of the ladder (of images) applies here, which one can leave behind when one has achieved that to which it leads.

This leads to the following phase in which the discipline of insight once again stands central. But now it does not function so as to make ego visible, but to reveal the true nature of our mind and experience; it makes the egoless or theocentric reality itself visible. It recognizes and acknowledges the space that surrounds ego or, better put, the space that is visible when ego becomes transparent. This second function (see the previous section) of the disciplines of insight is therefore concerned with pure vision without the support of any additional image or representation. In the famous text *The Mystical Theology* by Pseudo-Dionysius the Areopagite, this way of seeing is expressed as follows:

> And, Timothy, my friend, my advice to you as you look for a sight of the mysterious things, is to leave behind everything perceived and understood, everything perceptible and understandable, all that is not and all that is, and, with your understanding laid aside, to strive upward as much as you can toward union with him who is beyond all being and knowledge. (Pseudo-Dionysius 1987, 135)

The form of knowledge realized by the discipline of insight is a direct, nonconceptual form of knowing or experiencing that cannot be contained in the conceptual dualities of known and knower, of *experience* and *the one who experiences*. In the Eastern Orthodox Christian tradition, it is called *theoria*; in Zen Buddhism, *Shikantaza*; and in Vajayana Buddhism, *Mahamudra* and *Mahasandi*. It is this experiential knowing that reveals the ultimate nature of reality.

Many traditions emphasize that this form of experiential knowing is not a certain experience but rather a *way of experiencing*: an egoless way of experiencing. At this point, it is often said that no one has ever seen God. This is because, ultimately, God is not an object for our vision but rather like space: one can see the things *in God*. Along the same lines, it is said in the Buddhist tradition that the Buddhas themselves never saw enlightenment either. Enlightenment is not something that we can experience but a way of experiencing within which reality is seen as it is.

The order that we have given here appears to occur often in the practice of the contemplative life. But it is not absolute. There are, for example, stories of people for whom simply hearing a certain statement was enough for them to achieve the state of enlightenment or fulfillment, although according to the traditions, such people are rare. They are like people for whom it is enough to stop smoking when they hear that it is unhealthy. In other words, for them the practice of the intellectual discipline is enough to transform them existentially. For some, just seeing ego, if only for a second, causes them to drop their preoccupation right away. Therefore, they do not need to practice the disciplines of imagination that bring one to the point of giving up one's preoccupation with ego's world. They then may practice only the disciplines of mindfulness and of insight. They are comparable to people who first need to see an x-ray of a smoker's lungs before they can quit smoking.

Moreover, the emphasis that the traditions themselves lay on the use of the various mental disciplines differs. Zen

Buddhism, for example, makes only very sporadic use of the disciplines of imagination, whereas many Christian traditions give only a marginal place to the disciplines of mindfulness and of insight. Also, the relation between the mental disciplines and the disciplines of action and speech differ from tradition to tradition (see chapter nine).

This concludes our discussion of the mental disciplines. The division that we have used is based on the contemplative psychology of the mind that was outlined earlier. It is a *functional* division, in the sense that it rests on the mental functions that we discussed in chapters three and four. Instead of this psychological division, one could also divide these disciplines not according to function but according to their phenomenology. A good example of this approach is that by Naranjo (1990). Our approach, however, is different in that it gives an answer to the contemplative, psychological question of how the mental disciplines make use of our mental functions in order to foster the flourishing within.

NINE

The Disciplines of Action and Speech

INTRODUCTION

In this chapter, we will explore the disciplines of action and speech, to a certain extent. "To a certain extent" is an appropriate phrase, for there are so many kinds and types of these disciplines that we, by means of a number of typical examples, can at most give an impression of their *nature, function* and *form* and how they accompany the mental disciplines discussed previously. The simple reason that there are so many is that our actions and speech are multifaceted and that the situations in which we act and speak are also enormously varied. These situations differ, moreover, also with respect to time and culture and thus the form of these disciplines is also relative to their time and culture. Nonetheless, they do share a number of general contemplative psychological features. We will look at these in this chapter.

But let us first describe the disciplines of action and speech

in more general terms. The practice of these disciplines consists in observing guidelines directed at our dealing with the
world of phenomena: what to do and to leave undone and
when, how, and about what to speak or to remain silent. In
other words, they instruct us on how to conduct ourselves.
All great spiritual traditions include these disciplines of action and speech. The guidelines on which they are based have
to do with almost all aspects of our life.

The traditions trace the origin of these guidelines and also
often their justification to the sacred scriptures of the traditions and to the interpretation of these scriptures in the light
of the local culture. Thus the Jewish tradition has its *halacha*.
The verb *halach* literally means: "to walk, to go." *Halacha* is
the normative part of the Jewish tradition, as that has been
passed on in the written and oral Torah and in the course of
the centuries has been arranged in compendia or codices.
Islam calls the entirety of its guidelines on how Moslems
must conduct themselves *sharia'a*, which literally means: "the
path that leads to water." This entirety of guidelines, rooted
in the Koran and in the *sunna* (i.e. Mohammad's way of life),
has also, because of the cultures with which the tradition
came into contact, been expanded over the centuries into a
comprehensive aggregate of rules for life. A similar development can be seen in Christianity. On the basis of central ideas
in the Bible, such as the *Ten Commandments* and the *double
command of love* and on the basis of the example of Christ
himself, a system of rules for life has developed in interaction with its culture that is concerned with the social and
contemplative life. Hinduism also contains a plurality of pre-
scriptions for behavior, which together form a contemplative
way. This way is called *karma marga*, that is, the Way (*marga*)
of action (*karma*). This plurality is again an unfolding of ten
central rules for life, called *yama* and *nyama* (Akhilananda
1948: 105ff.) Both words have almost the same meaning:

to curb, to limit, to control. In Buddhism, the rules for life are established in the *Vinaya*. This term literally means: to lead away in the sense of taking someone away from some place. It includes all rules for laypeople and monks. The Vinaya is also a continuation of a number of central ideas: the *da'saku'sala*, i.e., the *ten virtues* (see, for example, Dalai Lama 1981).

From the viewpoint of contemplative psychology, it is not surprising that these traditions, despite theological differences, contain many similar rules for conduct. In the Ten Commandments, the ten *yamas* and *nyamas* and the ten virtues we find, with respect to action and speech, again and again the precepts not to kill, steal, not to conduct ourselves in a sexually impure way and not to lie. Obviously, the contours of a universal humanity are formulated here.

However, if we look at how the traditions have developed their guidelines further, then differences emerge. These differences are related to the time and culture in which the particular spiritual tradition is found. Two motivations come into play here. The first is to contribute to the local culture and its social life through binding the action and speech of human beings to ethical norms. The second is to bind action and speech to that which will help specifically in traveling a spiritual path. Elsewhere we have called this kind of action *contemplative action*: "contemplative action is compassionate or merciful action that awakens and brings to expression the contemplative perspective and way of life" (de Wit 1991, 216). In other words, it is a way of acting that causes our fundamental humaneness to flourish in every situation (de Wit 1991, 212ff.). There we explained in more detail that ethical action and contemplative action are not always the same. Think, for example, of a situation in which speaking the truth to an enemy who is looking for someone we have hidden in our home would lead to the death of this person.

To tell the truth about his hiding place is then nothing more than giving our inhumanity free rein. There are also many actions that are viewed as neutrally ethical, but that are very important for spiritual development, such as liturgical acts and many other religious practices (Vergote 1984, 283; de Wit 1991, 217ff.). They are subject to contemplative rather than ethical criteria. For this reason, many traditions have disciplines of action and speech that are based on precepts that do not have any ethical significance. We will see examples of this below.

The existence of these two different motivations, ethical and contemplative, also means that we can interpret and evaluate guidelines for action and speech in two different ways, namely in terms of their ethical value and in terms of their contemplative value. We can, for example, trace the commandment not to steal to our idea of justice or to the insight that stealing intensifies our egocentric experience of reality and thus chokes our fundamental humaneness. The importance that religious traditions ascribe to each of these motivations can vary to a great extent — both from tradition to tradition and within the traditions themselves. If we only employ an ethical interpretation, then judgment and condemnation and, in their wake, the theme of *guilt* and self-reproach are made central. There is little notice taken of the *educational power* of the disciplines for our fundamental humaneness. The tradition then receives primarily a moral function and its role is reduced to being a guardian of what is considered to be "good morals." If, in contrast, we apply exclusively a contemplative interpretation, this can lead to social alienation in that we no longer relate to the ethical norms of society.

However, for those who pursue a spiritual way of life, the contemplative value of the guidelines for action and speech are central. The value of these guidelines are measured according to the degree to which they promote the manifestation of our fundamental humaneness in word and deed. If we investigate the disciplines of action and speech from the viewpoint of contemplative psychology, we then also approach them from the perspective of the question of what their value is for the cultivation of the flourishing within and for its fruit in action and speech.

THE RELATION TO THE MENTAL DISCIPLINES

The contemplative approach to the disciplines of action and speech already shows that they are closely connected to the mental disciplines discussed previously. On the one hand, the disciplines of action and speech serve as a kind of support for the mental disciplines. After all, our experience of reality does not develop in a vacuum but in relation to what is happening in our concrete life situation. With respect to our attitude, this situation challenges us continually to go either in the direction of callousness and blindness or that of compassion and insight. The disciplines of action and speech give us instructions for meeting these challenges. And in that sense they produce, so to speak, the seeds of the flourishing within.

On the other hand, we can also see the disciplines of action and speech as the fruit of the flourishing within. We say: you shall know the tree by its fruits. We can see the way in which we act and speak as a kind of test of the genuineness of our internal flourishing. Of course, if it does not bear any fruit in our action and speech, something is wrong. One should then ask oneself whether such a "fruitless" internal flourishing is not a fantasy, something that occurs only in a spiritual fantasy world.

The disciplines of action and speech have something in common with the disciplines of the imagination, in particular.

For just as the images and representations have experiential value that can lift us up mentally, to follow guidelines also has an experiential value that influences the mind and can change our experience of reality. The situation that we create through our actions and our speech has an experiential value that either awakens our fundamental humaneness or does not awaken it. And that, in turn, can have an effect on our practice of the disciplines of the imagination — which can, in their turn, then influence our action and speech. Thus the Catholic tradition, for example, has had the discipline of *dedicating a sacrifice*, where one performs an action that he or she feels to be difficult but which can somehow benefit someone else that the practitioner cares about. In Mahayana Buddhism, a practice session is often closed by stating a wish that its merit may benefit all living beings. Thus we cultivate in ourselves a caring attitude. Within the devotional Way, there are many actions that are carried out as a sacrifice to God or with the intention that they please God. Because the disciplines of action and speech can be both the seed as well as the fruit of the mental disciplines, in almost all traditions they are practiced in conjunction with them.

THE FUNCTION OF THE DISCIPLINES OF ACTION AND SPEECH

In the introduction to this chapter, we have already touched on the function of the disciplines of action and speech. We will now investigate this function in more detail by means of this question: why do the spiritual traditions prescribe a certain way of action and speech?

As stated above, it is often thought that it is exclusively out of moral considerations: in that case it would concern becoming a morally good human being. We have seen that the spiritual way of life does emphasize primarily the ethical interpretation. A practical insight also lies at the bottom of this, namely that such a moral motivation — as the history of humankind shows — is far too weak to effect a real transformation of ourselves. Good intentions are only seldom strong enough — is the way to hell not paved with them? It is necessary that we feel connected to our own fundamental humaneness, Christ in us, our Buddha nature or whatever name the tradition gives to it and that we have the desire to cultivate this. We spoke about this in chapter five already in terms of conversion.

Within the spiritual way of life the answer to the question of the *why* of these disciplines is inspired by a fundamental insight: the restraint of ego is the most effective way to cultivate our fundamental humaneness, loving kindness and insight. Therefore, it is not that ego should be restrained because, according to some theory, it is *bad* or morally objectionable but because ego chokes our fundamental humaneness. It stands in the way of the flourishing within. The function of the disciplines of action and speech is to teach us to act and to speak in such a way that on the one hand ego is made visible and let go and on the other that our fundamental humaneness is uncovered and supported by them. Both are two ways of characterizing the function of these disciplines — like two sides of the same coin.

Two Perspectives on the Function of the Disciplines

The double function of these disciplines — the exposing and restraining of ego and the uncovering of our fundamental humaneness — also means that we can *experience* the disciplines of action and speech in two ways: from the perspective of ego and from the perspective of our fundamental humaneness. We will explore these two perspectives more closely.

Let us remind ourselves briefly what ego is and how ego is

246 Spiritual Practice and Development

manifested. We know that, in contemplative psychology, the term *ego* does not refer to a mental *entity* but to a mental *activity* that maintains a dualistic experience of reality. In that experience, the world of phenomena is the object of self-interest and thereby the object of hope and fear. From this dualistic mentality, as we said in chapter three, our *ego psychology* develops, in which greed, aggression and indifference are the dominant forces. These forces are manifested continually in our action and speech. How we then experience the spiritual disciplines is also determined by this.

The support that these disciplines in fact offer are then experienced as a restriction, a limitation, sometimes even as apparently hard and inhuman, as a "humiliation." They frustrate the self-exaltation of ego. It is for this reason that we can also characterize these disciplines *from the perspective of ego* as the practice of *humility*. The value of humility is emphasized by almost all of the contemplative traditions. In the Rule of Benedict, the whole contemplative development is sketched in 12 steps of humility. "Humility is the place of the ancestors dwelling" is a well-known saying from Vajrayana Buddhism. Here the term *ancestors* refers to the previous practitioners of the tradition who had attained enlightenment.

But the disciplines of action and speech do not only remove the space for self-exaltation. They equally go against ego's inclination for self-revilement, our self-hatred, our inclination to "destroy" ego. Therefore the disciplines are not only to be characterized as the practice of humility but also as the practice of *self-acceptance*, as the willingness to accept what we see in the mirror and to accept ourselves in friendship, who and what we are. This is not a conditional friendship which we acquire and preserve only through not disappointing ourselves or through maintaining a positive self-image. Rather, it is an unconditional one in which we accept ourselves with all our seemliness and unseemliness.

From the second perspective, that of our fundamental humaneness, the actions and speech that the disciplines prescribe are seen as the way in which a human being conducts herself in the state of fulfillment. By the state of fulfillment, we mean the state of mind that is free from the egocentric experience of reality. What are the features again of those moments when our experience of reality is free from ego and determined by our fundamental humaneness? As we already stated in the introduction to this book, these are moments in which we are not preoccupied with ourselves. These egoless moments are characterized by joy in life, compassion, effective action and insight.

At those moments we experience the disciplines of action and speech not as a limitation, not as disciplines that *guide* our action and speech, but as the *natural expression* in word and deed of our fundamental humaneness. All those actions that we usually think of as typically religious, ethical or spiritual are now experienced as the expression of freedom. This freedom is the *spontaneity of egolessness*, freedom from the *impulsiveness of ego*. Practicing these disciplines is now no longer experienced as a curtailment or renunciation but as a liberation and engagement. If others then judge us more often as morally highminded or good, this is, in a certain sense, a secondary issue. We have discussed this more extensively elsewhere (de Wit 1991, 139ff., 196ff.) and will return to it in the last section of this chapter.

The Function of the Disciplines as Mirrors

The disciplines of action and speech thus function, on the one hand, in such a way that they bring us into contact with the warmth and clarity of our fundamental humaneness by telling us to act and speak *as if* we were free of ego. On the other hand, it is precisely through this that our egocentrism becomes visible to us. After all, rather than leaving any room for the manifestation of ego in our words and deeds, the disciplines curtail such room. Because of this, ego, so to speak, continually comes up against the limitations that have been established. And the consequence of this is again that the form and forms of expressions of our ego become concretely visible to us. Ego is no longer simply another contemplative idea but has, through the practice of the disciplines, become an *experiential fact that can be localized*. Thus, these disciplines function as a kind of mirror, and that is, at bottom, the contemplative function of these disciplines. As a mirror, they show us the concrete contours of our ego, for whenever we have difficulty with the disciplines of action and speech, it is because at that moment we are confronted by one of the hard walls of ego's fortification. Our willingness to be humble or to accept ourselves enables us to work with ego instead of denying it or struggling against it out of hurt pride or self-hatred. In practical terms, this means that both in following *and* in trespassing against the guidelines that are contained in the disciplines of speech and action, the contours of ego become visible to us. In both situations, the disciplines work as a mirror. As long as we wish to travel along the Path, as long as our personal and deepest wish is to cultivate our fundamental humaneness, we learn as much (and sometimes even more) from our trespasses as from closely (and piously) following the guidelines that are contained in the disciplines of action and speech.

THE RELATIVITY OF THE DISCIPLINES

To a great extent, the function of the spiritual disciplines determines their form. We have seen that the mental disciplines have to do with transforming our egocentric experience of reality. The disciplines of action and speech are directed at *promoting* actions, including verbal ones, that give rise to an egoless experiential value and thus uncover our fundamental humaneness. In that way, they make us abandon actions that impress our egocentric experience of reality even more upon us. What we need to do and not to do for this purpose is thus *dependent on the form of ego*. Their form is relative both to the *phenomenon of ego* as such and to the actual *form of ego* that every person gives to it individually. The phenomenon and form of ego thus determine the form of the spiritual disciplines of action and speech.

Let us first take a look at the disciplines whose form is determined by insight into the nature of the *phenomenon* of ego itself. Ego and its dualistic experience of reality is a psychological phenomenon that appears in people in all cultures. It is neither Western, Eastern, Southern nor Northern. It is a general, universal psychological phenomenon. We discussed this in chapter three. The disciplines of insight are suited *par excellence* to rendering the phenomenon of ego visible — regardless of the form that ego has at a certain moment, in a certain time or culture. This is so because the disciplines of insight are *independent of the form of ego*. In that sense, they are universal, transcultural disciplines that can directly expose the illusion of ego in our experience of reality. Whether it is a primitive or a refined ego, the disciplines of insight expose both in the same way. The form of these discipline is determined by insight into the phenomenon of ego *as such*. In this sense these disciplines could be called *absolute disciplines*.

The disciplines of action and speech, however, do work with the *form* of ego. Why is that necessary? Because the form of ego can be so solid, so impenetrable and so dominant that it is impossible to see through it. We first need to do something about the form itself. For this, not only the disciplines of the imagination but also the disciplines of action and speech are appropriate. These disciplines are thus all *relative* in the sense that their form is dependent on (insight into) the form of ego and how it is expressed. We all make our own construction of ego by incorporating elements of the surrounding culture and elements from our individual histories. And this is what the relative disciplines work with.

Universal and Specific Disciplines

Although the disciplines of action and speech are relative, not absolute, disciplines, they are nonetheless partially universal in character. This is because the spiritual way of life springs from a soil that is transcultural, a soil of experience — the experience of our fundamental humaneness — that is given with our humanness itself and with which we are in contact to a lesser or greater degree. Because of this, we see a great many similarities in the guidelines for behavior that the different spiritual traditions formulate. This is because they encode the manifestation of our fundamental humaneness *in relation to* universal forms of ego. They encode what people in all times and cultures discover continually anew as authentic human action, such as: "respect for the views and feelings of others, patience, courtesy, understanding and responsibility for one another and compassion for the weak and underprivileged" (Queen Beatrix of the Netherlands 1992).

In addition to the universal guidelines, there are also *specific guidelines*. Again, we can distinguish different kinds. First of all, each tradition has *culturally bound guidelines*. Their relation to the culture consists, on the one hand, in prescribing how to let go of the *patterns in the local culture that confirm ego* and, on the other, in identifying and incorporating the patterns in that culture that are helpful on the spiritual path. No culture is spiritually so poor that a spiritual tradition cannot integrate a few values, and no culture is so rich that the tradition must not correct one or more of its features. The culturally bound guidelines of the spiritual tradition thus determine how the practitioner must deal with the cultural guidelines for behavior that he or she brings to the spiritual path. If the local culture, for instance, encourages greed or ambition at the expense of helpfulness, the spiritual tradition will be alert to the fact that greed or ambition will be an influential aspect of the ego of those entering this tradition. It will direct its disciplines at that point.

Secondly, there are relative disciplines that are based on *specific spiritual guidelines*. These disciplines work with ego on levels that are *not* rooted in the local culture but in the spiritual tradition itself. Here we can think of guidelines, for example, in liturgy and the form that is given to the way of life within contemplative communities. These guidelines are therefore relative to the tradition. We will give a number of examples of these in the section below.

A third category includes relative disciplines based on *individual guidelines* or *instructions*; these are concerned with the problem of ego on the level of the individual. They are relative to the individual and given primarily orally in the context of *personal guidance* (see the next chapter). The previously mentioned relative disciplines are often written down and are passed on in that form.

Together, all these relative guidelines determine the form of the disciplines of action and speech and thus the form of the spiritual way of life. Because of the relative character of the guidelines, the form of this life is not fixed for eternity. Its form evolves with the people who practice the tradition. People are bearers of the local culture and they have their personal history and outlook, their own attitude to life. These factors influence partially the individual form and manifestation of ego. If spiritual traditions are functioning well, they have insight into this and their disciplines are tailored to work with it.

The Form of the Disciplines of Action and Speech

What exactly do we mean by the *form* of ego? We mean egocentric patterns that a person has appropriated on the mental level and on the level of speech and action. The form is different for everyone and for every culture, and it determines, as we have seen, primarily the form of the disciplines of action and speech. We will now look at the form of these disciplines in more detail by means of two old sources: the *Rule* of Benedict and the *Vinaya* of Buddhism. Both sources are directed primarily at the *monastic* life. Of course, both the Christian and the Buddhist disciplines of action and speech cover a much broader area than just the monastic life, but we will discuss the guidelines for monks and nuns because the psychological function of the guidelines as a mirror can be seen here most clearly.

Examples from the Rule *of Benedict and the* Vinaya

In the Christian tradition, the spiritual disciplines have been formulated to an important extent in Benedict's *Rule* (1980). This text originated in the sixth century A.D. and is the basis for the monastic contemplative life in Catholicism. The Buddhist tradition possesses the *Vinaya*, a collection of guidelines and rules that began to take shape during the life of the Buddha and were written down after his death. Although the Christian and Buddhist traditions are quite different theologically, they nonetheless include very similar spiritual guidelines and precepts, both universal and particular, on how to behave and speak.

In chapter four of the *Rule*, which carries the suggestive title "The Tools of Good Works: What Are They?" Benedict lays down the Christian version of the universal disciplines: people are not to kill; not to commit adultery; not to steal; and not to do to another what one does not wish done to oneself; to discipline the body, to give new heart to the poor; to clothe a naked person; to visit a sick person; to be a support in time of trouble; not to repay wrong with wrong, but in fact to suffer patiently wrongs done to oneself; to suffer persecution for justice's sake. For the practice of the discipline of speech, Benedict gives a number of general precepts in the same chapter: not to bear false witness; to comfort one who is saddened; not to bring anger to a head, to utter the truth from heart and mouth, not given to criticizing; not to detract; to guard one's mouth from evil; to have no craving for controversy.

Because of their universal character, we find many of these precepts in the other traditions as well. In the Buddhist tradition, they are formulated in terms of *the discipline of refraining from the ten vices* (see, for example, Dalai Lama 1981, 53). The first three are directed at our actions: refrain from taking life; refrain from taking what has not been given; refrain from sexual misconduct. The next four concern speech: refrain from speaking untruth; refrain from slander; refrain from sharp words; refrain from drivel. Although the last three focus on our mental attitude, we cite them here for the sake of completeness and also because they instruct us to restrain the three basic emotions of ego (cf. chapter three) that tend to manifest themselves in our actions and speech: refrain from greed; refrain from malice; refrain from wrong ideas.

Next to these universal disciplines of action and speech, there are also a great number of *specific disciplines* in the

Rule and in the *Vinaya* that shape life in the contemplative community itself, precepts that specifically apply in the "workshop," i.e., in the "monastery enclosure" "where we labour diligently at all these things" (Benedict 1980, 65). There are rules governing action with respect to such practical matters as how monks should sleep: "They shall sleep singly in single beds. . . . If possible, let all sleep in one place . . . ." (Benedict 1980, 154). The *Rule* specifies whether the monks should possess any property: "let no one presume to give or receive anything without a directive from the abbot, nor to have anything of his own, absolutely nothing, not a book, neither writing tablets nor stylus, but nothing at all, for in fact they are not to have their bodies or desires in their own will" (Benedict 1980, 183). Benedict also indicates rules concerning daily manual labor, of clothing and shoes and of prayer. He also gives instructions concerning the place and function of the abbot and the prior and the monks' relation to the abbot: they are to love their abbot with an upright and humble affection. In everything, they are to be obedient to the abbot's orders, even if he himself — far be it from him to do so — acts otherwise, keeping in mind this command from the Lord: *do what they say but do not do what they do* (Matt. 23.3).

We find the same themes in the Buddhist *Vinaya* in the sections for *novices* (*sramaneras*) and monks (*bhiskshus*). The *Vinaya* was originally designed for wandering mendicants, but was later expanded to include rules of conduct for monks and nuns who lived in monasteries. To beg for food and in return to teach the *dharma* (the doctrine) was an important discipline in this. The *Vinaya* specifies from whom and when the monk or nun may beg for food. They were not allowed, for example, to beg for food from one another. It spells out what he or she may possess: the men may have three habits at most, the women five, a begging bowl for food, a razor (to shave the head and eyebrows), a needle, a belt (for the habit), a water sieve (to strain the vermin from the water so that they would not be killed when the monks would drink) and a sleeping mat. There are also rules about where he or she may sleep: always in a different place and not with someone of the other sex, etc. And, of course, the *Vinaya* contains rules that the shape the discipline of speech, such as instructions on how, when and to whom the *dharma* is to be taught, when and how to speak with one another and with benefactors, etc.

For life in the monastic community, Benedict formulated specific rules that also shape the disciplines of speech, such as: not to love much talking, to listen with pleasure to the holy readings which is for the good of our sanctification, to shun pride, to make peace with an opponent before sunset, not to associate with guests or speak to them at all when not given the task to do so. He devotes one chapter, of course, to the discipline of silence.

The Contemplative Psychological Significance

In our age, we often view the way of life sketched in the *Rule* and the *Vinaya* with a certain skepticism, if not with revulsion. But we should examine our skepticism. For what is the core of the *Rule* and the *Vinaya*? What is their psychological significance? It is precisely when we look at what these texts have in common that it becomes clear: both texts sketch a way of life that gives no room for ego to hide or establish itself. What these texts demand is the surrender of every form of *privacy*: the surrender of our inclination to safeguard ego and to keep the world (and especially one's fellow human beings) at a distance. And is it not precisely this inclination that has been exalted into a virtue in our time and other cultures? Is our skepticism and revulsion not partly rooted in that fact? And we must realize that privacy —

certainly as we know it in our culture — is a relatively recent "discovery."

The Buddhist tradition calls the person who has literally but primarily figuratively abandoned hearth and home an *anagarika*, i.e., one who is homeless: someone who has abandoned the struggle for privacy. Such persons practice being unconditionally and continually open to the situations in which they find themselves, and they do not withdraw physically or mentally from that situation. They unite themselves with their situations, thereby denying any room for the dualistic experience of reality ("me here" and "that there"). Caring for the self, then, becomes nothing other than caring for the entire situation. Such a withdrawing from the world of ego is the core of the contemplative life. In the Christian tradition, this withdrawing is called *anachorese*. That is why the first monks were also called *anachoretes*. Monastic life, as Benedict sketched it, is permeated by the surrender of privacy. We see this theme in almost all contemplative communities. Outsiders often suspect that such communities are a refuge for ego, a hiding place from the desolate outside world, but the reality of life in a contemplative community is very different: there is extremely little room for ego in this way of life.

One may, but does not need to, withdraw into a monastery or to the forest to lead a contemplative life. One could (and should) ask whether the disciplines of action and speech as described in the *Rule* and the *Vinaya* still fulfill their purpose in our time. Do they still bring about the surrender of privacy and the restraint of egocentric behavior? Do they still have the contemplative-psychological function for which they were intended? To investigate this, let us look us a number of disciplines of action and speech that are also practiced in our time.

Stabilitas Loci *and* Stabilitas in Congregatione

The first discipline we will explore for its contemplative psychological function relates to action. Many spiritual traditions contain the rule of not abandoning the monastic community or the place of retreat for shorter or longer periods (sometimes for life). If one follows this rule, it is almost always preceded by voluntarily taking a vow to keep to it. It is known as the vow of *stabilitas loci* (remaining in one place). This place can, for example, be where one goes into solitary retreat. The practitioner then vows not to leave this place of retreat before he or she has completed a specific spiritual practice or has attained a certain realization. This approach can be found in the Hindu tradition: the *yogi* draws a certain line around the place of retreat and vows not to step outside of it until completing a certain practice (*sadhana*) or until the *yogi* has reached enlightenment or death has come. A well-known example of this in the Buddhist tradition is, of course, that of the Buddha himself, who finally sat down under the *Bodhi tree* and vowed not to leave that spot until he had reached enlightenment. If the place is a contemplative community (*congregatio*), the term *stabilitas in congregatione* is also used (see, for example, Benedict 1980, 65). One then vows to remain in the cloister where one is.

Why do people do this? What is the function of such a discipline? The vow to stay in one place is the physical counterpart of the mental stability of which we spoke in chapter six. The contemplative-psychological function of this physical *stabilitas* and of the adherent vow is that we let go of the idea that we have an alternative, the possibility of withdrawing. One of the characteristic aspects of ego is namely that it always wants to have *alternatives* available: ego is the mentality that always wants to keep an exit open and therefore can never come to complete surrender and acceptance. Through the vow of *stabilitas loci* we surrender an important part of that mentality. We say: this is my place, my situation and that is what I want to work with, however it develops, *for better or for worse.* In a monastic community, we have not chosen our fellow brothers and sisters, and they offer us all aspects of human company — the nice and the irritating — and the willingness to work with that is expressed in such a vow.

Something similar applies to the situation of individual retreat where we are alone with the movement of our mind and our mental discipline. Our mind offers us all kinds of unpredictable aspects that we also did not and cannot choose: moments of restlessness, of desire, of joy and sorrow, confusion and clarity, etc., moments that sometimes seem to incite us to abandon the retreat. Our vow then entails that we are prepared to work with such moments on the spot. And when we do that, it appears that our situation and our mind are much easier to handle than we thought, precisely because we have made the vow not to evade them. The limitation that this discipline imposes upon ego proves to have something else within it: the flourishing of self-confidence and strength of mind and the room to be in the situation in which we live without any reservations. The experience of those who practice this discipline teaches us that it can bear these fruits.

Obedience

How do matters stand with the discipline of obedience that is so characteristic of monastic life? Its function as a mirror is to make the wilfullness of the ego visible. We practice a certain mental flexibility, the flexibility of going along with the demands that our situation makes upon us and of learning to recognize our egocentric impulses and to let them go. In its complete form, this flexibility is an unconditional obedience. This does not mean that we have to put up with everything and continually do what others tell us but that we develop the ability to be obedient in all circumstances to that which can bring our entire situation to flourishing instead of to that which will feed our ego.

Unconditional obedience seems to be asking a great deal, but we must also see the *discipline* of obedience as a way through the problem of obedience that ego raises. What happens if we are skillfully deprived of the room to follow our egocentric impulses? Our joy in life is then liberated from the captivity of our compulsiveness and regains its original suppleness and spontaneity. The apparently harsh discipline of obedience then proves to have a much different side to it which does not have anything to do with the subjection of the will of one person to another, even though it might look that way on the outside. To the contrary, it subjects ego to egolessness. This means, in fact, the creation of freedom, even though from the perspective of ego this is not readily apparent.

In the theistic traditions, the discipline of obedience is often formulated in terms of obedience to God. We see that, for example, in Islam and Christianity. The instructions for action and speech that are found in these traditions are also viewed as being of divine origin. Compliance to the prohibitions and commands formulated as rules are in a certain sense a means for rediscovering this humaneness and making it the basis for our behavior. Obedience to this then leads to the discovery of a deeper, underlying internal obedience: obedience to the voice of God in us, to Christ in us, to our Buddha nature. In contemplative-psychological terms, we can formulate this as being obedient to our fundamental humaneness. We can thus distinguish between two forms of obedience: an *external* form that is anchored in the following of rules formulated in language and concepts and an *internal* form of obedience that is not fixed in concepts but is anchored in our fundamental humaneness itself and its expression in word and deed.

Silence

It is also characteristic of the monastic disciplines of speech that the curbing of ego and the unlocking of egolessness are simultaneous. We can see this, for example, in the well-known discipline of silence. This discipline is widespread in the contemplative traditions and removes from us the possibility of and need for manipulating our situation by means of language for the sake of ego in order to establish, for example, a particular image or impression of ourselves in others. The function of this discipline as a mirror is to make our need for this visible. The interesting part of the practice of this discipline is that our relation both to our fellow practitioners and to ourselves begins to become separated from the fixed ideas and stories that we were accustomed to drape over ourselves and our past. We are forced to take a certain distance from that in our dealings with our fellow human beings. We throw our visiting cards away. When we have rid ourselves of them, then room for a form of communication arises that is nonverbal: we become acquainted with ourselves and others in a very immediate *perceptual* way, simply by experiencing one another. In the words of the Dutch poet Judith Herzberg: "We know each other for we have been silent together."

When we begin with this discipline, we often feel initially somewhat shut in and unsure. We cannot ask those who are practicing with us: "Who are you? Where do you come from? What did you do before you came here?" Neither can we "introduce" ourselves to the others in any way. We cannot pass on our inner agenda in which we have written down who or what we are. Therefore, we have no status in this situation, insofar as we derive this from our previous history. There is no longer any room for this. We can only see the others and pick up on the sphere that surrounds them. It is a very naked situation, which at first is often felt to be oppressive. But as we begin to rest more and more in the discipline of silence it proves to have its own space. It appears that we find that situation to be pleasant, that it can be a relief that we no longer have to sell our ourselves, our self-image, constantly. This makes our life situation very spacious, clean and pure. The discipline of silence thus proves to be very effective in making us conscious of the contours of our ego as they are manifested in communication with others. And it then appears that we no longer have to hold on to our ego, our self-image, in such a forced way nor to display it. Precisely because we have been able to see ourselves clearly, that image is no longer necessary.

Generosity

There are, of course, many disciplines that are practiced both in the monastic community and in ordinary life. They function, in fact, in the same way as the typical monastic disciplines. An example of this in the area of action is the discipline of generosity. This discipline also forces us to abandon the pursuit of self-interest. The importance of this discipline is also strongly emphasized by all spiritual traditions. In the practice of generosity, we go against our own inclination to hold on to what we think is necessary for ourselves in terms of time and possessions. Precisely through this, the practice of this discipline creates a sense of wealth in ourselves and our surroundings at the same time.

We are, of course, not talking about giving a bunch of flowers on occasion but about giving something that has real consequences for our own way of life: giving in a measure large enough to challenge us to let go unambiguously of our sense of self-preservation. That sense, which belongs to our dualistic experience of reality, is a source of fear and if we go through this fear in the act of giving, we notice that there is life outside of this fear. We experience that as a liberation and at the same time as the discovery of a fundamental, unconditional wealth: the whole world is given to us as wealth. This does not mean that we simply have to give everything away. It is not a moral *duty* but a practical matter: we can use the discipline of generosity to become acquainted with and to let go of our egocentric mentality that is manifested in a convulsive guarding of our own interests. This is the intention of this discipline and we thus (re)discover the fundamental wealth of the world and develop appreciation for it.

Speaking the Truth

An example of a spiritual discipline of speech that is not specifically bound to a monastic context and is found in almost all traditions is the discipline of *speaking the truth*. This discipline removes from ego the space to protect or exalt itself through lies of whatever kind. A little bragging, advertising oneself, belittling others, concealing our own shortcomings, our own awkwardness or mistakes — this discipline deprives us of the room to do this. Therefore this discipline also functions as a mirror for the manifestation of ego in speech. And however difficult the practice of this discipline might be, it leads to a form of peace and self-acceptance, to the understanding that we may be as we are with all our shortcomings and mistakes. We do not have to conceal them but can use them: we can loose upon them the disciplines that are necessary for rising above them. We can thus advance along the Path. But as long as we hide our short-comings out of shame or pride, we cut ourselves off from the Path, and our guide cannot help us.

The above examples of the disciplines of action and speech show that they have to do with practical issues. Each discipline has its own target area within our egocentric mentality, way of acting and way of speaking. It makes part of it visible and helps us to let go of it. They work, as stated above, as a mirror, whereas the use of this mirror is itself the wisdom and manifestation of our fundamental humaneness.

THE APPLICATION OF THE DISCIPLINES OF ACTION AND SPEECH

How are the disciplines of action and speech applied and when? Can or must all disciplines that the tradition contains be applied at the same time? Or are they gradually taken up by the practitioner of the contemplative life?

To that question the spiritual traditions do not give only one answer. On the one hand, the answer depends, namely, on the power of our *motivation* for wanting to liberate ourselves from our egocentric experience of reality and to cultivate our fundamental humaneness. On the other, it depends on our *insight* into the form of our ego and into the function of the spiritual disciplines. And, finally, the power with which we cling to ego also plays a role. If we have little insight and little motivation, we cannot bring ourselves to take up a contemplative life. If we have little insight but a great deal of motivation, we are of course capable of making progress on our spiritual path. Conversely, if we have much insight, we can also progress along the Path with a small amount of motivation. If we have both, we can progress more quickly. To a certain extent insight can compensate for motivation and *vice versa*.

Allow me to explain this by means of an example that I

have already used. Some people are capable of giving up a bad habit, such as smoking, as soon as they hear that it harms themselves and others. With others, this insight does not dawn on them by hearing but by feeling. Only when they begin to experience the consequences personally does insight dawn on them and they become motivated to give up the bad habit. They are then ready to impose a discipline on themselves that gradually frees them from this habit. Many of those who pursue a spiritual way of life have approached the matter in this way.

It is also possible that our life situation works, as it were, for us: in that case our daily circumstances do not allow us any other room than to let go of our egocentric experience of reality either entirely or partially. That happens, for example, when holding on to ego is too painful or too obviously foolish. Our life situation forces us into a contemplative discipline, without our being conscious of it or calling it that.

What all of this amounts to is that the measure in which we should take up the contemplative disciplines is different for everybody and that the choice for a specific form of the contemplative life — the monastic or so-called lay — is also different for everyone. A nice illustration of this is a classification found in Tibetan Buddhism. Here three kinds of practitioners are distinguished: those with highest capacity, those with medium capacity and those with lowest capacity. A famous text from the sixteenth century, written by the *mahamudra* master Karma Chagmey, characterizes the three as follows:

> The person of the highest capacity does not need to renounce worldly actions,
> But can practice while mixing mundane actions with the practice.
> This partaking of sense pleasures as the path, without abandoning them,

Is the example of King Indrabodhi.
The person of medium capacity abandons most worldly
    actions.
He practices while keeping the behavior of a monk.
Trying to acquire food, drink, and clothing
Is the lifestyle of most learned and accomplished masters of
    India and Tibet.
The person of lowest capacity cannot fulfill his aims while
    keeping two frames of mind.
He is unable to engage in both Dharmic and mundane
    pursuits,
And practices having to cast away concerns for the food and
    clothing of this life.
This is the lifestyle of such masters as Milarepa and
    Gotsangpa.

(Nyima 1989, 167–68)

It is interesting that Milarepa, the poet *yogi*, who lived as a
hermit and did nothing else but spiritual practice, without
worrying about food or clothes, is celebrated as one of the
greatest saints. At the same time, people like Milarepa who
spend all their lives and energy in liberating themselves from
the illusion of ego are called practitioners of the lowest capacity. Why? Because Milarepa's ego fixations were very
strong and unyielding, yet he was strongly motivated to free
himself from them. He devoted his whole life to this and it is
in that that his greatness lies.

King Indrabodhi did not have such a difficult and deep-
seated ego. The following saying applies to him: "Small
potatoes boil quickly." Under the guidance of his *guru*, he
continued to live in his palace and to take care of his subjects. Milarepa's *guru* Marpa was not a monk but a gentle-
man-farmer, a good businessman and was learned in the
dharma and many languages. He had a wife and children.

He loved to drink beer and was hot-tempered. But, just like King Indrabodhi, he was successful in finding his spiritual path because he was capable of using his worldly life situation to cultivate total openmindedness and unconditional compassion.

Between the contemplative life of the hermit Milarepa and the spiritual way of life led in the world lies the contemplative life of the person of medium capacity. In order to make progress on the Path, this person needs to simplify life down to the basic necessities. To this end, he or she withdraws from worldly life and lives as a monk or a nun.

Which way of life is suitable for us, and which spiritual disciplines could be beneficial for us, and when, are practical questions rather than ideological ones. Our self-insight and — if that is missing — our mentor's insight into us, our motivation and the circumstances of our lives are the determining factors. We will return to this in the last chapter.

THE PRACTICE OF THE DISCIPLINES OF ACTION AND SPEECH

Let us see, finally, if there are certain stages of development to be detected by examining the way in which the practitioner disciplines his or her actions and speech. We do, indeed, see that many traditions offer their disciplines of action and speech in a certain succession that seems to be guided by insight into the practitioner's development to that point. In many traditions, the emphasis lies primarily on disciplines that curb the manifestation of ego in word and deed — in other words, the freedom of acting out of ego is shackled. Just as the disciplines of mindfulness are primarily concerned with taming our mind, here the concern is primarily to tame our egocentric behavior. So the instructions for the disciplining of our action and speech have chiefly the character of *prohibition* — they advise against certain behavior:

do not do this and do not do that. Again, it is very tempting to give an ethical interpretation of these prohibitions — for they are often ethical — but from the viewpoint of contemplative psychology, the issue is not to be a good boy or girl. Rather, the intention is to make our egocentric blindness and emotionality visible by having them run up against the limitations imposed by the disciplines. The function of these disciplines as a mirror is central here. At the same time, we are thus deprived of the possibility of engraving our egocentric patterns of behavior even deeper. In this way, we plane ego down, as it were — knowingly if not willingly. That leads to what Meister Eckhart called *Gelassenheit*, a *detachment*, which contains an element of freedom: we do not, like an idiot, need to follow the impulsiveness of ego any more.

By curbing ego in this way, a certain room for further disciplines that are directed at the cultivation of egoless action and speech comes into being as a result. For our fundamental humaneness flourishes to the degree that our preoccupation with ego lessens. We begin to experience our fundamental humaneness more consciously and thereby become inspired to cultivate it by bringing disciplines into play that take our (experience with our) fundamental humaneness as their starting point. They therefore have more the character of *commands*: they positively advise certain actions. The discipline of generosity that we discussed above is an example of this. Formulated more generally, these disciplines contain instructions about how we can cause our environment to flourish.

Of course, the one phase does not follow the other in strict succession. It is more a question of shifting emphasis: the disciplines are directed first at acquiring insight into and refraining from egocentric behavior. After that, we add the disciplines that are directed at conducting ourselves in the world on the basis of this tamer state of affairs: we gain

practice in the doing of "good works." For without first taming our egocentricity to some extent, our ability to do good in
the world is very limited. We run up continually against the
borders of our ego, while not yet having developed the flexibility to open up these borders or at least to thrust them
back. Observing or not observing the commands then easily
becomes a source of self-exaltation or self-reproach and of
honor and blame — in short of internal, if not external, strife.
"Do good without expecting thanks" is still a utopia for us. We
then distance ourselves even further from the cultivation of
our humaneness and the chance is great that we are not inspired but *exhausted* by our service to others. We can even
lose the courage and faith that the cultivation of our humaneness is *at all* possible. However, whenever we mature in both
phases, then the prohibitions and commandments lose their
limiting character. The practitioner, as Benedict says,

> will begin to keep everything which hitherto he used to ob-
> serve not without fear, no longer now by fear of hell but by
> the love of Christ, and the good habit itself, and the delight of
> virtues. (Benedict 1980, 98)

Finally, in this change of attitude lies still another, third
stage of development. The more we become established in
the practice of the disciplines of action and speech, the more
they awaken the openness of the spirit from which the prohibitions and commands originally came. We discover that
we can live in that state of mind and begin to trust it. The
possibility of acting and speaking on that basis begins to open
up directly for us. That changes the character of our practice
of the disciplines in an essential way. The focus of this practice then shifts from an *external discipline* of following the
prohibitions and commands to the *internal discipline* of remaining in this open state of mind *during* our acting and
speaking. The discipline then consists in taking this egoless

state of mind as a starting point for all our actions.

At the beginning of this third phase, it is as if we are once again babies, as if we need to learn anew to walk and to speak. And "as if" is not even putting it too mildly: we must indeed learn to act and speak anew: to act and speak out of the open state of mind itself, to learn to act and speak not out of ego but directly out of our fundamental humaneness. At first we have little experience in this; we have to practice this and it is at this that the disciplines of action and speech are directed in this third phase. That seems to be a precarious affair. For letting go mentally of the security offered by the prohibitions and commands and resting instead in the state of intelligent gentleness and care for others and being guided by this gives us little certainty. We are now on our own and the only thing we have is our fundamental humaneness.

Precisely because we have barely learned to trust our fundamental humaneness and because this final phase of the disciplines of action and speech is precisely about acting out of this humaneness, this phase is often joined at first with an immense feeling of uncertainty and risk-taking. For our connection with our own fundamental humaneness is, as we have (re)discovered it in ourselves, at first like a young plant. Nevertheless, this young plant grows only when we give it room and expose it to our concrete life situation, with no guarantee that it will survive. Of course, it is not that the behavior which has been modelled by the prohibitions and commands has now disappeared. Rather, it is no longer guided by these: the behavior is now prompted by our fundamental humaneness and no longer by an *ethics of duty*. All our action becomes *contemplative action* (see De Wit 1991, 212ff.).

All of the spiritual traditions agree that this is the most advanced, most difficult and risky form of the disciplines of action and speech. It is risky because the discipline is no longer limited by the safety ropes of the guidelines. And it is extremely difficult not only because the practice is continuous, 24 hours a day, but because in this phase we practice not withdrawing into ourselves under any circumstances. This means being continually available to our environment: to our fellow human beings, to the situation that presents itself to us, and to doing without hesitation what the situation suggests will enable us to flourish. This is the discipline of action and speech that lies beyond guidelines and which has been formulated by Augustine as *Ama et fac quod vis*: love and do as you wish. Mahayana Buddhism speaks here of the practice of *unconditional compassion*.

This is no small task. We cannot bring this about because we have intended to do so, on a good or bad day, or on the basis of all kinds of moral considerations. We can bring this about only because we have learned that this practice causes the natural, nondualistic state of our fundamental humaneness to flourish even more, something we have discovered by means of earlier disciplines. In this state of openness, again, we and our environment are no longer two different entities that have to manage their mutual relationship as well as possible, but the two have merged into one whole.

In Vajrayana Buddhism, the practitioner who has completed this deepest discipline of action and speech is called a *siddha*. A *siddha* speaks and acts out of *crazy wisdom* — that is, out of a wisdom that is united with a completely uncompromising and unconditional compassion with respect to ego. This wisdom is free from every hesitation to subdue that which must be subdued, to destroy what must be destroyed, to care for that which needs care, as it is traditionally formulated. From the perspective of ego, the manifestation of this way of acting and speaking is completely unpredictable and incomprehensible: crazy. It works outside of the logic of ego.

The most well-known *siddha* in this tradition is *Padmasam-bhava*, who, as the embodiment of crazy wisdom, is called *Dorje Trolö*. He is most often depicted as riding on a pregnant tigress, who represents this uncompromising compassion:

> The symbolism of the tiger is also interesting. It is connected with the idea of flame, with fire and smoke. And a pregnant tigress is supposed to be the most vicious of all tigers. She is hungry, slightly crazy, completely illogical. You cannot read her psychology and work with reasonably. She is quite likely to eat you up at any time. That is the nature of Dorje Trolö's transport, his vehicle. The crazy-wisdom guru rides on dangerous energy, impregnated with all kinds of possibilities. This tiger could be said to represent skillful means, crazy skillful means. And Dorje Trolö, who is crazy wisdom, rides on it. They make an excellent couple. (Trungpa 1991, 174–75)

What this ultimate form of practice adds to the previous ones is this: we grow beyond the idea that spiritual success is guaranteed if we only closely and piously follow the guidelines. But that is not ultimately the way. Precisely because all actions can in principle be contemplative actions, the opposite is also true: actions that are prescribed in the disciplines can also become profane actions. There is no guarantee that the practice of the disciplines of action and speech will will have the intended effect. The decisive factor is not that we perform these actions but that we perform them with *insight into their contemplative function* and with the right motivation, the motivation to let go of ego and to manifest our fundamental humaneness. That is why Meister Eckhart says:

> We ought not to think of building holiness upon action; we ought to build upon a way of being, for it is not what we do that makes us holy, but we ought to make holy what we do. However holy the works may be, they do not, as works, make

us at all holy; but, as we are holy and have being, to that extent we make all our works holy, be it eating, sleeping, keeping vigil or whatever it may be. It does not matter what men may do whose being is mean; nothing will come of it. Take good heed: We ought to do everything we can to be good. (Eckhart 1981, 250–51)

TEN

Development and Guidance

INTRODUCTION

In chapter five, we explored to some extent the psychological nature of conversion. We spoke of the attitude that we often initially take toward the moments of openmindedness that break through our usual egocentric experience of reality and make it visible. In the subsequent chapters, we discussed the disciplines that take advantage of those moments.

We have seen that there are many kinds of spiritual disciplines. Thus, a question also arises as to when and the degree to which they can be applied in such a way that they bear fruit. Is the latter not different for each individual? These are practical matters that compel us to immerse ourselves in the theme of spiritual development and guidance. Every tradition gives its own name to those who offer personal guidance. The Christian tradition has its *abbas* and *magisters*, its pastors and elders. The Jewish tradition has its *rabbis*

273

and its *maggidim*; Islam has its *alim* (scholar, plural: *oelama*). Hinduism has its *gurus*. Theravada Buddhism has its *staviras* (elders) and Mahayana Buddhism its *kalyanamitra* (spiritual friend). Vajrayana Buddhism uses the term *guru* as well. Throughout this volume we will use the universal term *mentor*, which harks back to the Latin word *mens*, meaning "mind." A mentor is thus someone *who minds our business*, someone who is concerned with our mental growth.

Although each tradition has mentors, the position they hold varies from tradition to tradition. This has to do with the role that the traditions ascribe to the mentor. Some traditions say that God is the original — if not the only — mentor. In contrast, other traditions regard the human mentor as the only one who can render the spiritual path concretely accessible to us. Practical concerns also determine the position of the mentor: are there (still) good mentors available? What view does the local culture have of what it is to be a mentor?

The bond which, ideally, exists between mentor and student is also viewed diversely. Many traditions strongly emphasize the value of a *personal* bond. We see this, for example, in the Jewish (Chassidic) tradition as well as in Hinduism and Buddhism. Of course, it is not necessary to sit constantly on the mentor's lap; the quality (of openness) of the contact is more decisive than its duration. Because of this personal bond, the mentor is someone who knows us (our ego) well and can therefore instruct us personally. These instructions are not only given verbally but also through the mentor's exemplification of a certain way of being in that personal contact. The latter is often more important than formal instruction. This is how the statement made by Rabbi Loeb about his *maggid* (master) is to be understood: "I did not search out the *maggid* to get instructions from him, but to see how he tied and untied the shoelaces of his felt shoes" (Buber 1967, 142). In Christian and Islam traditions, we see schools in which the mentor occupies a very personal place (as in sufism and monastic Christianity) as well as schools in which the mentor has a somewhat more distant position. In the latter case, the emphasis is not so much on individual guidance as on instruction in the doctrine.

Whatever the case may be, some forms of spiritual guidance can always be found in the contemplative traditions. And it also always has the same goal: where there is growth, there can also be stagnation or lopsided growth; where there is growth, there is also the chance that the development will be hindered. The task of the mentor is to aid the practitioner in avoiding these obstacles where possible. There are many aspects to this and most spiritual traditions have access to an extensive contemplative psychological knowledge about the kinds of obstacles that can arise and about the disciplines that can help us to overcome them. For the most part, this knowledge is passed on orally in the contact between master and student, whereas some of it is committed to writing. We will direct our exploration here to two general themes: the nature and development of the relationship of trust itself between mentor and student and the way in which the mentor can help the student in dealing with obstacles along the spiritual path.

THE RELATIONSHIP OF TRUST BETWEEN THE MENTOR AND THE STUDENT

The mentor's most important task is to give the student instructions that are tailored to that particular student's needs. But are we, as students, prepared to follow those instructions under all circumstances? This raises the question of whether the mentor and the student are trustworthy and reliable. Usually we accept personal instructions only from those we trust. And trust is not something that can be decided on a good day (or perhaps even a bad one) — it is something that must grow (see de Wit 1991, 171ff.). Here we will look at other aspects of this theme on the basis of three quotations that discuss a number of universal themes concerning the relationship between mentor and student.

Three Quotations

The first quotation emphasizes the importance of mutual examination for the growth of a true bond of trust.

> Traditionally, it is said that the student should examine the teacher, and the teacher should examine the student. If a disciple fails to examine his teacher well and follows a wrong teacher, it will kill the life-force for liberation. Like blindly jumping off a precipice while holding someone else's hand, it is detrimental. If the teacher fails to examine the student well, and if the student is someone who will turn against him later on, this is the same as eating poison. Therefore, before entering a close relationship, it is extremely important that the teacher and the student both examine each other carefully.
>
> After finding that they can trust each other, the student should be very constant, and practice the teachings that he has been given with trust and confidence. (Nyima 1989, 127–28)

The second quotation concerns the possibility of judging the teacher's outward behavior and frame of mind:

> Of these, the frame of mind is the important aspect, though it is invisible. Although we can see how people behave, we cannot judge from this alone. Some Chinese ministers for example are experts in behaving nicely even in the face of the enemy. They will shake hands, joke, laugh and so forth, but we never know exactly what they keep inside their minds. On

the other hand, some practitioners or masters reach a certain level of realization and their outward behavior begins to change and sometimes becomes a little strange. Their actions don't really fit a normal human being's way of behaving. Sometimes it doesn't even fit a dharmic [spiritual] way of behaving. This may cause someone to wonder, "What is going on?" This sometimes slips out of one's mouth.

That's how it is. It is best to think, "Whatever he does is excellent, whatever he does is perfect," and to mingle one's mind with his. This attitude is very important, but difficult for a beginner. If one sees one's teacher doing something completely strange, then it is better to think, "This is beyond me, I don't understand," and not try to judge or evaluate his actions, but to leave the thought aside. One should not consider or judge him as one might an ordinary human being. (Nyima 1989, 129)

The third quotation concerns the development of the relation to the teacher:

A traditional teaching says that the master should first be a real person, a human being. Next, your teacher can be a book. Finally the master should be one's own mind. In order to have a book as a master, you must first have received personal instructions on how to practice according to the text from a truly qualified living master. Having heard these instructions, since staying continually near to a great teacher may not always be possible, you should take the oral instructions to heart and practice in solitude, using the text as a guideline. As you gradually become more experienced, you can follow along with the text trying to correct your own mistakes. Finally, the master will be your own mind, the naked awareness itself. (Nyima 1989, 189)

Unconditional Trust?

No one will disagree with the content of the first quotation concerning the need for the mentor and the student to get to know each other. It is relatively straightforward. It emphasizes that trust can only come about by getting to know each other well. The situation is comparable to that of an experienced mountain climber who begins a climb with an amateur. The two are connected by a rope. It is necessary that they know and trust each other's ability. They can thus decrease the risk of the climb, and the amateur is able to learn something.

In the second quotation, however, much more sensitive themes are brought to the fore. First of all, it states that such getting to know each other is not a simple matter — especially for the student. I have gone into this in more detail elsewhere (de Wit 1991, 206f.). There we saw that we should develop a certain degree of discernment in order to be able to recognize whether or not our ego is our advisor in this matter. But this passage introduces yet another aspect that makes such investigation even more risky and uncertain: the external behavior of the mentor is not simply the most important criterion. Put more strongly, the student's examination should focus more on the teacher's mental attitude of the teacher than on the teacher's external behavior. This passage touches upon a central point of the spiritual way of life with respect to the position of the teacher. Can we still trust Jesus if he violates the Sabbath by plucking grain (Luke 6.1–5) or heals someone (Luke 6.6–11 and 13.10–17), to say nothing of his beginning a fight in the synagogue (John 2.13–25)? Is it not actually unconditional trust that is involved here? Is everything that the mentor does good by definition? Conversely, can we continue to judge the mentor according to our usual standards? We often think that in our day and age we have become painfully aware of the risks involved in doing so. But were the Jews not very much aware of this in Jesus' time, and have not people always been aware of this? It would seem so, for this theme is present in all great spiritual traditions and in all times. There is a passage in the Buddhist songbook of the Karma Kagyü lineage in which the Indian *guru* Naropa speaks of this with his student Marpa before the latter returns to Tibet for good to resume his own work as mentor:

> In the view of some impure ordinary men, you will appear to gratify yourself in this life with sense pleasures. Your desires will seem unchanging, like carrying a rock, so solid and so great. On the other hand, since you yourself have seen *dharmata* [things as they are], *samsara* [the egocentric experience of reality] will be self-liberated, like a snake uncoiling. All the future students of the lineage will be like the children of lions and garudas and each generation will be better than the last. (Nalanda and Trungpa 1980, 141)

The *guru* Naropa thus has great trust in his student Marpa, in spite of the expected reactions of the ordinary person. But it does confront us with a dilemma: on the one hand, we cannot judge the mentor by conventional standards and, on the other, blind trust is not a realistic basis for one's relation to the mentor.

The Fear of Trusting the Mentor

Can we gain a better view of this dilemma from the perspective of contemplative psychology? To that end, we will now return to a central notion of this psychology: *contemplative action* (see the previous chapter's introduction and de Wit 1991, 212). Our dilemma arises because behavior can be interpreted in two ways: *politically* and *contemplatively*. In the political interpretation, human relations and behavior are viewed in terms of one's own interest and power relationships. This interpretation is based on behavioral criteria by which we determine abuse of power and unbridled self-interest. The political interpretation of what is humane is that the room for self-interest and power should be divided fairly among the people. We could also judge the mentor from this view. If we are accustomed to viewing human actions constantly and exclusively from this political perspective, then by *unconditional trust* we cannot imagine much else than a situation in which one person submits unconditionally to the power of another. We see the specter of a dictator and a totalitarian (sub)culture. Our fear of and hesitation regarding unconditional trust is thus justified. But there is also the danger that we absolutize this fear itself, so that it itself acquires the character of being unconditional: we believe that it is always and everywhere justified. We then live under the dictatorship of our distrust.

But, just as, for example, the practice of the discipline of silence is not political (it is not about silencing people, stripping them of their "right to speak up" or right to respond), neither is the relationship between student and teacher political. Rather, it is spiritual. When we interpret this relationship as only political, we miss its spiritual function. We are no longer open to seeing the mentor's action for what it is: contemplative action. This does not mean that we should ignore the political or ethical aspect, but that we must remain open to the spiritual function of our relationship with the mentor, even if that mentor behaves in a way that is difficult for us to understand. This can mean that there are moments when we must decide what we find to be more important: our own moral and political ideas, our thinking in terms of interest, power or "good manners," or our open relationship to the mentor which is not determined by our own familiar ideas.

Although care or compassion also manifests itself in the form of resistance to the abuse of power and unbridled self-interest, this is not to say that the only dimension that compassion has is political. In the words of Kuitert: "Everything is politics, but politics is not everything" (Kuitert 1986). Unconditional care is not bound to ideologies or political principles but springs from a soil that is separate from them. It precedes them because it originates in the experience of our fundamental humaneness itself. It is not our ideas but this experience that forms the basis for the relationship to the mentor. It is the foundation on which the mentor stands and the perspective from which the mentor guides us. The question is whether we dare to submit to this. If we ask ourselves this question we see that the issue of trust often lies even deeper. This question makes us aware that *trust itself is a major problem* for us. When we have lost contact with our own humaneness, we are no longer capable of trust from the perspective of this foundation. Our political and moral interpretations can then simply become attempts to gloss over this problem and we easily use such political notions such as *self-determination* and *independence* — which are valuable in their own right — in order to avoid trusting in the *spiritual meaning* of the mentor's action. Precisely because its spiritual function is too threatening, our egocentric mentality that strives for safety and security does not want any mentor at all, and certainly not a competent one.

Blind Trust

But the reverse can also happen: namely, that we gladly surrender to the mentor so that we are rid of our responsibility for our own lives, for what we do and do not do. This attitude is not based on openmindedness either but on ego, on the application of a premeditated strategy. We think that transferring the responsibility for our lives to our mentor is a convenient manoeuvre that enables us to sail through life. We can thus fool ourselves into believing that this is in fact what the mentor asks of us: did the mentor not ask for unconditional trust? And we may even be somewhat proud that we are able to display this.

This strategy is often paired with a form of hero worship (see also the last section), which to all appearances is "unconditional" but, in actuality, is blind. It is unconditional in appearance only because in reality it is *dependent* on a certain presupposition: "The mentor knows what is good for me; he is infallible. I must try to become like the mentor." Everything that we undergo in our dealings with the mentor are then no longer approached openly but on the basis of this presupposition. Whatever the mentor does or says is always met by a positive judgment. Nothing is too great to stand in the way of such a judgment, for much depends on it: our chosen dependence, our buttress, our certainty. This approach is also a political manuveur. In order to avoid the uncertainty of the open contact with the mentor, we choose in advance to view this relationship as a master-slave relationship (de Wit 1991, 209) and to conform to it. The mentor has not asked for this, but we have. Such an approach is blind because it encloses us in our own interpretations and hinders our growth in open insight and genuine trust.

The Awakening of Unconditional Trust

One of the spiritual functions of a true or genuine mentor is to make us aware of both political maneuvers — which are based on either blind fear of trusting or on blind trust. For that purpose the mentor thus creates psychological space in which we can free ourselves from our constant tendency to interpret our relationships with people in terms of interest and power (de Wit 1991, 209) — a space in which we are not caught by our positive or negative judgments about the mentor. It is precisely in this open space that our discernment, our discriminating awareness, can function. And it is this discernment that can lead to *unconditional trust* in the *spiritual* sense. It is this trust, based no longer on opinions or judgments, which Nyima's second quotation addresses. How does the mentor create this kind of psychological space? It is done by means of contemplative actions, not only in the form of giving personal instruction but also by creating situations in which we observe that our political interpretations have no sense or meaning. This is how the mentor's loving care becomes manifest to the student.

In contrast, a nonauthentic teacher takes advantage of our preconceived ideas and takes care to avoid shocking us. Such a mentor is always friendly, caring and predictable toward us. Such a mentor does not use a whip in the synagogue like Jesus did, and does not behave in a radical way against the *pandits* (scribes) as did Padmasambhava, the great Indian yogi, who converted Tibet to Buddhism. Such a mentor is, however, a visible support and anchor, a fixed point of certainty, an ideal ally for ego. Such a teacher is engaged in political rather than contemplative actions. Instead of uncovering our fundamental humaneness and awakening it, this mentor meets ego and nourishes (it by means of) thinking in terms of power and interest.

In short, an authentic mentor leaves no room for blind trust, since blind trust is not part of the spiritual path. But even if the mentor is *not* authentic, there is no room for blind trust, either. Blind trust is even more dangerous then because the "mentor" will not do anything to counteract it. So, in both cases, the student has to face this issue. In both cases, blind trust is excluded. And yet this does indicate a specific direction to us. In the first quotation above, this direction is expressed as the need to examine the teacher. In the second passage, which actually refers to a later phase of our relationship, it is worded as the need to remain open to the mentor's actions. This means that, after we have

completed our examination and our trust is beginning to increase, we do not apply our ideas to the mentor's behavior
but apply this behavior to our ideas.

In this way, we can experience the spiritual value of the
mentor's actions even more clearly. Then we can discover
and cultivate the example of the mentor within ourselves,
which is how, ultimately, we awaken the internal mentor
within us. This internal mentor (see below) is very different
from the mentality that has never learned to trust and says,
"I trust no one other than myself." It is not the mentality of
ego that plays it safe, but an egoless mentality that has gone
beyond striving for safety. Rather, this mentality has learned
to trust the world of the phenomena in its contact with an
authentic mentor and in doing so has discovered and learned
to trust itself. It is then possible, as the third quotation states,
that "finally the master will be your own mind, the naked
awareness itself."

DEVELOPMENT AND THE GUIDANCE THAT ACCOMPANIES IT

What role does the mentor's contemplative action play in
the development of the student once a realistic basis of trust
has developed between them? Naturally, this differs in practice from individual to individual, but nonetheless one can
indicate roughly what the psychological line is. This line
influences the way in which the mentor aids the student
in overcoming the obstacles along the spiritual path and in
developing a certain steadfastness or stability. We will now
explore this development further.

We have already characterized progress along the Path —
that is, the continual change of our experience of reality in
the direction of sainthood — in chapter five as a process of
ongoing conversion. This does not occur in a day. And although
there can also be moments sometimes of a more spectacular

nature, the process of conversion usually takes place almost unnoticed; it is only when we look back that we become aware that we have freed ourselves from a certain illusion or heartless attitude in life. This process has its high and low points as well, it own periods of progress and stagnation.

Expressed in Christian terms, the guidance of this process aims at creating room for the activity of the Holy Spirit, so that the student's egocentric experience of reality can be made transparent, and the Spirit's activity can be discovered in and work from the person's own heart. Therefore, in a very fundamental sense, guidance is also an expression of charity and of true care; and at the same time, guidance is an expression of insight into the psychology of the worldly person. As guides, we can give this kind of insight only if we ourselves are experienced in viewing our own egocentric experience of reality from the perspective of the open space of our fundamental humaneness. Our own egocentricity — our profane acting, speaking and thinking — then becomes, in a certain sense, an instrument, a valuable source of knowledge.

The student must, of course, offer a point of application for guidance to begin. In terms of the metaphor used in chapter five where we spoke of ego's fortification and the space around it, cracks must appear in the concrete of the fortification, and the student must be prepared to allow the mentor to see what becomes visible. But before the student dares to do so, there are many things that must have happened beforehand, and that is what we will look at first.

The Double-Sidedness of Moments of Conversion

In chapter five we discussed the first steps of the beginnings of conversion. Let us recapitulate a few points from that chapter. We discussed the fact that *moments of conversion* are double-sided. We can experience and describe that double-sidedness in many ways; such moments appear as moments of freedom, which makes us aware that we are being held captive. The fortification of ego begins to close in on us because we are aware of openness at times. Or we notice the staleness and despair within us because we experience the freshness of life, a moment of joy in life, briefly. It is at those moments when we feel warmth and compassion that we see how cold and callous we usually are. We begin to notice our continual and deep fear of life precisely because we experience moments of courage in life. And when we recognize and value moments of clarity, it is because at such moments we are aware of the fact that we are in a certain sense blind or go through life blinded.

This double-sidedness is characteristic of moments of conversion, which is how they differ from our usual experiential moments. Usually, we feel free or caring at one moment and later feel caught or indifferent. Our experiences usually cause us to go first one way and then the other. But at these moments of conversion, both sides are present *at the same time* and because of this we have in a certain sense *nowhere to go* — at least, not the usual places. At this point, the spiritual way begins. Expressed in Christian terms, we become sinners-in-the-process-of-conversion, a term that also expresses this double-sidedness. At this point, the profane world begins to lose its self-evident quality and the psychology of ego begins to crumble. We begin to sense that there is also another attitude to take in life.

The Development of External Stability

In chapter five we also discussed the fact that the result of moments of conversion is often initially great doubt — doubt in the sense of a very critical attitude that arises from the shocking awareness that we are fooling ourselves, that we have lived in a way that nourishes a lack of truthfulness. And, simultaneously, there is the desire not to become even more lost in this lack. This is how this critical attitude toward ourselves, our fellow human beings, the world and religiosity arises. This is primarily a very good and positive development.

But, in addition to this positive distrust, these moments of conversion also awaken an increasing restlessness because something deeprooted has been shaken. We begin to see our profane mentality and are shocked by it. In the first phase, we begin pay more attention to what we see than to the fact that we see. At that moment, we are already sinners-in-the-process-of-conversion, but we are more impressed by the "sinner" that we see than by the conversion. To use our earlier metaphor (from chapter seven), we grab the stick by only one end: the inadequacy of ourselves (our ego) and of the egocentric way of life. We see callousness, blindness, confusion and self-deception in ourselves and around us and the suffering that arises as a result. This leads to a critical attitude on the intellectual level and restlessness on the emotional level — restlessness in the sense of having no place to rest and not knowing where to look for it.

When someone in this phase knocks on the door of a contemplative tradition, the mentor will first of all say: "Stop. Take a break rather than pushing yourself further along the highway of life." This advice is like stopping the car on the shoulder of the road. When we get out, we see the sunlight and the blue sky and feel the wind brushing past our cheek and rustling the high, scented grass. Perhaps we see a wide, slow river and hear the sound of birds in the distance. The hectic and constricting pressure of our life project falls away briefly: we feel a moment of calm and have time to look around us. This is what the mentor can offer us in this phase. For some people, staying in a contemplative community or monastery with its fixed schedule and simple external order of the day may be a way of "getting out of the car": a way of entering into simply *being*. For others, it may be making room in their daily schedule for practicing a discipline of mindfulness, a time for doing nothing but resting wakefully in simply being. In both cases, we create room for catching our breath spiritually by putting ourselves in a situation of *external stability*. We stop and remain where we are, with ourselves.

What are the obstacles along the Path that appear in this first phase, and how do we work with them? In a certain sense, we experience our daily life in its totality as an obstacle precisely because we are unable to distance ourselves from it. We are obsessed by it. This is why in this phase it is often good for us to withdraw physically from our daily situation in life and to abandon the pursuit of all those matters from which we hope to attain satisfaction and gain a solid grip on life. We banish external obstacles temporarily. True, this way of dealing with obstacles has its limitations, but it is nevertheless helpful. After all, we first need to calm down and to slow down, which is the initial purpose of guidance.

The Development of Internal Stability

When this external stability has more or less acquired form in our lives by way, for instance, of a daily spiritual practice, room for further development arises. This development is instigated by the discovery that the restlessness and fear of life which we experience in our day-to-day life and ascribe to feared or threatening situations do not in fact arise from our external circumstances, but are created and maintained through our own mind. The extent and intensity of our inner restlessness and fear becomes more visible than ever, as it were, against the background of the external stability that the spiritual way of life already brought us.

This discovery can sometimes be shocking, albeit in a somewhat different way than we have already discussed: we are not shocked by the discovery that we live in darkness, in illusions, but by the fact that this darkness is of our own making. Having arrived at this point, we need a mentor more than ever and then in a very personal way. This mentor is no longer just someone who simply invites us to stop and helps us create an externally stable situation in our daily lives, but someone to whom we can and dare reveal ourselves. We need someone who knows the spiritual path personally — someone whom we can trust, who knows what we are talking about when we talk about our inner restlessness, about our fear of life, and especially our fear of ourselves, of our own mind now that it has proven to be the creator of our egocentric experience of reality with all its negative emotions and pain. We need a spiritual friend — and that is what the mentor now becomes.

The mentor provides not only friendship but also appreciation for students who dares to reveal themselves. In this phase, the mentor will point out that the discovery of our inner restlessness is valuable and necessary, *bona fide*, and can be trusted. This inner restlessness is manageable; we need not walk away from it. We need not be scared of ourselves, of our profane mentality. No matter how high the seas rise, they are of our own making, arising from our own energy, and that is why we are by definition strong enough to deal with them. We are as strong as those seas. In a certain sense, our practice of the mental disciplines is directed here at the discovery that we can work with that which we experience as *internal obstacles*. The more we discover this in our practice of the disciplines, the more *internal stability* takes root within us.

This internal stability is not the absence of restlessness but a mental steadfastness that can accommodate the turbulent movements of our mind. If we think back again to the metaphor of the stream in which we planted a stick, then internal stability is not the stability of quiet waters nor the absence of water, but rather the ability to keep the stick upright and, thereby, to feel the restlessness of the water. It is independent of the water. If we experience our stream of thoughts from the perspective of this internal stability, then the perspective is turned about: the greater our restlessness, the greater our internal stability. It is as though the turbulence of our stream of thoughts only plants the stick of our internal stability more firmly in the bottom of the stream. The stick changes into a rock.

The internal stability, which is only nourished by mental turbulence, is a fruit of our contemplative practice. It goes together with a mental reversal: a shift from being the *sinner*-in-the-process-of-conversion to being the sinner-*in-the-process-of-conversion*. That we can see and work through our profane mentality which was initially such a shock to us now becomes a cause for joy. We begin to feel increasing joy in our honesty with ourselves and the clarity with which we see our confusion.

At first we were shocked when we began to see in a very concrete way that we ourselves (our mind) were the creator of our egocentric experience of reality. This may have been accompanied by self-reproach, shame and guilt. We were disappointed with ourselves: we (= ego) had thought more highly of ourselves; we were so preoccupied with ourselves, so impressed by our egocentricity and its disastrous consequences that it escaped us that there was yet another side to it. Seeing ego also tells us that we as human beings have the capacity to see this ego. We can recognize our blindness and callousness, even though they are enormous, precisely because clarity and compassion are part of our being human as well. Or, as my mentor often put it, "The bad news is the good news." With this discovery, we arrive at the other side of the double-sidedness of our moments of conversion. Continuing with the metaphor of the stick, we begin to grab hold of the other end of the stick, the conversion end. Shame and sorrow about our profane attitude becomes a positive sorrow — a *felix culpa* that is free of every form of self-reproach and self-hate.

Thus the development of internal stability is not something cold and distant. On the contrary, it leads to another, more intimate attitude in life. A first characteristic of this stability is *honesty* with regard to our world of thoughts, our innermost feelings — an honesty that brings us ever deeper to our less visible emotions. A second characteristic is that it contains *self-acceptance*: we gradually become friends with ourselves as we are, with all our pettiness and magnanimity. We no longer need be ashamed of ourselves or behave differently so that others will not see how inferior we are. Tenderly and not without humor, we see the futility of promoting our ego and our endless service to ego's version of self-respect. In this way, this changed attitude in life also creates room for conceding or exposing our profane mentality to ourselves and/or to God. With this a third characteristic develops: *discernment*. As we mentioned previously, the Christian tradition calls this *diakrisis* and it enables us to see what comes from our profane mind and what comes from the Holy Spirit. The Buddhist tradition calls it *prajna* and it enables us to discern between that which promotes ego and that which uncovers egolessness.

Diakrisis or *prajna* gives us a sense of direction for the first time. We are no longer groping about in complete darkness but can see how and where we must go to cause our fundamental humaneness to flourish. This introduces the manifestation of a fourth characteristic of internal stability in our attitude in life: a sense of trust in the Way and in its concrete viability. The Christian tradition uses the old Greek word *pistis* for this, a good translation of which is "faith." The Buddhist term *sraddha* is usually translated as "faith," which means the following: "a conviction in the qualities of meditative stabilization and its fruits" (Hopkins 1983, 72). Its function is to serve "as the basis for generating an aspiration for wholesome qualities that have not yet been generated" (Rabten 1992, 125–26).

Together, all these characteristics of internal stability make our egocentric mind manageable and thus another attitude toward our surroundings arises. We gradually discover that the obstacles do not lie in our surroundings, in the people and objects toward which our egocentric emotions are directed, but in these emotions themselves. We see that we do not need to avoid certain situations as much as we did while developing external stability. We discover that our internal stability creates the ability to work with our egocentric emotions and representations *directly*, that is, to see through them and to free ourselves from them. When our internal stability begins to develop, we are able to work with our mind directly rather than indirectly by avoiding or seeking out certain situations. We can tackle our jealousy rather than the object of our jealousy. Instead of trying to conquer or eliminate our enemies, we find it much more important to conquer our own aggression. Instead of avoiding things that might arouse our greed, our discipline consists of recognizing our greed and letting go of it on the spot in order to be able to step back into the open space of egolessness. Our everyday situation — which used to be an external obstacle for us — now becomes fertile soil for our practice.

Our surroundings — every last aspect of them — used to fill us with fear — the fear of losing control. We thought that the profane world existed outside of ourselves and that it was better to avoid it. Now we see that this world exists only within our mind (and in the minds of others). If we want to free ourselves from that profane world, avoiding certain external circumstances is then no longer that important. The fact that we have egocentric attitudes that dominate our mind, speech and actions to the detriment of ourselves and others is important.

Of course, certain situations still trigger certain egocentric emotions, but now we can use them to overcome those emotions. We can overcome those emotions only at the moment that they occur and not by avoiding situations that trigger those emotions. That such a thing is possible is a wonderful discovery, because it means that uncovering our fundamental humaneness in this phase is no longer a utopia but a very concrete mental skill by which we systematically begin to leave our egocentric emotions and ideas behind. Because of this, the world of the phenomena no longer appears to us simply as the object of these emotions. It does not appear exclusively anymore as that with which our ego is involved but reveals itself more and more in its original nakedness. We begin to have an inkling as to what the spiritual traditions mean when they speak of the fundamental sacredness of the world (see de Wit 1991, 194f.).

The Changed Attitude toward the Mentor

When our internal stability begins to develop, our relationship to the mentor changes as well. Then we also begin to see that the mentor lives in this original nakedness and that his or her instructions are given from that perspective. This causes our trust in the mentor to acquire a different quality, moving from the kind of trust that we have in a good friend to devotion and admiration.

Admiration is a very ambivalent thing. In the mentality of ego, it easily takes the form of hero worship, which is always followed by jealousy and, sooner or later, revilement of the hero. Ego's version of admiration therefore has no stability. In addition, it does not inspire us to see ourselves as we are but prompts us to show ourselves as good as possible or even, for that matter, as helpless as possible to the one that we admire. Then we often try to get as close as possible to the object of our admiration so that that which we admire may perhaps rub off on us and we may even be admired to some extent by others. To that end, depending on what seems to be the best strategy, we put our best or worst foot forward. What actually happens here is that we try to charm the mentor without giving up the fortification of ego. We try to manipulate the mentor: "I admire you very much and value your guidance. In gratitude I offer you a hospitable welcome in my fortress. Please, come live with me." Or the student says: "I trust you so much that you may approach my fortification. To make it easier for you, I have set a bench in the open space close to it." If the mentor should fall for such a proposal, a situation would arise that would no longer be fruitful because the possibility of guidance would be thwarted. Guidance would then occur under the student's conditions. But a genuine mentor does not not fall for this. These forms of manipulation are known to the mentor, and he or she does not respond to them but works around them. The mentor does not take a fixed position with regard to our ego and at the same time remains unmoved. The mentor only asks what is going on with that foot of ours that does not come forward.

But admiration in the spiritual sense evokes something very different: trust, surrender and, in particular, readiness to reveal ourselves as we are. We no longer put our best or worst foot forward, but our admiration manifests itself as naturalness, as simplicity in conversation, as complete, unarmed nakedness. Only then is true contact with the mentor, and the mentor's world, possible. In this contact, we also see the extent of the insight and care that the mentor employs in working with the manifestations of our ego. Our mentor exemplifies this for us. We gradually see the degree to which the mentor lives from the perspective of fundamental humaneness and is its embodiment. Then we begin to realize that our admiration for the mentor is none other than our dedication to and longing for our own true humaneness.

The Development of Stability Within

Thus, when our internal stability develops, we gradually develop skill in working with our ego and internal obstacles along the spiritual path. We make good progress along the Path. We become familiar with the ins and outs of our mind and adept in the disciplines that we practice. But all this, too, can become a routine. For, even though we execute this contemplative skill scrupulously, it seems that there are always new obstacles or, rather, situations and attitudes that we experience as obstacles. The feeling that we are making progress slowly disappears, and our spiritual ambition and trust in the Way is no longer nourished. And thus a new kind of disbelief or uncertainty arises: will we ever reach our goal? Whatever goal we may have set, and even if we have embraced the idea that there is no goal, the question of whether there is a Path at all now returns.

Many spiritual traditions say that when this occurs we enter into a phase or possibly only a moment of despair. All forms of the tradition — its approach and insights, its disciplines that we have appropriated — are as familiar to us as the backs of our hands. Everything seems too familiar, stale. Or perhaps we cling to the forms of the tradition and feel that we ourselves have become stale. It is as if there is no

longer any sense of moving forward in our spiritual development. Then it is easy for an attitude of nihilism to arise: we
think nothing of the disciplines, of the spiritual way of life.
Or it may be the other way around: we do find something in
the spiritual life but think nothing of ourselves. We are first
testy and then desperate, first aggressive and then depressed.
We experience the Path as an dead end. Externally we may
still hold on to its forms even if it is only out of habit or for
something to do, but deep in our heart we have lost faith in
the whole affair, ourselves included. It may still look good
and convincing on the outside, and we still work internally
with our obstacles as we should, but deep in our hearts we
no longer believe in it.

One can express it better, perhaps, in the following way:
our disbelief is not a disbelief in something but disbelief
as such — disbelief without an object. It is disbelief as a state
of being — a state of despair that exists on its own, for there
is no longer something to which we can turn. And we can
no longer choose to follow a spiritual path to do something
about our disbelief because we are already doing that. Nor
is quitting an alternative, because we have the feeling that
that is exactly what we have already done. Caught between
a rock and a hard place, there is nothing toward which we
can direct our disbelief, no object for our disbelief and no
possibility for shrugging the whole thing off. It is as if everything to which we had so fully applied ourselves has fled,
as if our spiritual path has expanded itself into an endlessly
wide landscape. We cannot say that we have arrived at the
end of the path because we have not seen an end anywhere.
Nor has the Path ended, but its contours and its direction
have disappeared from sight. There is no longer a Path to
see. We do not know what to do when we discover that there
really is no (longer a) Way.

In connection with this, the Greek Orthodox Christian

tradition speaks of *akèdia*, despair — despair with no way out, because there is nothing about which to be despairing. It is despair in the sense of an unfathomable mental low. In this tradition, *akèdia* is viewed as a great sin. And it is certainly a great existential problem for the practitioner, because this total despair is nothing other than *complete openness* with no buttress whatsoever, but it is not yet recognized *as such*. To arrive at that recognition, the spiritual traditions say, it is more necessary than ever to persevere in our discipline, which is what the mentor will most certainly advise. We no longer have, it is true, any inspiration nor do we know why we should persevere. But if our mentor tells us to persevere, then we do so, even if only because we see no other alternative. We have nothing better or worse to do. Then it is possible that we discover that this mental low, this insecurity only appears as such because we still see it in a very subtle way from the perspective of a remnant of ego, a remnant of spiritual ambition and expectations about the Path. The Path itself and our ambition to make progress along it are the *hidden obstacles* before which we now stand. The experience of despair is the flipside of this subtle ambition. When we let go of this ambition it becomes possible to rest in this complete openness. Our internal stability then deepens even more into what we could call *stability within* or *hidden stability*.

In theistic terms, this stability lies very close to the hidden intercourse with God, to the hidden activity of the Holy Spirit within us. The first two forms of stability are relevant to the progress along the Way, to working with our profane side and rising above it. But this stability is a state of being — not as it appears in contrast to ego but as it appears to itself. Many traditions use the term *sacredness* or *holiness* for this, but this term also stems from the perspective of the sinner in the process of conversion. From its own perspective, this state is not experienced as sacred or spiritual, which is exactly why it leads to so much despair. What has happened is that, without our noticing, we have begun to live outside the ruins of ego and thus also outside every spiritual path, since that path exists only as long as (and because) ego functions.

When we still lived within the fortifications of ego we saw that which was outside as light because it was so dark within. Now, however, we stand in a blinding light that initially appears to be darkness because it is blinding. This darkness was good enough for John of the Cross because it was nothing other than the light of the Holy Spirit. Mahayana Buddhism uses the term *dharmamegha*, cloud of dharma, for this phase. In this phase we no longer identify ourselves with the doctrine, with the path or with the technique.

> The bodhisattva doesn't identify himself with the path any longer because he has *become* the path. He *is* the path. He has worked on himself, trod on himself until he has become the path and the chariot as well as the occupant of the chariot, all at the same time. He is vision, energy, skillful means, generosity, knowledge, panoramic consciousness. (Trungpa 1988, 123)

In this sense, there is no path to see any more because the light (Sanskrit: *prabhasvara*) of our Buddha nature (or whatever the traditions call this fundamental state of clarity) now shines unhindered.

In terms of contemplative psychology, we have called resting in the state of complete clarity and openness *stability within*. When we learn to rest in it, its fruits also become freely manifest in the form of unconditional, unsolicited joy in life, courage in life and compassion because that is its nature — just as it is the nature of the sun to give light and warmth and thus cause the earth to flourish and just as it is the nature of flowers to bend toward the light, not because they have made that their goal but because it is their nature.

Many traditions speak about this stability within in terms of the internal mentor, the *magister interior*, the internal *guru*. When it has developed and we dare to trust in it, it becomes our guide. Prior to that we would like to trust it, but it is still too much drowned out by the voice of ego. But now we can understand the wordless speech of the *magister interior*.

We then also discover that there is no difference between our mentor, the *magister exterior*, and the internal mentor. This fills us with eternal gratitude for the ingenuity and goodness of the mentor and the tradition. For they turn out to be none other than the manifestation of our own fundamental humaneness in the world that is hopelessly caught up in ego's callousness and fear of life.

Ultimately, that is, from the final perspective of the stability within, the Path and ego are illusions. Thereby all contemplative psychology is an illusion as well. But it is precisely because of this truth that we value and should value the spiritual traditions, which through their psychological insight, and out of compassion, have developed powerful and effective spiritual disciplines that can free us from these illusions.

BIBLIOGRAPHY

Akhilananda, Swami. (1948). *Hindu Psychology: Its Meaning for the West*. London: Routledge and Kegan Paul.

Amaladoss, M. (1990). "Mission: From Vatican II into the Coming Decade." In *Vidyajyoti, Journal of Theological Reflection* 54: 269–80.

Augustine, *Confessions*. (1983). Trans. J.G. Pilkington. *The Nicene and Post-Nicene Fathers, First Series*. Vol. 1. Grand Rapids: Wm.B. Eerdmans Publishing Company.

Bataille, G. (1981). "Méthode de méditation." In *Oeuvres Complétes*, Vol. 5, 191–228. Paris: Gallimard.

Beatrix, Queen of the Netherlands. (1992). "Kersttoespraak koningin." *NRC-Handelsblad* (28 December).

Becker, G.J. (1968). "Crime and Punishment: An Economic Approach." *Journal of Political Economy*.

Benedict of Nursia. (1980). *The Rule of Benedict: A Guide to Christian Living*. Trans. Monks of Glenstal Abbey. Dublin: Four Courts Press.

Bennington, Geoffrey, and Jacques Derrida. (1993). *Jacques Derrida*. Trans. Geoffrey Bennington. Chicago and London: The University of Chicago Press.

Buber, M. (1967). *Chassidische vertellingen*. Cothen: Servire.

Bulhof, I.N. (1992). "Spiritueel humanisme." In *Streven: Cultureel maatschappelijk Maandblad* 59: 1254–65.

Burms, A. (1990). "Fictie, zelfbedrog, contemplatie." In *Tijdschrift voor filosofie* 52: 3–16.

Campbell, J. and Bill Moyers. (1988). *The Power of Myth*. New York: Doubleday.

Chadwick, O. (1958). *Western Asceticism*. Philadelphia: The Westminster Press.

Chödrön, Pema. (1991). *The Wisdom of No Escape*. Boston/London: Shambhala Publications.

Claxton, G. (1986). *Beyond Therapy: The Impact of Eastern Religions on Psychological Theory and Practice*. London: Wisdom Publications.

The Cloud of Unknowing. (1957, rpt. 1983). Trans. Ira Progoff. New York: Dell Publishing Co.

Dalai Lama. (1981). *The Opening of the Eye of Wisdom*. Illinois: The Theosophical Publishing House.

de Bruijn, J.T.P. (1987). "Vroomheid en mystiek." In J. Waardenburg. *Islam: Norm, ideaal en werkelijkheid*. Weesp.

de Groot, A.D. (1969). *Methodology: Foundations of Inference and Research in the Behavioral Sciences*. The Hague: Mouton.

de Wit, H.F. (1989). "Over de (on)kenbaarheid van de psychologische werkelijkheid." In M.C. Doeser and A.W. Musschenga (eds.). *Werkelijkheid van de wetenschap*. Kampen: Kok.

———. (1990). "Psychotherapy, Buddhist Meditation and Health." In *Journal of Contemplative Psychology*, Vol. 7. Boulder: Naropa Institute.

———. (1991). *Contemplative Psychology*. Trans. Marie Louise Baird. Pittsburgh, PA: Duquesne University Press.

Diekstra, R.F.W. (1982). *Ik kan denken / voelen wat ik will*. Lisse: Swets and Zeitlinger.

Dorje, Wangchug. (1978). *The Mahamudra: Eliminating the Darkness of Ignorance*. Dharamsala: Library of Tibetan Works and Archives.

Drewermann, E. (1990). *Beelden van verlossing*. Zoetermeer: Meinema.

———. (1991). *Dieptepsychologie en exegese*. Zoetermeer: Meinema.

Duijker, H.C.J. (1980). *Psychopolis: Een essay over de beoefening der psychologie*. Deventer: Van Loghum Slaterus.

——— et al. (1968). *Leerboek der psychologie*. Groningen: J.B. Wolters.

Duintjer, O.D. (1988). *Rondom metafysica — Over 'transcenden-tie' en de dubbelzinnigheid van metafysica.* Meppel: Boom.

Eckhart, Meister. (1981). *The Essential Sermons, Commentaries, Treatises, and Defense.* Trans. and intro. Edmund Colledge, O.S.A. and Bernard McGinn. Classics of Western Spirituality. New York/Ramsey/Toronto: Paulist Press.

Epstein, M. (1995). *Thoughts Without a Thinker: Psychotherapy from a Buddhist Perspective.* New York: Harper Collins Basic Books.

Evagrius Ponticus. (1987). *Geestelijke geschriften.* Monastieke Cahiers 34 and 35. Bonheiden: Uitgaven Abdij Bethlehem.

Evans-Wentz, W.U. (1927). *The Tibetan Book of the Dead.* London/ Oxford: University Press.

Fortmann, H.M.M. (1974). *Als ziende de onzienlijke.* Book 1. Hilversum: Gooi en Sticht B.V.

Giri, Nityananda. (1992). "Mediation in Hinduismus." *Dialog der Religionen* 2.

Gleitman, H. (1986). *Psychology.* New York/London: Norton.

Guenther, H.V. (1973). *The Royal Song of Saraha.* Boston: Shambhala Publications.

Hellings, J., S.J. (1942). *De geestelijke oefeningen van den H. Ignatius van Loyola.* Amsterdam: H. Nelissen.

Hermans, H.J.M. *et al.* (1985). *De grondmotieven van het menselijk bestaan: Hun expressie in het persoonlijk waarderingsleven.* Lisse: Swets and Zeitlinger.

Hopkins, J. (1983). *Meditation on Emptiness.* London: Wisdom Publications.

IJsseling, S. (1990). *Mimesis. Over schijn en zijn.* Baarn: Ambo.

Inada, K.K. (1970). *Nagarjuna: A Translation of his Mulamadya-maka-karika with an Introductory Essay.* Tokyo: The Hokuseido Press.

Jaeger, W. (1992). "Kontemplation — der christliche esoterische Weg." *Dialog der Religionen* 2.

James, W. (1981). *The Principles of Psychology,* Vol. 1. *The Works of William James.* Cambridge MA/London: Harvard University Press. First published in 1890.

———. (1977). *The Varieties of Religious Experience.* Fount Paperbacks. Glasgow: Collins. First published in 1902.

John of the Cross. (1963). *Ascent of Mount Carmel*. Trans. E. Allison Peers. Electronic Edition. Christian Classical Ethereal Library. Wheaton, Ill. Website: http://ccel.wheaton.edu/john_of_the_cross/ascent/ascent.html.

Jung, C.G. (1938). *Psychology and Religion*. New Haven: Yale Univerity Press.

Kaufmann, P. (1971). "Imaginaire et imagination." In *Encyclopaedia Universalis*, Vol. 8. Paris. Pp. 733a–39a.

Ketelaars, Thijs, OSB. (1986). "Met U: in zelftucht, trouw en moed." In *Benedictus Tijdschrift* 47: 57–58.

Koenen, M.J. and J. Endepols. (1960). *Verklarend handwoordenboek der nederlandse taal*. Groningen: J.B. Wolters.

Komito, D.R. (1987). *Nagarjuna's 'Seventy Stanzas': A Buddhist Psychology of Emptiness*. Ithaca, NY: Snow Lion Publications.

Kongtrul, Jamgon. (1987). *The Great Path of Awakening*. Boston/London: Shambhala Publications.

Kouwer, B.J. (1963). *Spel van de persoonlijkheid*. Utrecht: Bijleveld.

Kuitert, H.M. (1986). *Everything is Politics but Politics is not Everything: A Theological Perspective on Faith and Politics*. Trans. John Bowden. London: SCM Press.

———. (1993). *I Have My Doubts: How to Become a Christian Without Being a Fundamentalist*. Trans. John Bowden. London/Valley Forge: SCM Press, Ltd./Trinity Press International.

Kwee, M.G.T. (1990). *Denken en doen is psychotherapie*. The Hague/London: East-West Publications.

Kwee, M.G.T. and T.L. Holdstock. (1996). *Western and Buddhist Psychology: Clinical Perspectives*. Delft: Eburon.

Lopez, D.S. Jr. (1997). *Religions of Tibet in Practice*. New Jersey: Princeton University Press.

Louf, André. (1992). *Tuning in to Grace: The Quest for God*. Trans. John Vriend. Kalamazoo: Cistercian Publications.

Mindel, N. (1985). *The Philosophy of Chabad*. New York: Kehot Publication Society.

Moyaert, P. (1983). "Over het ik bij Freud en Lacan." In *Tijdschrift voor Filosofie* 45: 388–420.

———. (1985). "De structuur van de mystieke liefde bij Theresia van Avila." In Ed. D. Hutsebout. *Over de grens*. Leuven: Universitaire Pers Leuven.

———. (1988). "Mystiek en liefde." In *Mystiek en liefde. Wijsgerige Verkenningen*, Vol. 5. Eds. J. Walgrave and P. Moyaert. Louvain: Universitaire Pers Louvain.

Nalanda and C. Trungpa. (1980). *The Rain of Wisdom*. Boston: Shambhala Publications.

Namgyal, T.T. (1986). *Mahamudra: The Quintessence of Mind and Mediation*. Boston/London: Shambhala Publications.

Naranjo, C. and R.E. Ornstein. (1972). *On the Psychology of Meditation*. London: Allen and Unwin Ltd.

Nishitani, K. (1982). *Religion and Nothingness*. Berkeley: University of California Press.

Nurbaksh. (1989). *The Paradise of the Sufis*. London/New York: Nimatillahi Publications.

Nyima, Chokyi. (1989). *The Union of Mahamudra and Dzogchen*. Hong Kong: Rangjung Yeshe Publications.

Perrot, M. (ed.). (1989). *Geschiedenis van het persoonlijk leven*. Amsterdam: Agon B.V.

Podvoll, E.M. (1990). *The Seduction of Madness*. New York: Harper-Collins.

Proust, M. (1954). *Swann's Way*. Trans. C.K. Scott Moncrieff. New York: The Limited Editions Club.

Pseudo-Dionysius the Areopagite. (1987). *The Mystical Theology*. Trans. C. Luibheird. New York: Paulist Press.

Rabten, Geshe. (1992). *Mind and its Functions*. Le Mont-Pelerin, Switzerland: Edition Rabten Chöling.

Reynolds, J.M. (1989). *Self-Liberation Through Seeing with Naked Awareness*. Barrytown, NY: Station Hill Press.

Rilke, R.M. (1993). *The Duino Elegies*. Trans. Leslie Norris and Alan Keele. Columbia, SC: Camden House.

Sanders, C. *et al.* (1989). *De cognitieve revolutie in de psychologie*. Kampen: Kok Agora.

Sartre, Jean-Paul. (1972). *La Transcendance de l'Ego. Esquisse d'une description phénoménologique*. Paris: Librairie Philosophique J. Virn, 1972.

Shantideva. (1997). *The Way of the Bodhisattva*. Boston/London: Shambhala Publications.

Shapiro, D.J. and R. Walsh. (1984). *Meditation: Classical and Contemporary Views*. New York: Aldine.

Shotter, J. (1975). *Images of Man in Psychological Research.* London: Methuen.

Steggink, O. and K. Waaijman. (1985). *Spiritualiteit en mystiek.* I. Inleiding. Nijmegen: Gottmer.

Suzuki, D.T. (1970). *Zen and Japanese Culture.* Princeton, NJ: Princeton University Press.

Theisen, J., OSB. (1993). "In de marge of in het hart. Over de plaats van de monnik in kerk en samenleving." In *Benedictus Tijdschrift* 54: 2–15.

Tolstoy, L. (1954). *Anna Karenin.* Harmondsworth: Penguin Books.

Trungpa, C. (1969). *Meditation in Action.* Boston: Shambhala.

———. (1973). *Cutting Through Spiritual Materialism.* Boston/London: Shambhala Publications.

———. (1976). *The Myth of Freedom and the Way of Meditation.* Boston/London: Shambhala Publications.

———. (1986). *Shambhala. De weg van de krijger.* Cothen: Servire.

———. (1991). *Crazy Wisdom.* Boston/London: Shambhala Publications.

Tydeman, N. (1991). *De plaatjes van de os.* Amsterdam: Karnak, 1991.

Van der Lans, J.M. (1980). *Religieuze ervaring en meditatie.* Deventer: Van Loghum Slaterus.

Van Kaam, A. (1983–92). *Formative Spirituality.* Vols. 1–5. New York: Crossroad.

Vasubandhu. (1971). *L'Abhidharmakoija.* Trans. Louis de La Vallée Poussin. Brussels: Institu Belge des Hautes Études Chinoises.

Vergote, A. (1984). *Religie, geloof en ongeloof: Psychologische studie.* Antwerp/Amsterdam: De Nederlandse Boekhandel.

———. (1987). *Het meerstemmige leven: Gedachten over mens en religie.* Kampen: Kok Agora.

Vroom, H.M. (1989). *Religions and the Truth.* Trans. J.W. Rebel. Amsterdam/Grand Rapids: Rodopi/Eerdmans.

Walker, S. (ed.). (1987). *Speaking of Silence.* New York: Paulist Press.

Writings from the Philokalia: On Prayer of the Heart. (1972). Trans. E. Kadloubovsky and G.E.H. Palmer. London: Faber & Faber.

Zegveld, A. (1991). "Gebed en leven." In *Benedictus Tijdschrift* 3.

INDEX

Academic psychology, 35, 38, 52-53, 119, 122, 207
Akhilananda, Swami, 187-88
Allah, 32, 80
Amaladoss, M., 13
Ambrose, Bishop, 18
Anthropology, 31, 57, 94
Apophatic spirituality, 217-19
Aquinas, Thomas, 110
Arjuna, 179
Art, 28-29
As You Like It (Shakespeare), 125
Ascent of Mount Carmel (John of the Cross), 192
Augustine, Saint, 17-18, 90-91, 107, 114, 166, 270

Bataille, G., 157
Beatrix, Queen of the Netherlands, 116
Becker, G. J., 84
Behavior, 32, 35, 41, 50, 115-16, 266-67
Behavioral psychology, 30, 194
Benedict, 254
Bennington, Geoffrey, 70
Bhavanakrama, 131
Bible, *See* New Testament; Old Testament; individual Gospels
Bielecki, Tessa, 191-92
Blickfeld, 126
Brahman, 32, 90
Buddha, 17, 172, 179, 190
Buddha-nature, 32, 57, 91-92, 159, 163-64, 230, 245, 259, 298
Buddhism
  and ego, 90-91, 155
  and four attitudes of, 180
  and insight, 64, 143, 146, 150, 218, 292
  psychology of, 31, 70, 97, 106, 112, 126, 135
  and spiritual disciplines, 172, 191, 204, 208, 218, 256

Sutras of, 80
theories of, 18-19, 54, 83, 157, 176-77, 180-84, 188, 206, 214, 230, 237, 241, 252-57
in Tibet, 195, 264, 283.
  See also Mahayana Buddhism; Theravada Buddhism; Vajrayana Buddhism; Zen Buddhism
Bulhof, I. N., 13

Campbell, J., 94
Carmelites, 85, 191
Cassian, Saint, 210
Catholicism. *See* Christianity
Chadwick, O., 131, 210
Chassidic tradition. *See* Jews and Judaism
Chinese, 219, 276
Chödrön, Pema, 49
Christ. *See* Jesus
Christianity
  Augustine on, 17-18
  Drewermann on, 120
  and Holy Spirit, 57, 92, 225, 230, 285, 291
  and knowledge (diakrisis), 82, 144, 177, 179
  Kuitert on, 63-64
  and mental disciplines, 33, 54, 96-98, 155, 173, 181, 191-92, 206
  and mentor, 275
  and monastic life, 155, 179, 275
  Orthodox practice of, 206, 237
  practice of, 19, 82, 130-31, 187, 190-91, 210, 217, 232, 237-38, 292
  and sin, 56, 98-99, 160, 286
Clarity of mind
  and consciousness, 4, 13, 15, 127
  and experience of reality, 37, 65-73
  and humaneness, 12, 54, 130
  and openmindedness, 128-29, 164

and humaneness, 86, 92-93, 109,
115, 245-50, 269, 283, 293, 299
and humanity, 45-46, 48, 94, 108,
116, 290-91
and joy, 91, 164, 298
mental movement of, 102-07, 111,
115-16, 155-59, 255-58, 284, 294
and mentor, 278, 281, 283, 295, 299
and metaphor, 103, 158-61, 163, 294,
298
and perspective, 91, 99, 111, 148,
153, 156, 158-60, 221, 231 270, 297
as profane, 92-93, 109-09, 113, 184
psychology basis of, 58, 86-89, 92-94,
102, 108, 112-13, 115-17, 252, 286
and self-image, 93, 105-09, 112, 158-
59, 161, 164-65, 183, 199, 246-48,
261, 287, 290-93
and spiritual traditions, 87, 89-95,
98, 108-09, 114-17, 182, 185, 250-51
vulnerability of, 100, 106-08, 164
Egocentricity
absence of, 96-97, 293
and emotion, 48, 111-15, 262, 292
and expectation, 45-46, 83, 167, 267-68
and experience of reality, 70, 104-08,
111, 139-41, 145, 160-65, 182,
200, 214, 226-28, 235-36, 285, 289
structure of, 56, 96, 109, 113, 134,
141, 189
Emotions, 3, 48, 111-15, 187-88, 235
Ephesians, Book of, 122
Epistemology, 142
Experience of reality
and absolute reality, 70-71
aggression, 71-72
awareness of, 68, 75-76, 79, 87-88,
141, 176, 218
and childhood, 67-69
and clarity of mind, 37, 65-73
and consciousness, 63, 97-98, 125-28,
284
and contemplative psychology, 38-39,
69, 122, 139, 146
and disciplines, 68-70, 181-82
and dualistic split, 111, 139, 184, 249
and egocentricity, 70, 104-11, 139-
45, 160-65, 182, 200, 226, 235-36,
247, 285, 289
and guidance, 80-81
and perspective, 65-66, 73, 157, 226
and self-image, 71, 76, 80, 89, 154
and spiritual growth, 59-61, 63, 244
and spiritual traditions, 39, 66, 71,

79-80, 149, 162, 165-66, 193, 233
and stream of experience or thought,
38-39, 74-75, 128-29, 136-38, 142,
181, 212
terms for, 66
totality of, 79-80
and Western culture, 68

Fear, 48, 55, 93, 100-03, 262, 280, 288-
89, 292
First-person perspective, 35-40, 42-45,
49, 54-56, 86-87, 117-18
Formative sciences, 38
Formative Spirituality (Van Kaam), 38
Fortmann, Han M. M., 26, 100, 147-48
Freedom, 33, 72, 110, 154, 213, 215, 259,
286
Freud, Sigmund, 24, 50
Fundamentalism, 161-63

Generosity, 261-62
God
and experience of reality, 71, 185
and Holy Spirit, 164, 297
image of, 45-46, 54, 57, 148-49, 163,
167-68, 179-181, 184-89
kingdom of, 56, 210, 224
Louf on, 82-83
as mentor, 274
and Muslim tradition, 92
relationship with, 50, 61-62, 159,
184, 218, 229-32, 244, 259, 291
and vertical religiosity, 63
wrath of, 163
Zegveld on, 233-34
Gratitude, 184-85
Greek Orthodox Christianity, 296-97
Guidance, 80-85, 154, 196-97, 275, 285,
294, 299. See also mentor

Hammarskjöld, Dag, 2, 18
Happiness. *See* Joy
Hedonist psychology, 50-52
Hermans, H. J. M., 37
Hermeneutics, 66
Herzberg, Judith, 260
Hillesum, Etty, 2
Hindu Psychology (Akhilanada), 187-88
Hinduism
commandments of, 240-41
disciplines of, 176-77, 180-81, 191, 232
and openmindedness, 155
traditions of, 19, 80, 90, 146, 187,
206, 218, 257, 274
Holdstock, Robert, 195